THE NATURE OBSERVER'S HANDBOOK

"An excellent resource for those who want to learn how to explore the outdoors. This comprehensive guide will help people make nature study a fun and important part of their lives."
— Jerry Bley, Education/Research Coordinator,
Natural Resources Council of Maine

"Dr. Brainerd's book will help people get in touch with nature and understand it well, wherever they wander, be it across their back yard or around the world."
— Charles E. Roth, Chief Naturalist/Educator, The Massachusetts
Audubon Society, and author of *The Wildlife Observer's Guidebook*

"Brainerd's book is an invitation to explore the *patterns* in nature: a trickle of a water drop down a window pane or the meandering of a great river, the weeds in a sidewalk crack or Amazon forests. The author's curiosity and enthusiasm are infectious. The invitation will be difficult to refuse."
— Chet Raymo, author of *The Soul of the Night*

"His rich guidance leads you to farms, roads, canals, and even towns and cities, tempting you to follow, observe, and enjoy."
— Herbert S. Zim, respected author of numerous children's science books

"Reading *The Nature Observer's Handbook* is like taking a leisurely trip with a congenial and knowledgeable traveling companion. It will make you feel like hitting the road—or the hiking trail or the bike path—with your eyes wide open and your senses attuned to the natural world."
— Gale Lawrence, author of *A Field Guide to the Familiar: Learning to Observe the Natural World* and *The Beginning Naturalist*

THE
NATURE
OBSERVER'S
HANDBOOK

Learning to Appreciate Our Natural World

by John W. Brainerd
illustrations by the author

An East Woods Book

The
Globe
Pequot
Press

Chester, Connecticut 06412

Cover photo by C. R. Wyttenbach, University of Kansas/BPS

Library of Congress Cataloging-in-Publication Data

Brainerd, John W. (date)
　　The nature observer's handbook.

　　Bibliography: p.
　　Includes index.
　　1. Natural history—Outdoor books.　　2. Nature study.
I. Title.
QH81.B768　1986　　508　　86-22824
ISBN 0-87106-824-9

Manufactured in the United States of America
First Edition/Second Printing, October 1987

CONTENTS

PREPARING FOR YOUR TOUR
  1. Time for Adventure   3

NATURE'S PATTERNS
  2. The Sky   21
  3. The Lay of the Land   26
  4. Rocks   31
  5. Soils   38
  6. Natural Vegetation   43
  7. Wetlands   50
  8. Streams   60
  9. Lakes   68
10. Seashores   75
11. Seas and Oceans   86
12. Wildlife   93

PEOPLE'S PATTERNS
13. Farms   105
14. Rangelands   112
15. Forests   121
16. Quarries and Mines   129
17. Trails   136
18. Bicycling Ways   143
19. Roads   149
20. Bridges and Causeways 158
21. Canals   163
22. Yards and Gardens   167
23. Towns and Cities   173

TECHNIQUES

24. Recording Your Observations   181
25. Reading More   191

Bibliography   209
Index   239

PREFACE

Nature is often best observed while you are stationary, still, and quiet, perhaps sitting on a stump or looking out a window. But many of us these days are on the move, and fast, so this book was conceived primarily to help people observe and appreciate nature more while "on tour." I've coined the term *nature touring* to draw attention to the importance of sensing nature while traveling, be it around the yard, around the block, or around the world. Indeed, this book might have been called "Nature Touring."

Nature touring can be a worthwhile activity in its own right. We often hasten to arrive at a destination when we would do better to slow down to admire the landscape along our way, to observe nature's remarkable patterns, the over-arching skies, the mountains, valleys, and seas, and, when we take time to look closely, nature's fascinating details. We do not need to dash to "collect" national parks, our magnificent heritage of very special areas. (The average visit to all the national parks is less than six hours, and 97 percent of the visitors do not go more than 300 feet from the car.) Let's purposefully look for nature wherever we tour, along the way.

Touring thus can give us meaningful experiences with the

natural world, from which we have all evolved and into which we must willy-nilly fit. By *nature* I mean sky, earth, and sea with all their living things, the plants, the birds, and you and me. And while dealing herein with things natural, I shall not neglect entirely things artificial. No artifact exists that has not been artfully made from nature's gifts. Too bad to see cold steel without sensing its precursing molten metal and the mountain or plain from which its iron and coal were mined.

Touring to me suggests that in going from here to there we should have some purpose for our trip, the travel not so direct, however, but that some wandering is allowed. Indeed, the sideways amble and the backward glance are much to be recommended, whatever our reasons for touring. It is wise to have your own *personal* purposes even though a companion or group may have outlined or organized your tour.

While your wheels roll or your feet plod, the travels of your mind are what really concern me as I write, for through them you will receive your most meaningful rewards. My reward in writing this book is the thought that with ever-increasing appreciation of nature you will help adapt people's patterns to nature's patterns. In that respect, we all have far to go.

How long a trip may constitute a tour? In the Victorian nineteenth century, Americans and Britons who had enough money would take an extended "grand tour" of continental western Europe, visiting museums, spas, and other places considered proper for the cultured. By contrast, Henry David Thoreau, a philosophical pinch-penny, restricted his touring to his native New England, mostly hiking and canoeing, and wrote that he had traveled widely in Concord, his home town! John Muir went even farther in mini-travel, recounting his experience at the tip of a giant California sugar pine climbed during a storm, its swaying top carrying him back and forth from here to there, there to here, in a great adventure.

I hope this book encourages you to gain nature-touring tips from the accounts of other travelers throughout written history, from Odysseus to the latest authors who share their journeys by words and pictures so you can experience their travels vicariously. The writings of others can take you on journeys of the mind far beyond the boundaries of this book, so be sure to use the final chapter, "Reading

More," and the bibliography. But realize that your own purposeful tours, maybe just around your yard or along a city street, can be highly rewarding and worth sharing with others.

Because my own travels have given me great pleasure and added to my understanding of my own life and the lives of others, I have included in this book some of my experiences while touring with an eye to nature. I hope you may benefit a bit from them. I want this book to be a personal one not only for me in its writing but also for you in its reading.

I do not know you. I wish I did, for then I could share with you more effectively and no doubt even more joyously. I recognize, though, that if you have read even this far we have a common interest in nature. Good! If you like things simple, the opening paragraph or so of most chapters is designed with you especially in mind. If you want somewhat more information and ideas based on my philosophy of nature touring, then read on.

Whatever your personal purposes, modes of travel, routes, and destinations, may you have many joys while observing nature.

I

PREPARING FOR YOUR TOUR

1 TIME FOR ADVENTURE

All outdoors awaits you! Sooner or later the time approaches when you can break with routine and journey out into the natural world. Perhaps you will explore new roads or trails. Perhaps you will forsake all beaten paths. Or perhaps you will follow the same old routes but with new eyes, indeed with all your senses sharpened for new experiences . . . for an hour, a month, a year.

When was the last time you toured your yard on hands and knees to see what the ants are doing? Or checked on the pavement cracks behind the grocery store for curious weeds? Have you been to the beach lately in a gale or snowstorm, or discovered the highest place in town and stood tall upon it? If not, chances are you need an escapade. Let nature aid your escape, not only as added zest to your adventure, but as its basic goal. For nature is right under our feet, always, whether under city pavement, in a suburban yard, or in the wheat fields outside Chugwater, Wyoming.

Adventure always involves problems. Your first may be just breaking away from routine. Repeating today what you did yesterday is the easy habit. But take a little time to think about a trip, too.

How long a trip? How risky? What will the neighbors say if they notice you face-to-face with the ants in your yard, or if they suddenly get a postcard from you from, say, Scrag, Washington? Perhaps you should alert them and maybe make them a bit envious. For any considerable time away, you will of course have pretrip problems. Your house plants may die without you, unless you arrange for a plant-sitter or give them away. Your dog? Perhaps it is ready for adventure too; or it can be safely left with a relative, friend, or kennel. Farm animals of course require someone to care for them regularly at your farm, unless you sell them and start with new ones on your return. If you are not self-employed you need, of course, to make arrangements with your employer.

So, like everybody else, you have pretrip problems, no doubt including financial ones. But if they seem insoluble at the time, at least dream of a fantastic tour, a "someday-trip" when, with only a minimum of qualms, you can break away.

Company?

About that yard tour: You may learn most about ants if you tour your yard alone, but two sets of eyes and two brains may be better than only one. Perhaps ask a child to join you. Often small children have helped me see what I would otherwise have missed, especially things near the ground. Local teachers can perhaps suggest a student to accompany you, a young or not-so-young person in need of a project for science, art, or language; why not a study of ant-ways while you contribute your yard and enthusiasm for nature? Of course a university entomologist can be a noble co-crawler!

For an extended tour, be sure to pick a companion who will wear well. I do recommend people for companions, but Robert Louis Stevenson traveled with a donkey and John Steinbeck with a french poodle. People with a ready-for-anything attitude and a good sense of humor can help you adapt to the bizarre happenings you will surely encounter. Also, a good companion will leave you psychologically alone at times even though physically right beside you, knowing that the most important part of a line of music may be the rest between notes. If you really need continual solitude, travel alone, but snap out of yourself at times to enjoy the people you chance to meet in your travels.

Some travelers derive more pleasure if the trip is one taken with the family. Taking children and spouse may provide scant rest from a busy home life, but it does provide respite from routine in the familiar environment. Of course some kids get motion sickness, but applied psychology, well-spaced intervals of travel and stops, and minimal medication, if necessary, can often mitigate that problem. The joys of sharing an adventure with loved ones can more than compensate for annoyances.

Helps in Planning

If touring, in nature or otherwise, seems beyond your planning ability, do ask for aid from an experienced person, a friend or relative who has enjoyed traveling. Or consult one of the many helpful travel agencies; they can suggest places to go, routes, seasons, fares, timetables, lodgings, clothing, and budgets. And don't fail to get a librarian's help for pretour reading. A book about ants? One on painting wildflowers or on photographing landscapes? A history of plantations of the Old South? A field guide to birds of the American West, Swiss Alps, or wherever? Regional magazines, trade magazines of auto makers; bus, train, and airplane publications; and travel sections of newspapers can help you plan what you might want to see and do.

Some of the best tours are not only professionally planned but also are conducted by professionals. Travel agencies, travel companies with buses, trains, and/or ships, automobile associations, and some oil companies, can provide a wealth of possible trips ranging from local tours to around-the-world voyages. Professional and amateur societies also provide opportunities. I'll never forget my 3-week study tour of Bavaria, Austria, and Switzerland with a group of forty foresters; I was the only non-forester along, and what a lot I learned! Advertisements from garden clubs, Audubon societies, and photographic organizations offer tantalizing tours, as do those for senior citizens.

Some Whys and Wheres

Although a need for change may be a primary reason for touring, you should also have other purposes in mind. Do you wish to travel widely to experience the contrasts of windy plains, high mountains, dark forests, and wave-buffeted shores? How about visiting historic sites, places that take your thoughts back in time, helping you know better the natural and cultural environments from which your roots grew? Or would you rather explore the play of light and shade across nearby woods and fields, perhaps photographing or painting them at different times of day and season, or writing about them—and being home in time for supper? Perhaps you would like to take one of my dream-trips for me, following the autumnal flutterings of monarch butterflies from Canada to the mountains of Mexico.

Before you decide on a tour, let your mind wander; an unexpected locale may come to you. Or try the old game of opening an atlas, with eyes closed, and letting your index finger fall somewhere; then open your eyes and say, "That's where I'm going!"

Walking

For short tours, walking gets you closest to nature, although some of us naturalists go one step "shorter": we creep or crawl as when studying ants, rosette plants, or microclimates near the ground. Along with time, rate, and distance factors, you should consider detail versus breadth of observations of nature. If you have enough time, you can, with other limitations disposed of, walk across a continent. Great!—but you'd probably do it only once in a lifetime, whereas you could take almost daily walks down to the river year after year and learn an awe-inspiring amount about earth, sky, water, and the living things therein. You could walk briskly and tape-record your observations on such daily tours; or on daily tours you could linger here and there to jot down notes and make sketches. (See Chapter 24.) Of course walking poses limitations: time, leg power, foot comfort, and the cost of feeding your healthy appetite. The rewards of walking, though, can be immense.

Perhaps you are physically and mentally ready for backpacking in wilderness. Although I can sometimes get a feeling of wilderness in an urban park, that experience is different from being neighbor to loons on a northern lake. Unfettered nature, unpaved and plastic-free, provides ultimate experiences for adventurous people. Knowing that wilderness is there is salutary for all of us, even for the severely handicapped and house bound who can rarely go. Actually being in wilderness should be a privilege earned by careful preparation of body and mind, as well as spirit, for entering nature as a caring part of it, and leaving it unspoiled.

Cycling

Cycling, like walking, gives excellent contact with nature. I recommend it especially for birding when you want to see a variety of species within a limited time, as during migrations and censuses for wintering or breeding birds, and in a limited area where good roads or bikeways give easy access to various habitats. Repeated cycling tours in and around a small town offer efficient data-collecting outings, and provide valuable information to share with other birders. The quietness of bicycling allows you the joy of approaching wildlife without disturbing it, the better to observe its normal behavior and admire its beauty. Bicycling also makes stopping easy for listening to bird songs and calls. Entomologists, botanists, and other naturalists can also profit from local bike tours. Longer cycling tours can give you an unexcelled feel for larger landscapes, their ups and downs, weather, vegetation, wildlife, and land use. Whenever possible avoid roads with heavy traffic, and watch out for grilled manholes and bridges, broken bottles, and other trash. Obey all traffic laws, of course.

Prepare yourself physically, pace yourself carefully, and choose equipment and clothing with care much as you would for wilderness camping. Be well versed in bike repair. Chances are that you will wish to camp most of the time, but a motel or bed-and-breakfast stop may be wise occasionally.

A student of mine bicycled across the United States and sent me a report on a postcard each week, finely printed, describing the types of vegetation that he was experiencing. Another biked the West Coast from Canada to Mexico taking photographs to tell me of her travels.

Motorcycle touring increases your range along with cost, power, noise, and risk. Because helmet and machine will separate you from nature more than when bicycling, it will behoove you to stop frequently to savor natural phenomena, or to make longer stops at special nature sites, for example to enjoy evening and early-morning birdsongs. As a motorcyclist you may reach faraway places that a bicyclist might never experience.

Driving

Touring in your own car permits taking more equipment and supplies. A larger wardrobe may be desirable for varied habitats such as city and country, mountains and shore; but avoid nonessentials, to leave room for geographic guides, natural history reference books, and other reading to help you understand and enjoy your new surroundings. Photographic and sound-recording equipment, paints, and writing materials also need assigned space in a naturalist's auto. Some hard choices must be made to avoid clutter, not only in small cars but also in vans and trucks.

Touring by auto may involve tenting or staying at motels and/ or hotels, or accepting invitations from forewarned friends. Whatever way you travel, take a first-aid kit, safety signals, repair tools, flashlights, and dark glasses. If camping, package your tent, sleeping bags, cooking gear, and food compactly and keep them in order. Plan carefully. Make lists. Your enjoyment of nature will be commensurate with camping skills that leave time to explore your environment or to relax and let the nature around you seep into your consciousness.

Recreational vehicles of many types provide a roof over your head wherever you are, obviating setting up and taking down a tent, often irksome chores in inclement weather. Efficient housekeeping in a trailer or motor home leaves time for enjoying nature's wonders, but the vehicle tends to seal you off from more intimate contact with nature. At times that's great, as when mosquitoes coat the screens or desert dust screams by in a hot wind. Realize, though, that your mobile home must stay mostly on roads and parking sites. Too many fragile environments are being denatured by thoughtless drivers. Vehicles off the road can give wildlife grief and destroy vegetation. Even faint wheel marks on slopes can initiate gully erosion in grasslands and arid lands, and upstream erosion creates harmful deposits downstream, perhaps sedimentation of a reservoir or burial of fertile agricultural soils under sterile ones. To enjoy nature off the roads, leave your wheeled vehicle; take a canoe, kayak, horse, mule, or donkey, or go by "shank's mare" (your own legs). Tread lightly on our precious Planet Earth.

Public Transport

Public transportation by bus, train, plane, or boat is often desirable, especially if only one or two of you are touring. You leave to others the worries of the road. Meeting people is often facilitated. Often you can read, write, sketch, and photograph as you travel, along with making acquaintances, who may or may not share your interests in nature. Or snooze. Spending nights on public conveyances can be tiring, unless you can find (and afford) a berth. Such transport often deposits you in a city, where you may wish to establish a base in a hotel. Although all cities have some nature to seek and enjoy, you will probably want to plan trips from your hotel to surrounding countryside. Rent a bicycle, car, or recreational vehicle, or strike out on a backpacking trip. Sometimes it is money well spent to hire a taxi for a half-day or a day with a cautious driver willing to stop at sites you may choose for sketching, photographing, collecting (with any permits needed), or just exploring. Being driven has special advantages in foreign countries with strange ways of operating vehicles.

Ferry boats can be a delight on harbors and bays. Cruise ships, especially those catering to naturalists, can take you to naturalists' paradises. (So can a canoe!) In one of my wildest dreams I sail a little ketch along the coast of Maine, follow the Inland Waterway to Florida and the Caribbean Sea, and just before I awake to reality, I loll in South Pacific atolls before sampling the breath-taking harbors of New Zealand and Australia. May you dream too; that is part of planning any good nature tour.

Clothing

Appropriate clothing helps make nature tours efficient and enjoyable. Consider well the climate(s) you will visit and the weather you can expect at the season(s) you will be there. Choose durable, easily cleaned clothing. "Earth colors"—various shades of browns and greens—show soil minimally and tend to camouflage you in many environments (but not in snow). Shades (darker) show soil less in most environments than do tints (lighter), which are usually most appropriate in deserts and along many sandy shores. For hazardous places such as alpine mountains and remote barrenlands, bright reds and oranges may help teammates or search-and-rescue parties find you. (You will not embark on foolhardy ventures that put others at risk.) During hunting season in the country, wear brilliant red or orange to avoid being shot, and don't pull out a white handkerchief, which a careless or inebriated hunter might mistake for a deer's white tail.

Light-weight clothing, worn in layers when cold and shed when warmer, is preferable to fewer heavy garments. A light-weight hooded jacket or parka and pants which are rain-resistant, perhaps cheerful red or yellow for dark rainy days or for photogenic conspicuousness, can also make good wind-breakers on sunny days in exposed situations such as mountains, seashores, and deserts. (Sailors refer to such protective clothing as "foul-weather gear.")

Footwear poses problems. Rugged terrain suggests rugged boots, which are heavy and bulky. In my old age I favor moccasins; but when sharing country with poisonous snakes, I watch where I set each foot! If you cannot be that careful, wear tall leather boots. You probably know what type of footwear gives you comfort, but I'd avoid sandals in most outdoor environments. Reserve barefootedness for your own lawn, sandy beaches, muddy shores, and occasionally other places where your feet can bring you safe and intriguing sensory messages about land under foot.

Food

Food? For a day's outing traveling light, good nourishment can come from sandwiches, granola-type cereals, cheese, chocolate bars, raisins, and other dried fruits. If visiting a region with chemically different water, or if unavoidable long drives make life too sedentary, prunes can usually counter constipation. In cold weather, concentrated sweets provide quick calories. On lengthy tours, home diet may not be possible but may be good as a basic plan to modify. Try to fit your diet to your degree of activity so you maintain your normal, healthful weight. Be experimental, a bit cautiously, with strange foods in strange places. If you insist on trying to find only your customary foods, you may miss much of the fun of travel. Regional specialties can be a delight. A student of mine hiked throughout Europe eating regional foods and photographing where they were harvested; on returning to college, he gave us a wonderful slide show. Food is more than energy.

If you carry your own food on trips, be prepared to avoid food spoilage, which can be both wasteful and dangerous. If keeping food cool poses problems, buy perishables in small quantities only. Use ice when available and/or canned coolants in insulated containers kept clean. Or avoid perishables by using dehydrated, freeze-dried, and/or irradiated foods. When camping, provide storage inaccessible to wildlife, including ants and bears! Food, like clothing, is personal, a combination of whim and practicality. Emphasize the latter—and learn from mistakes, some of which in retrospect may be hilarious.

Water

Plan for your drinking water. Good water is less and less available in our overcrowded, overconsumed world. For day trips, you may wish to carry a small plastic water bottle, or in arid regions a cloth-covered

11

metal canteen or cloth water-bag that cools by evaporation. But water is heavy, so you should consider carefully any sources available along your route.

Water in different regions contains different chemicals; it may be "harder" (that is, with more lime or related salts) or "softer" (more acidic, with less calcium or other basic materials and more free hydrogen ions). Our body chemistry often needs time to adjust to such differences. When touring by car to a different region, I take a large container of "home-water"; as I use some of it I add new water at new places. Thus the water's chemistry changes gradually by dilution, permitting my body to make gradual adjustments. In uranium-mining areas and other places where wastes may not be adequately disposed of or where disease-causing organisms are prevalent, it is wise to drink bottled waters or other processed beverages. Disinfectant tablets are advisable for camping trips, and boiling water for a few minutes kills most harmful germs. But uranium nuclides, PCBs, and other hazardous wastes in water bodies or groundwater cannot be so readily eliminated—if at all.

Touring with Children, Elderly, and Handicapped

Taking young children on nature tours brings special rewards to both you and them. Most children delight in outdoor scenes, animals, and flowers when they have had positive experiences with them, and to sense their delight increases your own enjoyment. If you are new to parenting or to teaching other people's children at schools, nature centers, or camps, you will profit by reading some of the excellent books on nature study and environmental education, such as Dorothy Shuttleworth's *Sharing Nature with Your Child* and Joseph Cornell's *Sharing Nature with Children*. But here are some preliminary thoughts:

Try to balance what you expect to derive from a tour with what you wish the child to get from it. *You* may wish to add more species of birds to your life list. Fine. But there may be times when *the child* may have much more fun watching a common house sparrow rather than chasing after a bird it is not interested in. Be prepared for some self-sacrifices while remembering that children should not be overindulged.

Consider a child's attention span. You may like to take a half-hour to watch a sunset, but your youngster may enjoy it for only one minute and then want to play hide-and-seek. Being prepared with a picture book, pad of paper and crayons, cards, or a simple boxed puzzle may permit you to contemplate your sunset a little longer. Portable magnetic chess or checkers sets are enjoyed by many older children and afford good interplay with adults.

Some people tour with radios and portable televisions to serve as children's entertainers. Youngsters should be taught to play them at sound levels that do not interfere with enjoyment of the out-of-doors by others. Electronic games are available in miniature these days, portable enough even for some backpacking. But if your reasons for nature touring include developing in your child a sensitivity for and attachment to nature, you will probably want to minimize technology and emphasize resourcefulness and imagination in playing with objects in the natural environment. Our forebears' games such as Pick-up-sticks (also called Jackstraws) and Odd-or-even, played with pebbles, acorns, or any little natural objects, obviate having to truck along gadgetry and also can teach lessons about nature in a delightfully informal way.

When children are old enough, having a hand lens along for special observations can be a treat. Make sure it has a sturdy cord to go around the child's neck each time it is used; a bright plastic tag at the top of the loop helps prevent its loss between uses. Thirty seconds of peeping through it may suffice for a 3-year-old. A 6-year-old boy may want to keep it for 10 minutes, perhaps just to feel important. A 12-year-old girl genuinely interested in nature may be responsible enough to have her own hand lens, and the lifetime of pleasure studying natural history that goes with it.

A monocular field glass or pocket telescope adds little burden on a trip and can contribute immensely to fun and knowledge. Children at first need help in using these: Teach them to look first at the object to be observed and then put the instrument to their eye while doing so, rather than look first through the glass and then wiggle it around trying to find the object. Practice before a tour can give a child a feeling of helping with the preparations. Binoculars should be similarly used. As described later, both monoculars and binoculars can be used in reverse position to serve as a magnifying glass.

Cameras are wonderful tools for helping young people focus on scenes and their environmental components. Again, helping a child learn to use the camera before starting on tour is beneficial. The child should appreciate the cost of film and prints as well as the initial cost of the camera. Some light-hearted informal instruction with the camera can greatly increase the satisfaction that picture taking gives.

For all the paraphernalia of books, crayons, paper, games, and optical equipment, adult help will be needed to plan packing, transportation, and use. Suitable containers must be devised, preferably light in weight, sturdy, and easy of access. Milk cartons cut partially open sometimes make efficient containers for carrying and storage in cars and even backpacks. But when on tour, most children will need regular help to keep their things in order.

What children eat depends on the age and health of the children. Foods range from mother's milk to large amounts of peanut butter for fast-growing teenagers; and home-cooked meals in a recreation vehicle are different from dehydrated, partially prepared foods carried by backpackers. Between-meal snacks can ease the tedium youngsters sometimes feel on trips. Dried fruits are recommended. Chocolate bars are good for special times when a quick energy stimulus is called for, but sweets usually need careful monitoring. One family I know who drives a lot in late spring and early summer takes fresh peas still in the pod; the children like to shell them and nibble en route. The pods can sometimes be scattered at the destination to lay out a follow-me trail through natural habitats or even an old-fashioned, but biodegradable, "paper chase."

Liquids are important for children as well as for adults. Oranges are often too messy in cars or other conveyances, but juicy apples are fine if cores are put in litter bags or, when hiking or biking, tossed well away from the trail for the benefit of wildlife. Fruit juices in individual cartons can be prechilled in a freezer for short warm-weather trips. And children can be helped to appreciate just plain water, a precious and refreshing natural resource.

If you are traveling by car and eating many meals at restaurants or picnic tables, you may wish to use a commercially available

14

small-child's seat that clamps onto almost any table. A portable stroller also makes a safe seat for a little one. A child's harness and leash can help keep toddlers out of danger and slightly reduce adult supervision. With a recreation vehicle, you may decide to take a playpen along for a toddler.

Small children may need special arrangements for wheeling. Bicycles can be equipped with a seat over the rear wheel; front seats make steering more hazardous with heavier children. For walks around town or in museums and nature centers, a portable stroller increases the child's security and comfort; it also can free your hands for shopping, handling literature, camera, binoculars, whatever; the stroller can sometimes also hold packages or a shed garment as the day warms. A folding luggage cart such as used in airports can do double duty as a small child's stroller if equipped securely with a sturdy box of suitable proportions, perhaps a carton from a local market or package store.

Small children on the trail often need to be carried. When our firstborn was between the ages of 2 and 4, she spent many hours afield on my shoulders while I was doing ecological research for my thesis. Fortunately she was a dainty little thing. We had good companionship though occasionally I would forget she was up there. Today one can buy excellent strap-on carriers for babies and small children to be worn in back or in front. I see many on the trail and often wish I had had one years ago.

Elderly people often have needs somewhat different from those of younger adults with whom they are traveling. Perhaps having experienced much already, these older people may be less concerned with new adventures than with the feelings of security that come with a more reliable schedule. Also a slower pace befits their lower energy levels. If you are younger, you will need to balance their needs and yours, perhaps making more reservations in advance or planning a shorter tour or one with more frequent rest stops and longer pauses. Older people are often more willing to linger and enjoy a scene, if they are comfortable, being less desirous of dashing off to see one new thing after another.

As we age, we often become more conscious of our microclimates. With reduced circulation and lower intake of energy from food, we may feel cold more. We may notice a draft that younger people won't notice. We may need an extra wrap, or express the desire to move out of the wind. Or conversely, we may seek the shade when others are playing in the sun. Exercise can help stimulate circulation and other body functions. When driving or being driven, we should take a stretch or a little walk about once every hour. In a bus, train, or plane, a stroll up and down the aisle is recommended.

When starting out on a trail, as at a nature center, an elderly person may well be concerned about how long a walk lies ahead and whether there will be steep grades or other rough going. He or she may choose to start back over the same route while the rest go ahead. In that case, an understanding should be reached about a comfortable meeting place at an agreed-upon time. (We older people are prone to worry when people do not arrive when expected!) Perhaps one of the party should elect to escort the older person back.

Older persons may need to take more medicines than younger people do. We may or may not want to be reminded to take them but will probably appreciate having a small plastic bottle or covered cup handy for a sip of water when taking a pill. When traveling out of state or in a foreign country, we should have enough medicine for the entire trip; pharmacists often cannot give out medicines prescribed by doctors whom they do not know. And it is good to have prescriptions, anyway, to show a doctor consulted on tour. Prescriptions for eyeglasses also should be taken on trips, in case they are broken or lost. When removing eyeglasses at home, we have well-established habits for setting them down and later retrieving them. On tour, we have to give extra thought to such matters. (At night when camping, I put my glasses in my right boot or moccasin and my flashlight in my left. Thus I cannot walk away shod in the morning forgetting these important items!)

Because a person's bladder becomes less accommodating with age, an older person may like to be near a bathroom or portable toilet at night. When camping, a sleeping bag that will unzip at the bottom without having to unzip the side makes for a more convenient and warmer trip to the latrine because you can walk in your sleeping bag. (Someday I want to have a sleeping bag with a pocket for my flashlight, but my eyeglasses will still go in my boot.)

Handicapped people find touring somewhat easier than it once was, because of today's widespread understanding of their needs and the availability of better facilities such as ramps and restrooms. A travel agent can help plan tours that ensure such facilities. I once had the privilege of camping for a week with a young person who was totally blind. We shared a wonderful experience. I described to him what I saw, and he told me of all he could hear and smell and feel. For both of us that week together extended our awareness of the nature around us—and of each other. May you have a similar happy experience some day.

Some people can get up and go without planning. That may seem easier than planning carefully, but the hardships will probably come later. Nature-sensitive people want to be alert to possibilities, to be prepared, indeed to be sensible. A healthy attitude adds to the richness of any tour. Be prepared to meet nature on its own terms, to merge with it while recognizing that you are a part of it.

II

NATURE'S PATTERNS

2   THE SKY

When I let my cat out the door, he stops halfway out to look around, for dogs probably. His ancestors had to be aware of wolves, coyotes, and other cat-grabbers. But he never looks at the sky overhead. My rooster does, though, cocking his head so that one eye scans the heavens as if watching for hawks. When I step out the door, I usually glance at the sky, not from fear that some animal may eat me, but in joy that the sky is deep blue or smooth gray or puffed by white clouds or, at night, moonlit or sprinkled with stars.

When I lived in cities amid tall buildings, only a crack of sky would show high above the street, scarcely enough to let me know in which direction any clouds, smoke, or flags might be blowing. Then when I went to the suburbs or country I could get a better view of the sky and would rejoice in taking a deep breath of cleaner air. City sky, though, can seem extra precious because there is less of it to be seen, unless you make a trip to a rooftop or visit the waterfront.

We usually think of sky as being high above us. When we have to turn on the windshield wipers, however, we are reminded that actually the sky is all around us, its raindrops telling us that as air is cooled the water vapor in it may be precipitated. At 55 miles an hour on the highway, we sense that we are pushing against invisible gases having considerable density. After pulling into a campground on a clear evening, we may reach for a sweater or other wrap as cool air settles in the valley, cool air being heavier than warm air. A little down-valley breeze, gentle as a zephyr, may waft our barbecue smoke so that we move to the opposite side of our fire, and it may bring to us the aroma of onions in the stew on a neighboring camper's up-valley stove.

If on a summer evening we are cruising by boat, becalmed a mile or more off shore, we may suddenly smell the fir trees or other shore vegetation as the air over the land cools and slides down across the water. This land breeze may begin to fill our idle sails, gently nudging our craft into renewed motion. Camping on a beach on a hot day, we may feel the coolness of a little sea breeze coming over the water as the land heats its overlying atmosphere, thus causing it to rise and suck ashore the heavier, cooler air over the water.

Most of us spend our lives at the bottom of the sky, aware of air when it is too hot or cold, too wet or dry, too windy or too breathless for comfort. When touring, we should seek relaxed moments to enjoy the air when it is just right, perhaps sampling with our noses the intimate air an inch from a rose flower or fragrant viburnum blossom. Sky amid petals? Yes! Big things are always made of little things. The "big sky country" of Montana is made of molecules. Can the grandeur of a complete half-bowl of heaven over the Great Plains be matched by the exquisite perfume of a flower? Perhaps.

Being a New Englander, when not touring I live in Earth's Zone of Prevailing Westerlies, the wind blowing from the west. The sky each day reveals the nature of whatever air mass is riding eastward on these circumplanetary winds. The air mass is a great swirl of gases made more or less visible depending on the amount and condition of the water it holds—in short, either clouded or cloudless. Usually my first minitour of the day is from bed to window for a look at the sky, and sometimes to gaze at the ground to note any new gifts from the sky: dew, frost, puddles, snow.

Today as I write I am in Australia. Opening the trailer ("caravan") door, I was greeted not by yesterday's all-cerulean sky with hot wind from the continental Outback, but by gray clouds borne by a cool south wind from the Tasman Sea. This afternoon sporadic sun shines through gaps between soft-edged cumulus clouds such as one expects in sea-margined climates of New England, old England, New Zealand, Netherlands, and Japan. Clouds give clues to climate. To travel from one climate to another without cloud watching is comparable to visiting a restaurant and failing to sniff the aromas of its kitchen. Why miss the fun, not to mention the useful information imparted by one's senses? As travelers, people on the move, we have many choices to make, for instance about destinations, routes, and suitable clothing. New Englanders touring to the Zone of Prevailing *Easterlies* (or to the Horse Latitudes) had better think at length about what they will need to wear—or not wear! Pretrip study of geography prepares us for sky watching as we go, like roosters, heads cocked with an eye to the sky.

The midcontinental climate of North America is noted for its summer thunderstorms. Midday hot air will pick up water from the Gulf of Mexico, transpired dampness from fields of cotton and corn in the Mississippi Lowlands, or moisture from the Great Lakes. By mid-afternoon, gray-bottomed cumulus clouds may develop into "black-bellies" as updrafts of humid air hump higher and higher to form turreted castles. Their white tops flatten in the gleaming sunlight of cold upper air, but the column of tumultuous air-water has a deeply shadowed bottom, sometimes a threatening purple or even greenish black. Lightning may zag against the increasing darkness as a curtain of rain sweeps down across the countryside. Black-bellies are worth watching and not only for their beauty. They sometimes form tornado funnels. If one ever comes swirling-roaring toward you, get to the best shelter you can. If in a car, drive with cautious speed at right angles to its apparent path of approach; if about to be caught, crawl into a culvert!

Expect fog when warm air passes over cool water, as in the Gulf of Maine or Puget Sound. After a long drive to the coast you may feel car-cramped. A ferry ride or tour boat cruise gives a good change of pace and a chance to watch gulls fly-swim gracefully through their ocean of air. But if you need to stretch your muscles and swivel your joints, rent a rowboat and go rowing. But expect fog.

Fog is a visual softener, obscuring edges and making masses loom mysteriously. Colors lose their intensity. Sounds come from misty nowheres. Odors hitchhike to your nose on tiny water particles that facilitate the remarkable chemistry of smell. Your cheeks sense the chill of the water transmitted by the air. Rest on your oars; feel the fog. Enjoy it.

But fog, this cloud surrounding you, is like the thunderhead and many other aspects of nature: It should be respected. And at times feared. Controlled fear is a healthy emotion designed by evolution to keep us out of trouble. When on fog-prone waters, it is foolish to go without a compass and the knowledge of how to use it. Set a course by it *before* the fog catches you. Realize that fog may trick you. You may think you can gauge the approach of a gray or white fogbank a mile or more away, so that you can reach a harbor before it comes; but while you watch its distant edge, it may also be sneaking in overhead unnoticed until it suddenly shuts down all around you, obscuring all visual clues about direction—except perhaps the set of waves immediately around your boat. Sailors must always keep one eye on the sky as well as on the water. They lead a lilting life on the edge between the ocean of air and the ocean of water, enjoying and fearing both.

A common error when touring is to spend too much of a day in driving or other mechanized travel. An early stop enables you to find the most suitable accommodations for the night and to get a bit settled in your new environs. Then you have time to explore. In a city, I have a naturalist's tendency to head for a park, zoo, aquarium, botanic garden, or natural history museum, perhaps first stopping at a news stand, book store, or library to read a bit about the local possibilities for studying the area's natural resources. But sometimes I just walk, because nature is everywhere and does not have to be jammed into collections open to the public. Sometimes I poke down narrow alleys or inspect the markets to see what fruits, vegetables, and meats are local produce. But often I do the opposite. I search for sky.

One memorable afternoon I arrived in Munich, Germany, and spotted an ancient church. I found the sexton, and he gave me permission to climb the old stone steps to the belfry where I could watch the sun set over the Bavarian city spread below me. What a glorious scene, and what a sky.

Save time for sunsets, especially when in open country. If Earth rotates into its own shadow just at suppertime, perhaps you

24

should take a picnic supper to some hilltop, shore, or center of a field with maximum view of the sky. Bread, cheese, chocolate, and water can in simple manner satisfy while you watch the western horizon tip upward to hide the sinking sun. Clouds lighted from the bottom look delightfully different from those seen during the middle of the day, and of course their colors are redder as the sun's rays are sorted out while going thickwise through Earth's atmosphere, much as a pane of glass may look green when looked through edgewise.

Often the best of a sunset is to the *east*, especially when that is where the clouds are, as when a thunderstorm has rumbled eastward at the close of a hot summer day. Then the last rays of the sun may strike across the landscape to illumine brilliantly some church spire, willow, tasseled corn, or mountain peak seen against the darkness of the black-belly. Nor is the show over then. Linger to watch the fading afterglow.

Twilight invites us to enjoy the night sky with its incredible beauty. After spending all day inside a car, a motel room is in its own way refreshing and relaxing; a country inn can provide hostelry with local culture; your bunk in your trailer or motor home is comforting; but in good weather a sleeping bag spread underneath the sky can be a magic carpet extending your travel of the mind, guided by the star myths of ancients or the most recent reports of astronomers researching planets and galaxies beyond galaxies beyond galaxies. Fall asleep feeling very small and very happy to be touring space on Planet Earth.

3   THE LAY OF THE LAND

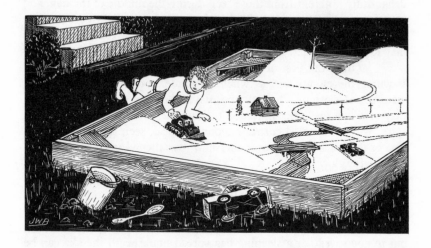

I still like to play in sandboxes, especially if they are not too cluttered with toy cars, odd pieces of wood, rusty pails, and spoons stolen from the kitchen. "Play" is not quite the right word, though, when one has to get the sandbox clean for a fresh start. The one I most recently played in had been long neglected. Not only were witchgrass runners sneaking into it under the wooden sides, but sharp thistles also thought it a good place to grow.

A clean sandbox is a great place to lay out a tour. First level the sand so it is flat and smooth. Then sit and think. How about a mountain? Perhaps one big, perfect volcano all by itself—or a mountain range or two? Maybe low, rounded mountains like the ancient Appalachians; maybe jagged ones like the youthful Rocky Mountains, the Cascades, the Andes, and the Alps. After a little planning, get to work with a spoon and a toy bulldozer and change that flat sand into a world of hills and valleys, with straight roads crossing the valleys and twisty mountain roads climbing up through passes between the low-lands, and a plain reaching to a far plateau in the northwest corner by the clothesline. If you don't have a small toy car to tour the roads you've made, get a stick about the size of your thumb, climb into its driver's seat, and off you go. Tomorrow add dried weeds for trees, stones for buildings, and lots more.

Basic to any landscape of course are its flats, ups, and downs. Even Kansas, eastern Colorado, the Texas coastal plain, and the Australian Outback are not all flat, nor is the yard behind your house or the paved road in front. Water poured on an almost-flat area, if it doesn't sink in, will find low spots and form a temporary stream or puddle. If you have a family with small children, you can have lots of fun planning a tour with road maps (or navigation charts for sailors!) and then making a minirelief map in the back yard with soil or snow, to help the youngsters visualize what landforms and waterforms to look for on your tour. If there is no yard to mess up for educational purposes, perhaps you can get to a beach for castle building. No beach? Then try a microscale model made of chocolate pudding, with streams and lakes of milk.

If you just do not have time for a pretour study, perhaps you have a youngster who will delight in researching the landscapes toward which you are heading and then will rejoice in being the "landform authority" during the tour.

Landforms, both big and little, have more or less distinct outlines, often best seen when the sun is low in a clear sky and casts long, dark shadows. If there is a small ant hill in your yard or a neighboring parking lot, watch it at different times of day. If nobody is around, or if you don't care what any onlooker may think, get your face down nearly to ant level and look sideways at the hill to note the *angle of repose* of the grains from which it is built. Particles of different size and shape have typical angles of slope, and they cannot be piled steeper than this angle without slumping (at least when dry). Be prepared to enjoy the many slopes you will see in your travels, including road cuts, sand dunes, stream banks, and mountainsides.

Nature has two ways of making landforms, by *construction* and by *destruction*. Ant hills and volcanoes are built up; so are many other kinds of mountains such as the uplifted Front Range of the Rockies in

27

Colorado and the Wasatch Range in Utah. But no sooner is a landform pushed up but nature begins its destructive carving by wind, water, animals, and gravity. The destruction, however, is itself creative, making landform patterns such as deltas, alluvial fans, and the jumbled rock piles called talus or screes on the sides of steep mountains. So as you travel, you can watch for *constructional landforms* and *destructional landforms*, plus of course many which combine the two, for example an old volcanic cone furrowed by erosion, or a plateau of sedimentary rocks once smoothly deposited on an ancient sea bed but later uplifted by heavings of Earth's crust and now dissected by down-cutting streams. Indeed there is much to watch for!

Hiking with a heavy pack gives us a feel of the landscape's ups and downs; our leg muscles and leaning bodies relate steepness of a grade even better than do our eyes. Bicycling too feeds us excellent information when we need to downshift gears or tug harder on the handlebars as a level stretch of road almost imperceptibly becomes a rise, or when we bend lower with rested pedals to swoop down a hill.

Driving an automobile is an exciting way to explore landforms. In the 1920s our ancient Model T would occasionally require a low gear-ratio to conquer a hill. The foot pedal would be thrust down, attended by much rattling and grinding of gear teeth, and the car would slowly climb. For a very steep hill it might require turning the Ford around and crawling up backwards in its very low-geared reverse! Sporty little modern cars can give us the fun of manual shifting as we, the car, and the topography attain a happy feeling of unity. Cars with automatic shifts and other computer-programmed controls remove much of our sensitivity to the ups and downs of roads; foot pressure on accelerator and brake may be minimal and thus deprive us of sensory messages to our consciousness. On the other hand, riding as passengers we are freed entirely from operating the vehicle and happily are at liberty to use our eyes to look around far more than would be safe for a driver to do.

Although few memories ever survive earliest infancy, probably our earliest perceptions of three-dimensional form are of a mother's contours when we were nursing babies. My earliest recollection, however, comes from a little later during a crib-confined day. Bored with my bottle, I turned my attention to the adjacent wallpaper on which I somehow dribbled the remaining milk to make a darker pattern. Behind it the softened plaster became gougeable even for my infant finger. In my memory I can see that hole now, my first appreciable altering of my environment beyond the confines of my crib. Sculpting—in spite of my first remembered scolding—has enticed me ever since, especially when observing the natural carvings and modelings of Earth's surface. Follow the brief suggestions below for observing constructional and destructional landforms, and you may enjoy them more as you travel.

Watch for the levelest lands that are almost as flat as an ocean horizon. Absolutely flat land is rare, even when smoothed over and hard-topped by road builders. A good road has a crown, the highest part, usually in the middle with gentle slopes to the side to ensure that water falling on it flows at right angles to the traffic rather than creating problems by running along it. Even a well-made parking lot is not truly flat; it tips slightly to a storm drain or well-vegetated area where the runoff will not make a gully, a destructional landform. The most level landforms have been deposited by water, for example the lake beds (playas) in arid regions like Arizona. They make people want to race cars.

Watch too for the nearly level floodplains of mature streams. ("Stream" is the geologists' term for any flowing water, be it river, brook, or dribble down a windshield.) A mature stream has been around long enough to loop along, carving sideways into its banks and in the process leveling the land. When a mature river or brook floods over its banks, friction with the earth slows the current, reduces the energy for transporting sediment, and makes it deposit some of it. The bank may thus be built up as a natural levee while beyond it and lower than it the floodplain is enriched by a fresh deposit of silt. These floodplain soils are excellent for agriculture because of both their fertility and their levelness. Floodplains are fine also for outdoor recreation, parks, playgrounds, wildlife sanctuaries, and boat-launching and swimming areas, but floodplains should *not* be used for permanent buildings. ("The floodplain belongs to the river" is not a well enough known saying.) The river will probably flood again, perhaps disastrously for people who have used its floodway foolishly, and nobody can tell just when. Many a mobile home has been demolished by floods—tourists' trailers and tents too!

If you must camp on that temptingly flat floodplain, be ready to pull out at very short notice. In arid regions, a heavy thunderstorm on ground little protected by vegetation may spawn a flash flood miles away, without a cloud as a warning to you. In such country it is wise never to camp on a floodplain, or a dry streambed, or on a *low* natural terrace ("bench"), even if others are doing so. They may be from humid regions where flash floods occur only in hilly areas. Sensitivity to nature's patterns may mean not only joy but also survival.

Great diversity of landforms may be encountered when you travel long distances, as when crossing a continent. To deal with the many kinds of landscapes, geographers speak of *physiographic regions*, extensive areas with similar landforms. For instance, in touring from New Jersey to California, you pass through the Eastern Coastal Plain, Piedmont, Appalachian Mountains, Central Lowland with its Mississippi Valley, Great Plains, Rocky Mountains, Great Basin, Sierras, Central Valley of California, and Coast Ranges. Each is interesting and beautiful. But even on short trips within one physiographic region you can note lesser landforms, rejoicing in the snugness of little valleys and the open-to-the-sky exaltation of small hilltops, no two of which are just the same. Individual landforms are like individual people: They are special when we take the trouble of seeing them as special.

4 ROCKS

One of my earliest remembered explorations, when I was between 3 and 4 years old, took me to a rock outcrop about 50 feet behind our house. It was a scramble-up-and-jump-off sort of place, about 5 feet high, gradually sloped on the east but steep to the west. Also it had a mystery hole, about one fingerwidth wide and one fingerlength deep, sometimes with water in it and sometimes with a spider! That was my first meaningful rock. Later we children played King of the Castle on it—high adventure. When older, I concluded that the hole had been drilled by an early farmer quarrying the granite for a stonework, because many times in touring to other places I saw similar signs of how old-timers bored into rock outcrops to split off slabs for foundations, doorsteps, and hearthstones.

Pebbles as well as outcrops are pieces of Planet Earth's rocky crust, bits broken off and ground up by nature's many methods of turning big pieces into little ones. One of my earliest lessons in architecture and home design occurred on our gravel driveway. In late spring, my father raked it to repair the minigullies of the March mud season. Smoothed places were ideal for laying out rows of pebbles, the walls and partitions of little houses built for imaginary inch-tall people who, no doubt, lived in the oak woods behind the stone wall flanking the driveway.

That stone wall ran all across our New England town, marking the boundary of a grant from the king of England. I didn't know that in my early teens when I carelessly tumbled the stones aside to please my collie so that she could exchange teeth-barings with a dug-in and very defensive woodchuck. I didn't think then of all the sweaty labor Seth Mason and his neighbor had invested in piling those rocks some 250 years before, building probably an average of 16 feet of wall a day with the help of an ox and chain.

Stone walls are more meaningful to me now, after studying geology and mineralogy, and after noting an almost infinite variety of walls on three continents. I have often wondered about the rocks they were composed of and the people who constructed them. May wall watching give you as much joy as you travel as it has me.

If you are hiking or biking, you can easily pause to inspect a gray stone wall. Its stones, though, may not be gray! Its color may depend more on the kinds of lichens growing on it. Crusty gray lichens and speckled black ones may be oversplotched with spangles of gray-green parmelia lichens or orange wall lichens, and perhaps with the more velvety green mosses on the stones' shadier and moister surfaces. If—without vandalizing the wall's beauty and integrity, and with the owner's permission—you crack open a stone to see what it is made of, you may find a bright pink granite, a blue shale, or a white limestone. (When breaking rock, always protect your eyes with glasses or goggles.)

If you are touring by car, bus, or train, watch for walls that parallel your line of travel. Watch especially along old roads that have evolved along aborigines' trails, paths later fenced to restrain settlers' livestock being driven along country lanes to pasture or market. You may have to look long and intently to spot a stone fence paralleling a modern multilane highway! Watch for walls angling off from your travel route. If they could talk, they would have their own stories of property ownership and land use; perhaps you can guess their reasons for running as they do.

Rocks

Travelers who tarry to question hear many a good story. If there is a rock wall or brick wall where you stop to camp or lodge, perhaps you can locate people with a little time to share their knowledge about its recent history or maybe even about its geological past. Your listening may be rewarded by some fascinating information. "My great, great grandfather brought those bricks from Ireland in his clipper ship, as ballast for his load of linens." Yes, bricks are reconstituted rocks, manmade recyclings of clays triturated long ago by rushing torrents of mountain brooks or glacial streams. So do ask about brick walls as well as about rock fences.

Human history has always been based on Earth history. Trails and older roads have of necessity adapted to any formidable rocks along their way, winding among outcrops and boulders, seeking low passes through mountains, or following up a ravine to conquer an escarpment. While touring such routes, it's fun to imagine the first people to pioneer these paths and roads, to note the rock structures that they had to skirt. One extreme example is Raton Pass in Colorado; the first covered wagons going west had to be eased with ropes down the very steep slopes.

Whether on old roads or new, the major landforms you see are formed of rocks, though often not visible because covered by soil, vegetation, or human culture. Sometimes they form eternal-looking masses, great portions of continents, for instance the Laurentian Shield of very ancient rocks in eastern Canada, the Deccan of India, and strings of mountain ranges like the Rockies, Andes, and Himalayas. But, given geologic time, rocks can be comminuted to gravels, sands, silts, and clays and deposited as sediments along streams and in beds of lakes and oceans. With more time the particles may be reconsolidated to form new rocks: *sedimentary rocks, igneous rocks,* and *metamorphic rocks,* more or less visible to passersby.

How fast you pass of course partly determines what you see of anything, rocks included. Wheeling along without stopping you can often note the grandeur of rock formations of the three major kinds, though details must wait for more leisurely, closer admiration. From high-speed highways you can watch for major landforms and for outcroppings at road cuts where modern engineers have refused to be intimidated by nature's rock.

33

Igneous Rocks have been born of Earth's internal fires (compare the word *ignited*) deep below the crust. Some igneous formations, granites for example, have cooled slowly while buried and insulated by overlying rocks. Their minerals have had time to grow large crystals. Outcroppings at the surface today have been unburied by geologic ages of erosion or by upheavings of Planet Earth's mountain-making processes. In humid climates, mountains called *monadnocks* are sometimes made of granitoid rocks resistant to erosion; they stand conspicuously above the countryside of less durable rocks and thus are visible to fast-moving travelers.

In contrast, some igneous rocks have formed at Earth's surface, poured out as flows of volcanic lava congealing into such rocks as dark-colored basalt, cooled so fast that only small crystals have formed. Perhaps somewhere you can spot a basalt cliff with its long, vertical joints created as the rock cooled and as weathering enlarged the cracks. Or someday you may see the grotesque rocks of the "channeled scablands" of the Columbia Plateau in eastern Washington State.

Other igneous rocks have been hot-hurled into the air by volcanoes to settle as ash, pumice, or a glass called obsidian. These may be harder to note in passing but do outcrop here and there. But if you stop and look more closely at any naturally outcropping rocks, in time you may spy the large crystals of granites and veins of minerals that often streak through them, or spot the volcanic glass, perhaps vitreous "Job's Tears," that fell from the sky during an eruption.

Sedimentary Rocks are those most easily recognized as you move past them fast. Their layering is often conspicuous, showing coarser and finer textures of sands and gravels deposited by water whose rates of flow varied with circumstances of weather and season. Some sedimentary rocks were formed of wind-deposited particles that similarly reveal layering ("bedding"). The strata may be nearly horizontal, even for many miles, as under Kansas and eastern Colorado; or gently tipped as in the Cincinnati Dome of southern Ohio and northern Kentucky; or markedly slanted in areas of tilted uplift as in the Black Hills of South Dakota and in many other mountains of the western United States. Perhaps you can find sedimentary rocks that are cross-bedded, with some strata at angles to other beds because of changing environmental conditions during their deposit.

Textures of sedimentary rocks are used to classify them. *Conglomerates* include gravels; *sandstones* are made mostly of sands; *shales* (also called mudstones) have come from silt and clay; and *limestones* have been derived from shells of aquatic organisms. Limestones appear massive, with little visible layering, as one passes by them. Formed as they were under water, weather and seasons affected them less markedly in their more constant environment.

Metamorphic Rocks include any which have been markedly altered by heat, pressure, and/or chemical changes. They may previously have been igneous, sedimentary, or metamorphic rocks in an earlier stage. Their contorted strata and their varied patterns of color and light and dark minerals may easily catch your attention and lead you to look more closely. When you have time you may want to study geology and mineralogy to satisfy your new fascination with the history of our planet's crust. Typical metamorphic rocks are "schists" and "gneisses."

As I write this paragraph, I'm sitting in my favorite writing place, a nook in a cliff on the edge of Penobscot Bay in Maine. This niche perches in a little indentation of the shore between two rocky points about 30 feet apart, forming what I call "Hesperides Cove." I'm tempted to describe the rocks surrounding me here, the massive, rusty-painted igneous felsite shot through with horizontal "sills" and vertical "dikes" of metamorphic rocks. It is a place so special in form and color, so lichen-decorated above and seaweed-festooned below; it is so adamant in its stance against the sea, yet so fractured, chipped away by frost and crashed against by storms. This rocky Hesperides Cove typifies uncounted other rocky places, ones just as special if only you take time to give them close attention.

You can delight in rocks because of their shapes and surfaces, perhaps seeing imaginary faces in their profiles or imagining a "queen's bathtub" hollowed in a streambed where a stone has tumbled around for many centuries. You can rejoice in the rusty, iron-oxidized yellows and reds of a level-topped desert mesa or a slant-topped cuesta and watch them turn from purple to black as the sun sets. Such experiences may make you an enthusiastic lifetime rock watcher.

But maybe you want to get to know rocks more intimately. Geologists say never try to identify a rock until you have cracked it open to observe a fresh surface. If your curiosity impels you to thus study a fragment of Planet Earth, be *sure* to protect your eyes with glasses or goggles to avoid any blinding splinters. Then as you gaze at the freshly exposed surface, you may realize that you are looking at something never before seen by human eyes. You don't have to find a gem inside to value it, nor do you have to join the "pet rock" faddists. You may want to analyze your rock by using geologists' tests for hardness, weight, luster, and color—including the color when it is powdered by scratching it on a white "streak plate." If your specimen cooled slowly enough to have crystals, you may become absorbed with the crystalline angles used by mineralogists to classify minerals.

For one reason or another you may wish to take a rock home. Think twice, though. Can the place where it lies spare it? Suppose others also take pieces. Will the place be visually defaced? Will it suffer increased erosion? In some states, New York for instance, it is illegal to remove stones from along the highway. Nor are stones to be removed from most parks and Indian reservations without permission. As an example of thoughtfulness, you can help protect our natural resources, which so often suffer from the need and greed of Earth's ever-growing population.

An old saying among geologists is that every beginner needs a truck. Perhaps nature can spare here and there a stone large enough to add to your souvenir garden wall. But whenever possible collect only what geologists call a "hand specimen," usually one not more than 1 to 2 in. (2 to 5 cm) on each side. If you cannot find a loose piece of such dimensions, cut one off a larger rock by using a hammer and cold chisel (and of course wear glasses or goggles). A hammer alone is less suitable; the chisel is needed because it permits a cracking pressure to be applied at precisely the desired spot, avoiding damage to a valuable crystal or especially pretty surface. Each specimen should be wrapped in paper, with a label giving date and site, and be carefully placed in a bag or box for the trip home. You should not need a truck!

I well remember the lake shore in Montana where my wife and I first caught "agate fever." Wading at the edge admiring the pebbles in the water, she called me—"Come see!" Here and there a pebble of exceptional color, pattern, and glassy luster, indeed translucence, showed its beauty unlike that of the duller stones familiar to us on our

New England coast. Above the waterline the pebbles looked less al-luring—until we wetted them with saliva, a practical method though not genteel in some surroundings. Agates, quartzy stones named after a river in Sicily, are hard to resist capturing, but I have enjoyed taking color pictures of them as they lie in very shallow, calm water, leaving them to decorate the shore.

Pebbles do not need to be agates to be collectible. When you return home you can put a few pet pebbles in a glass dish of water as a centerpiece, a change from flowers; but like flowers they need fresh water to keep them sparkling and to avoid cloudiness from dust and bacteria. Some people exhibit their souvenir pebbles dry after coating them with a varnish or lacquer. For permanent shine, you can buy a rotary tumbler with grinding powders to polish your little stones.

A naturalist couple whom I know has toured the United States, Canada, and Mexico many times. As they travel, they easily make acquaintances with curious youngsters—under the supervision of the children's parents, of course—and delight them with gifts of a few polished pebbles. They accompany their gifts with a little story about some phase of mineralogy or geology, hydrology or climatology, or the like, often with some spider lore thrown in for added intrigue if they find spider-egg cases on nearby rocks. This kind couple has positively touched innumerable youngsters. Perhaps you can do the same, helping others to see more and appreciate more of the nature around them.

5 SOILS

You don't have to go far to find soil. Right now there may be a bit under a fingernail, or in the dirty-clothes hamper, or in a corner of the window sill, or on your cat's fur where she is licking it. A little tour around the house, even a very clean house, may reveal more soil—or should we say "dirt"?

One definition of dirt is "matter in the wrong place." The word "soil" is best saved for the ground-up rock that plants grow in, as in flower pots, gardens, fields, and forests. So in this book, soil means ground-up rock, preferably in "the right place."

But soil is more than bits of rock. Between those little pieces is air or water, usually both. When water fills all the little pore-spaces between the grains of rock, we say it is "water-logged" or "saturated." Only rarely is there only dry air between the rock particles. Usually at least an invisible film of water coats the bits of mineral matter, enough to let some very specialized plants, for example beach grasses of sand dunes, get the water they need to live.

In addition to bits of rock, air, and water, most soils have organic matter, that is, dead materials from plants and animals—perhaps the wing-cover of a ground beetle, the after-breakfast droppings of a rabbit, rotting oak leaves, or acids from wet pine needles. Most soils also include living organisms, but many are too small to see without a microscope. Some larger animals spend a part of their lives in soil—gophers, woodchucks, and earthworms.

Of course, the roots of plants live their hidden lives down in soil, holding on for dear life and drinking from the soil's water the chemicals they need. Plants are an important part of almost all soils where there is water enough for life. Often in humid regions they completely cover the soil and prevent our seeing it.

So to see the soil when you travel through humid regions you have to watch for places where nature or people have removed some of the concealing vegetation. Watch for streambanks where water has cut into them, giving a side view of the soil. Soil scientists (pedologists) call such a section a *soil profile*. Over the years, the bank-top vegetation and animals have probably contributed enough organic matter to make a layer of *litter* (not the unsightly kind discarded by too many tourists). In grasslands, instead of litter we use the word *thatch* for the accumulated organic matter.

In a bank's soil profile, beneath the litter or thatch, a layer of soil has probably been darkened by organic materials washed down from above or dragged down by earthworms and broken down by the life processes of the multitude of little soil organisms. Here, where the organic matter is well incorporated with the mineral particles, pedologists call the material *humus*. Roots of most plants are very happy in the humus layer. Often rich in nutrients, it enables soil to hold a good balance of air and water.

A streambank profile if cut deep enough may show lower layers of soil composed almost entirely of mineral particles (plus whatever air and water may occupy pore-spaces). These "subsoils" may either have developed from the weathering of underlying rock, making *residual soils*, or they have been deposited on the underlying rock by streams, by water near the bottoms of ponds, lakes, or oceans, by wind, or by ice during some past glaciation; these are *transported soils*.

You may find a place where an eroding stream has revealed the underlying bedrock from which residual soil has been created or on which a transported soil has been deposited.

Along roads you can often see soils exposed in roadcuts where contractors have lowered the grade to make for easier travel. If freshly dug, the profile may be similar to that of a stream-cut bank. But soil thus exposed tends to erode unless covered, so road crews may have mulched it with hay, straw, coarse gravel, or netting; or it may have been seeded with grasses and legumes (pulses); or planted with trees and shrubs; or riprapped with stones to stabilize it. Of course all such treatments of roadcuts will more or less hide the soil, as will nature's own methods of replanting them with spores, seeds, and invading roots. As you tour you can watch banks for both the destructive and the healing processes carried on by nature and people.

Soils of cultivated fields reveal much about the land through which you are touring. For instance, consider their colors. In school teachers used to tell us, "Color the sky blue. Color the grass green. Color the earth brown." Many soils certainly are brown, which is a dull kind of orange. Some soils are yellower, and some redder then strict orange; some are lighter and some darker then pure orange at its brightest, most intense hue. When you have learned to observe many of the subtleties of brown (orange!), then you notice much about soils that you were unaware of before.

But wait! All soils are not brown. Soils range from red to blue. Some are green, some purple (even though faintly so). Where I am now writing at Hesperides Cove, "down east" in Maine, I am looking at blue-gray soil where storm waves have excavated the bank from under the huckleberry bushes and spruces. These ash-colored soils (*podzols*) are typical of areas under cone-bearing trees where acidic soil waters have removed the rusty iron compounds or where a cold climate has prevented the iron in the soil from becoming rusty by contact with the oxygen of the air. You can sometimes find thin layers of similar light gray to white soils farther south, as under pitch pines on sandy Cape Cod in Massachusetts and in New Jersey.

You can find the reddest soils in hot climates. There, oxygen combines readily with the soil's iron to create almost blood-red *laterite* soils. But red soils in cooler climates have most likely developed from sedimentary rocks deposited long ago when the climate was much hotter, times in earth history that geologists call periods of "redbed formation"—for instance in the Triassic Era when dinosaurs left footprints in the red muds of the Connecticut River Valley and other hang-outs of those "ruling reptiles."

Soils that are dark brown to almost black have originated where grasses have held sway for centuries, as in the prairies and plains of central North America, central Europe, and the pampas of South America. Rich soils are excellent for agriculture and grazing, for example the black earths of South Dakota and Iowa, called *chernozems*, and the *chestnut* soils to their south. You can look for the gradual soil transition zones if you tour from the podzols of northern Minnesota southward to Texas and New Mexico.

In hot, dry regions such as the deserts of Arizona, the soils are for the most part pale, strongly reflecting the day's intense sunlight under the brilliantly blue sky. In places the pebbles, often with the finer soil particles blown away by desert winds, have a lacquered appearance known as "desert varnish," their surfaces having been long exposed to solar radiation. In some places, especially in dry lake beds, the soil is white with alkaline salts glaring back at the cloudless sky. Occasionally a bank's profile shows a horizontal band of white indicating where lay an ancient lake bed later covered by darker sediments.

Much of the great visual beauty of deserts derives from the colors of their bare rocks and barren soils unobscured by vegetation as in humid regions. For best viewing of a desert, I recommend being alone outdoors in it for 24 hours. You will see that the color of rock and soil, far from constant, changes with the quality of sunlight at dawn, midday, and dusk, and of moonlight or starlight at night. Yes, in summer it does make some sense to dash across a desert at night when it is cool, to sooner enjoy the mountains or the ocean on the far side. But that is a little like gulping down a juicy steak so that you can the sooner enjoy ice cream. There is much to enjoy in deserts, including their beautiful soils. Linger if you can.

Indian cultures of the American Southwest have produced artists with great sensitivity to their surrounding nature, of which they so wisely feel an integral part. Through their religions, which recognize the wholeness and holiness of their environment, they have for centuries expressed their perceptions of nature through their sand paintings. Tourists are fortunate when they can buy a plastic-protected sand painting to remind them later of the beauty of desert soils and of the Native Americans who have developed such meaningful cultures on them.

Eurasians brought a metal culture to North America, and it largely supplanted the mostly stone culture of Amerindians. One major result has been the development and wholesale use of metal tools and machines to remove much of the native vegetation. As metal saws have felled the forests, so have metal plows destroyed the prairie turfs. Now as you tour our continent you can observe hundreds of square miles of bared soil. The same is true of other continents where lands once grazed by native animals and imported livestock have subsequently been plowed for cropland. Depending on the season and planting schedule of the farmers, these lands readily reveal not only their soil colors but also the values and attitudes of those who cultivate them. Sometimes they are influenced primarily by traditional folkways, but often they are ruled by the relentless pressures of short-term economics and the debilitating struggle for financial survival. Today the resulting desertification threatens the lives of millions of people in Africa, South and Central America, and Asia, people who share our Planet Earth.

As you travel across farmlands, look for soils that are well cared for, protected by cover crops, mulched, or left fallow when not planted to a productive crop. Watch for grassed waterways through tilled fields that let stormwater and meltwater trickle instead of run down hill, which causes erosion of priceless topsoil. Keep an eye out for rows of trees and shrubs making windbreaks in open country to minimize erosion of soil by wind. Be aware of mistreated land where little rills of water are beginning to form gullies in the fields and where subsoil thus removed from them is fanning out over good topsoil in low places or is silting in ponds.

Have regard for soil as you travel. Think of it not as ground-up rock which just lies there. Appreciate it as a life-giving, dynamic mix of bits of rock with its components of air, water, organic matter, and living organisms—a very thin and complex mixture to be handled gently when the native vegetation is removed.

6 NATURAL VEGETATION

Secret places! For children, Hide-and-Seek combines the excitement of stalking and of being chased with the surprise of being found. The "seeker" hunts for the "hiders"—Where are they? Maybe under the bed? In the corner behind the bureau? Behind daddy's coat in the coat closet? And the out-of-doors has many more possibilities, especially for country children. Tall grasses can hide little folk; and even mid-grasses can permit crawling trails. Highbush blueberries, rhododendrons, viburnums, and many other shrubs give secretive cover to older children whose primitive instincts relish ambushes more elaborate than the toddler's delight in saying "Boo!"

Natural vegetation also provides children with outlets for sequestering instincts. How satisfying it can be to find some natural spot in which to be alone for a time, undisturbed, unregulated, unsupervised by parents or teachers or peers. I still like to curl against the base of a forest tree, to stretch back-to-ground amid prairie grasses, to slip my canoe into a curtaining stand of cattails, or to climb a tall pine and thus be removed, remote, relaxed, especially after a long walk or bike trip through city and suburbs to reach the country, or after a day's drive on busy highways.

Natural vegetation can thus be relished intimately, much as our most distant ancestors evolved with the plants supplying their psychological needs along with food, fiber, and medicine. Today the Earth's crowding populations need wilderness more than ever. Of course we often like best what we are accustomed to. Many tourists from cities favor a trailer camp with close-packed recreation vehicles, bright lights, and television. If you are such a person, here is a challenge: After supper some evening seek the most natural corner of your trailer park, perhaps the boundary fence on which you can lean with your back to the noise of human bustle. Listen to the crickets; watch the birds go to roost in a tree; and maybe linger until the stars shine.

Plants are less than intimate when seen from a jet plane 30,000 feet or more above them. But often the big patterns of our world are triggers to our curiosity. Far below we note indistinctly the blue-gray of forests or the orange-red of deserts, in patches or expanses determined by climate, landforms, and human activity. When thus flying from city to city we may resolve to travel the route some day by auto or bicycle to appreciate the vegetation at closer range.

For many of us living in the United States, the plants we live among are ones introduced from other lands, for instance sidewalk plane trees and lindens from Europe, flame trees from Africa, lawn grasses from Europe, or corn from Central America. Many wildflowers brightening our roadsides have come from Europe: daisies, dandelions, hawkweeds, chicory, several clovers, and many others. To find native American vegetation, we may have to go to areas specially set aside in parks, sanctuaries, and wildlife refuges; in these protected places native plants live in their natural communities with native animals, for instance the national parks among the Florida Everglades, the California Redwoods, and in the Great Smoky Mountains.

Fortunately many other smaller, relatively natural areas have been dedicated for preservation. If you are not already acquainted with the parks of your own town, a quick tour to find them is recommended; or if you live in a large city, you can start by contacting its park department and asking for a map of its parks and other recreation areas; then you can visit them to look for relatively natural vegetation. You can also ask your community library for any materials written about local natural areas, including wildlife and wildflower sanctuaries.

After such preliminary touring around town or city, you may decide on one area in which to search for plant communities that seem to represent natural assemblages of plants. What to look for will of course depend upon the region where you live. In Florida you would hunt for remnants of subtropical forests, sawgrass everglades, mangrove swamps, or stands of bald-cypress. In Maine, where vast areas of coniferous forest still exist, you would seek near your town or city places that might have escaped the successive lumberings, which gave Maine the name "Pine Tree State." In western Washington State, you might discover locally a patch of giant Douglas firs and sitka spruces, and in southern Arizona the grotesquely beautiful saguaro cacti. And in between these four corners of the United States, countless other types of native vegetation invite your inspection and enjoyment.

Looking for still-natural places is treasure-hunting! What is so precious about natural areas? For one thing, we tend to appreciate what is rare. You remember the old saying about not appreciating water until the well runs dry? Today the supply of natural vegetation is diminishing fast. Time is short for experiencing nature as our forebears knew it, even as tiny remnants. So now is the time to get up and go look for these treasures, these living museums.

When we tour we are seeking change. Natural areas supply change of a special sort: They present us with landscapes that have not been designed by people. They are "doing their own thing" in the miraculous ways that nature has evolved. They present us with sights, sounds, smells, and feelings that are not being bought and sold. Although we may get tired traveling to natural areas, the chances are we shall come away refreshed by experiencing them.

Fortunately there are organizations to direct you to these special places. To be sure to include some natural areas in your travels, you can first find out where some of them are and read about them. The following sources will be glad to help you.

International Governmental Agencies

To find out about government-controlled natural areas in countries other than the United States, a first step is to contact their embassies.

National Governmental Agencies

In the United States, federal agencies with tracts of natural vegetation include the U.S. Department of Agriculture's Forest Service and the Department of the Interior's Bureau of Land Management, Fish and Wildlife Service, and National Park Service. Their publications are on sale from the U.S. Government Printing Office, Washington, DC 20242. Write the GPO well ahead of your tour and ask as specifically as possible for literature about natural areas in the region you expect to visit. It will mail you a bibliography from which to choose the appropriate publications; you then send an order to the GPO. A sometimes quicker method is to contact local or regional offices of these agencies, finding addresses in a telephone book. They can supply information about your locale or region and may be able to give you addresses of offices in other regions where you expect to tour.

State governments increasingly have agencies responsible for natural areas. Again, a telephone book is a good first step toward locating them and finding what information they can provide about native vegetation.

Private International Organizations

Friends of the Earth has branches in over twenty different countries. Contact its office in San Francisco, listed in the next section under private U.S. organizations.

The Internationl Union for the Protection of Nature and Natural Resources has its main office at Avenue du Mont Blanc, 1196 Gland, Switzerland, with its Commission on National Parks and Protected Areas (CNPPA). It can supply the names and locations of over

150 unique areas on the World Heritage List, which was initiated by a UNESCO convention in 1972.

The Nature Conservancy (see under private U.S. organizations) has an International Office at 1785 Massachusetts Avenue, N.W., Washington DC 20036 (202-483-0231).

The Sierra Club (see under private U.S. organizations) has an International Office at 228 East 45th Street, New York, NY 10017.

Private United States Organizations

The American Forestry Association is "dedicated to the protection and intelligent use of the nation's forests and related resources." It publishes the popular monthly *American Forests* and has regional representatives in Beaverton, Oregon, and Atlanta, Georgia. Contact the Association at 1319 Eighteenth Street, N.W., Washington, DC, 20036 (202-467-5810).

Friends of the Earth has for its motto a quotation from poet Robinson Jeffers: " . . . the greatest beauty is organic wholeness, the wholeness of life and things, the divine beauty of the universe. Love that, not man apart from that . . . ," indicating the organization's concern for natural areas. It publishes a monthly newsmagazine, *Not Man Apart*. Contact: 1045 Sansome Street, San Francisco, CA 94111 (415-433-7373).

National Audubon Society publishes the well-known *Audubon Magazine*, which often includes articles about natural vegetation and its wildlife. It also has offices worldwide. Contact: 950 Third Avenue, New York, NY 10022 (212-546-9100 & 212-832-3200).

National Parks & Conservation Association "focuses on defending, promoting, and improving our country's National Park System while educating the public about the parks." Contact: 1701 Eighteenth Street, N.W., Washington, DC 20009 (202-265-2717).

National Wildlife Federation has over 4 million members in its state affiliates. It publishes *National Wildlife* (202-797-6800), and *International Wildlife*, with this editorial creed: "To create and encourage an awareness among the people of the world of the need for wise use and proper management of those resources of the earth upon which our lives and welfare depend: the soil, the air, the water, the forests, the minerals, the plant life and the wildlife." It also publishes *Ranger Rick* for young people. Contact: 1412 Sixteenth Street, N.W., Washington, DC 20036 (202-797-6800).

The Nature Conservancy has thirty-six regional offices in the United States in addition to its International Office (see above). It has the world's largest program for " . . . preservation of natural diversity by protecting lands and waters supporting the best examples of all elements of our natural world." It has completed over 3000 projects preserving more than 2 million acres of areas with natural vegetation and wildlife. Projects are beautifully described bimonthly in *The Nature Conservancy News*. Contact: 1800 North Kent Street, Arlington, VA 22209 (703-841-5300).

The Sierra Club " . . . works to restore the quality of the natural environment and to maintain the integrity of ecosystems." It has fourteen club offices in the United States as well as many local chapters. Its journal, *Sierra*, is published bimonthly. Contact: 530 Bush Street, San Francisco, CA 94108 (415-981-8634).

The Wilderness Society has over 50,000 members devoted to keeping wildlands natural. Contact: 1901 Pennsylvania Avenue, N.W., Washington, DC 20006 (202-842-3400).

In addition to the aforementioned international and national organizations, there are uncounted regional, state, and local groups concerned with preservation of natural areas, for example the New England Wild Flower Preservation Society. You can find such groups by asking at libraries, nature centers, natural history museums, and botanic gardens. They can help you discover natural vegetation in their locale. Sometimes a local person may, if not too busy, be delighted to show you a favorite natural area.

But if you find yourself on tour without having asked about natural areas ahead of time, keep your eyes open as you go. Driving across Iowa the first time, we spotted Sheeder Prairie on our Shell road map. We were thrilled to find it just north of Casey, a preserved fragment of original tall-grass prairie with Big Bluestem grass higher than our heads, just as described by the pioneers penetrating it with their covered wagons. Since then we have sought other preserved prairies, most recently The Nature Conservancy's Konza Prairie in the Flint Hills near Manhattan, Kansas. Indeed a treasure, this great expanse of grassland is an excellent site for encountering the historic environment of our Plains Indians and white pioneers, as well as for the study of natural vegetation and wildlife.

When you become familiar with such a preserved natural area, you learn to recognize the native plants and can look for them in areas that have not been set aside as reserves. For example, plants formerly very extensive in the Midwestern prairies can sometimes be spotted along railway embankments. They have persisted there largely because the train right-of-ways have been maintained by burning, thus creating environmental conditions similar to those of olden days. Prairie fires—usually kindled by the lightning storms typical of summers in the Midwest—had burned over the land repeatedly ever since the climatic change that had originally created the prairies, the French word for the beautiful natural "meadows" discovered by French voyageurs centuries ago.

Look also in the old cemeteries for the grasses and showy wildflowers that so often delighted the Indians and early settlers. As you contemplate the plants amid the tombstones, let human and natural history merge in your mind. Remember the Robinson Jeffers poem, a fragment of which is the motto of Friends of the Earth, quoted above.

My first day touring in New Zealand, I asked at a grocery store where I might park our rented campervan for the night. I was directed to a campground that, by good fortune, was adjacent to a nature reserve of subtropical rainforest. There I was thrilled to see for the first time tree ferns living in their natural environment. Had it not been for the efforts of the local chamber of commerce of the Town of Orewa, cooperating with the Eaves Bush Reserve's Puriri Park preservationists, these beautiful tree ferns and their associated puriri trees, nikau palms, and giant kauri trees festooned with lianas would not have been preserved to delight not only local people but also travelers from another hemisphere. Perhaps you on returning from a tour can help safeguard a natural area near your home to bring joy to folks from both near and far.

7 WETLANDS

Rain is much maligned. As the saying goes: "Rain, rain, go away! Come again some other day." But what delights would be lost without rain. After the rain come: mud pies for toddlers; puddles to splash through when we are older; then ponds with frogs. As we mature we learn the multitude of pleasures and ecological values of wetlands. Although the United States Fish and Wildlife Service estimates that only 46 percent of our nation's original wetlands survive, that leaves us still some 99 million acres in the lower forty-eight states; and if you go to Alaska in summer, you'll find millions more acres, abounding and afluttering with wildlife. Perhaps too you will venture to foreign wetlands, maybe the Camargue region in southwestern France, or even the vast Amazon basin with its thousands of miles of tropical watercourses threading through rainforests and jungles.

However, a wetland may be awaiting you just a few blocks away, one which even in a city has survived drainage, filling, siltation, pollution, and dumping. If you are so fortunate, a short walk may take you to a picnic spot where marsh grasses, shrubswamp bushes, and/or treeswamp trees tell you of the moisture that makes a wetland possible. There you can munch lunch while watching for wildlife for whom the wetland is home.

A bicycle can take you on a lunch-hour tour of one or more wetlands near your workplace, or on a supper-hour search for solitude where water reflects a sunset. Or perhaps you choose to invite some young bikers along. Your enjoyment may be enhanced by sharing their delight in watching ducks, herons, marsh wrens, muskrats, predacious diving beetles, or who knows what.

Of course it is water that makes a *wetland*, usually not enough to make a permanent pond or lake but enough to encourage some plants and exclude others. The U.S. Fish and Wildlife Service classifies water bodies over 6.6 feet deep as *deepwater habitats* rather than wetlands. Most wetlands will rarely if ever be flooded to that depth. Many will only occasionally show water on top of the soil.

Water table is the term applied to the surface of water in saturated soil. It may be deep; it may be shallow; it may be at the surface of the ground as visible water. Often the water table goes up and down depending on rainfall, snowmelt, drying winds, and even on how much water plants are drinking. So as you travel, you will sometimes see water in wetlands and sometimes you will not. You learn to spot many wetlands not so much by looking for water as by looking at the vegetation that indicates a relatively high water table.

How about a cross-country tour to look for wetlands? Just as some bird watchers take a trip primarily to see how many different species they can find, you can go searching for different kinds of wetlands. Although not dubbed "species" they have been classified, so you can make a list and check them off. No matter what corner of the United States you explore, you can find a *buttonbush swamp*; but if you want to "get" a *pocosin scrub-shrub wetland*, you will head for the Southeastern Coastal Plain in North Carolina!

One popular classification is based on the most conspicuous plants in a wetland. *Marshes* have predominantly grassy-looking plants, soft-stemmed ones called "herbs." These include the true grasses and their relatives called bulrushes and sedges, and also many not quite so closely related such as the cattails, burreeds, tules, and rushes. Short or tall, stout or thin, they give a meadowy look to the landscape,

51

sometimes in little patches or fringes along shrublands or treelands, sometimes in broad expanses as in the Florida Everglades and other coastal areas, for example the "merses" along Scotland's firths. Marshes are often classified by the freshness of their water, as saltwater marshes, freshwater marshes, or brackish marshes (with a mixture of fresh and salt water).

Saltwater marshes provide special delights. As tourists we like to go to sea beaches. Often these are on so-called barrier beaches, long stretches of more or less insular sands that protect the mainland from onslaughts of ocean storms. Salt marshes usually lie between the barrier beaches and the mainland; they are often neglected by recreationists because the ocean side of the barriers is so obviously attractive. But if we turn our attention to the salt marsh and trouble to investigate the lively natural happenings amid the cordgrasses, not only do we meet the plants adapted to the comings and goings of the tides, we come face to face with the vibrant life of the animals balanced between the incursions of salt water from the sea and the influx of fresh water from the hinterlands.

But in fact a salt marsh may be inland, even in a desert! In arid lands there is little vegetation and its resulting organic matter to hold whatever rain may occasionally fall. Whatever water does not evaporate almost at once may make its way down into the soil and cracks in the bedrock. Over a long time some of the water slowly gets back to the surface. Often it brings up with it salts that it has leached out of the rock and soil. When the upward movement of salts is greater than any downwashing of them, salts accumulate at the surface. Whenever and wherever enough water accumulates to make a wetland, it will likely have salt marsh plants. At times the alkaline water will form a "playa," a temporary desert lake; when it dries up, caked salts will persist on its flat surface and marsh plants will make a dormant fringe or lie sleeping as seeds deep in the mud cracks. . . . So, to add a *playa salt marsh* to your list, go to the desert.

Brackish marshes can be found inland where there is enough rainfall to balance to some degree the amount of salts in the soil, as in many parts of the semiarid American West, for instance in the Great Basin of Nevada and Utah and in the high plains east of the Rocky Mountains. You may not see any crust of brine but can discern a slightly salty taste. (Do not drink brackish water; it may have poisonous selenium in it.)

You can often find brackish marshes at the landward edge of salt marshes where fresh groundwater filters into them or surface water flows down into them. *Estuarine marshes*, along the estuaries where rivers flow into the sea, have zones of salty, brackish, and fresh water; they blend and vary with the tides and seasonal runoff from the land.

Freshwater marshes are typical of humid regions. In the slightly humid areas of the grasslands and wheat fields of our Great Plains east of the Rocky Mountains, you can add *prairie potholes* to your list of wetlands visited. Rainfall is limited and the land windswept; few trees and shrubs can grow, but the low-to-the-ground grasses flourish. Depressions left by glaciers, dimples mostly less than 2 feet deep, accumulate runoff from surrounding land. Grasses, sedges, and rushes hold sway in somewhat circular marshes. In spring they are alive with migrating waterfowl; many stay to nest, especially in the wetter years. Then after the fall migration has swept south, the winds of the Great Plains rustle the dried grasses while snow and ice lock the land for another winter.

In south-central Canada and north-central United States, there are some 300,000 square miles of this pothole region. But of the 7 million acres of original wetlands in the Dakotas only about 3 million remain for you to admire—the others have been drained, filled, or flooded; and Iowa has only about 1 percent of its natural marshes left.

Many freshwater marshes lie along rivers and smaller streams or along the fringes of lakes where brooks enter and deposit silt in their triangular-shaped deltas. These *riverine marshes* are often best explored by canoe. You can paddle Indian-style, without lifting the blade of your paddle from the water to drip noisily; thus in silence you can round a channel bend through tall grasses and cattails and perhaps see a great blue heron before it sees you, or maybe spot a spotted sandpiper teetering on a muddy bank. If you plan your tour to be in Minnesota during the wild-rice harvest, you may be able to find an Indian who can show you the time-honored way of gathering the seeds by shaking the ripe fruiting heads into the canoe.

Swamps have conspicuous woody vegetation and therefore lack the marsh's meadowy look. *Shrubswamps* have bushes predominating.

Because they have often developed from the gradual filling in of marshes or the abandonment of wet meadows, they may still have considerable patches of grass. Tree seedlings may start among the shrubs and with time grow up above them forming a *treeswamp*. As this gradual succession of vegetational stages continues, more and more organic matter accumulates on top of the soil and in the water; eventually the forest becomes drier and may give scant evidence of having begun as a wetland swamp.

Buttonbush shrubswamp, mentioned earlier, is a good one for your wetland list. Buttonbush is the most widely distributed shrub in North America, but look for it where it starts in shrubswamps with deeper water than most. The seeds from its round fruits (like old-fashioned buttons) can germinate and grow at a depth of two feet or more, eventually emerging from the water as scraggly bushes in which red-winged blackbirds like to nest. During their nesting season redwings themselves make it worth a trip.

If you can go hunting for shrubswamps in autumn, look for *highbush blueberry shrubswamps*. Their flaming red foliage will make you reach for your camera and color film, especially where the shrubs grow at the edge of a quiet reflecting pond. Noting their location while they are so conspicuous can help you find these shrubswamps in midsummer, when you can harvest the delicious berries. Learn, however, to recognize the thicker-stemmed poison sumac bushes with their compound leaves and clusters of white berries sometimes living among the blueberries. Because blueberries need an acidic rather than an alkaline soil, look for blueberry shrubswamps in the New England states or other places where native rocks like granites form acidic soils.

While enjoying the Rocky Mountains, you can add *willow shrubswamps* to your list; you find them growing on gravelly soils along streams. Willows like cool regions with limey soils so they are happy here in the mountain valleys. And they make bees happy, blooming as they do while snow still clings to the slopes above.

Shrubswamps are thus named by their most conspicuous kinds of bushes, though often many other plants coinhabit with them. For example, *viburnum shrubswamps*, which can be seen abundantly from New York west to Illinois, commonly include dogwood bushes with reddish stems and elderberry bushes with flat-topped clusters of white flowers in early summer. By contrast, *alder shrubswamps* found in the northeastern United States grow with few associated shrubs. The alders invade wet pastures no longer grazed; New Englanders say "The alders have a mortgage on the farm and before long they'll own it." Look for alders along the low edges of meadows and along streams. These shrublands are beloved by woodcock, who often probe the soft, moist ground for the earthworms that till the soil there.

The *pocosin swamps* of the Southeastern Coastal Plain, especially in the Carolinas, are called *scrub-shrub wetlands* because of the scattering of scrubby evergreen trees, mostly pond pine and bay trees, which project above the shrubs of wax myrtle, fetterbush, and titi. Many other acid-loving shrubs and herbs are mingled with them plus fascinating wildlife; but as you explore, realize that some of the snakes in pocosins are poisonous. A herpetologist makes a good companion on your forays there to look for plants and animals. The great Dismal Swamp of Virginia includes pocosins, but it is not nearly so dismal to today's naturalists as it was to those who named it.

Treeswamps are some of the most beautiful. If you want to see bald-cypresses and their associated wildlife you will do well to head for the Gulf Coast of the United States. So-called *cypress swamps* (not closely related to the true cypresses of the Mediterranean region) are perhaps most beautiful when the trees have their feathery foliage rather than in winter when they are bald; but even then the trees are both imposing and intriguing. They often stand in shallow, open water quite far from any visible shore, and their odd-shaped "knees" emerging from the water close to the buttressed bases of their trunks are curious. For even more beauty, note the festoons of the gray-green "Spanish-moss" and, in summer, prothonotary warblers with their brilliant yellow plumage; and listen at night to the background music of chorus frogs and grunting nutrias raising their furry families at the bases of the cypresses. This is a scene worth searching for, even if you fail to see an alligator or the endangered Florida panther!

While touring along the Gulf of Mexico, you may want to visit the *mangrove swamps* of the south Florida coast. Here the many-stemmed mangroves standing in the shallow salt water trap sediments from the along-shore currents and help Florida grow in extent, albeit slowly. They also protect the shore from hurricanes surging out of the

Caribbean. Look for minnows among the stems and organic debris in the water, for the mangroves provide excellent nurseries for many kinds of fish that later swim to open water as potential prey for pelicans, frigate birds, and many other forms of wildlife as well as for sport and commercial fishermen.

The *bottomland hardwood swamps* on the floodplains of the Lower Mississippi Valley are quite different from the softwood cypress swamps. A great variety of oaks, gums, beech, sycamore, and other deciduous trees grow on the alluvial (river-deposited) soils and provide habitat for many animals. These forests are shrinking because their short-term ability to produce dollars when converted to farmland is greater than their apparent dollar value for timber, flood control, and wildlife. Add this type of wetland to your list while you can; only about one-fifth of its original extent remains. If you visit these wetlands in autumn, look for wood ducks fattening on the fallen acorns of pin oaks.

Red maple floodplain swamps are easy to find in the Northeast of the United States and southern Canada where they are the predominant hardwood treeswamps. Often they occur as riverine strips along floodplains with other hardwood trees including silver maple, elms, sycamore, ashes, willows, swamp white oak, and some birches. On slopes away from the river floodplains and their terraces, you can look for *red maple seepage swamps* where little tributary valleys may not have any visible surface water but are moist with groundwater seeping through the soil. Because red maples turn brilliant reds and oranges in the autumn, that is a good time to identify seepage swamps by their color as you look at hillsides; they turn color earlier than do the vermilion sugar maples on the better-drained slopes. When the leaves have fallen, red maple swamps, on flats or slopes, lend a smoky gray color to the landscape, a cooler tone than do the twigs and branches of oaks and birches of adjacent areas.

Most attempts to classify natural phenomena face the problem of intermediate types, for instance hybrid species. With wetlands, we have categorized the pocosins referred to above as scrub-shrub wetlands because of their mix of bushes and trees. Treeswamps near the northern limits of tree species also have scattered trees, mostly larch and black spruce, intermingled with northern shrubs, grasses, sedges, mosses, and other cold-tolerant plants. These live in wetlands called *muskeg* in low places where water accumulates. In northern Canada and Alaska the muskeg is underlain by permanently frozen ground, the permafrost. Farther south wet openings in the spruce-fir forests may be thawed out for only a brief summer when arctic and subarctic wildlife, from mosquitoes to moose, thrive there during the long summer days.

And finally we arrive at the wetlands called *bogs* and *fens*. These wetlands hold stagnant water, the bogs acidic and the fens basic alkaline. Many are probably best classified as scrub-shrub wetlands; some with few if any trees, however, have mostly only those bushes adapted to the climate and water chemistry, and some may have only herbaceous plants. Warning: some people get hooked for life on the fascination of bogs. They abound with highly specialized organisms able to survive in the acidic environment. In a *sphagnum bog*, sphagnum moss colonizes at the surface of waters accumulated in the undrained kettle-hole depressions left by melting icebergs of glacial times. The sphagnum spreads a mat in which leatherleaf, Labrador-tea, and other shrubs can establish, along with lovely orchids and insect-devouring sundews and pitcher plants. In time the sphagnum creates deposits of peat (hence its common name of peat moss), used as fuel in northern countries lacking sufficient wood fuel and as a soil additive for horticulturalists. Once you get interested in bogs you can recognize varieties such as *leatherleaf bogs* and the commercially developed *cranberry bogs*; include them in your tour itineraries at the most appropriate seasons to enjoy them. On a crisp autumn day you can savor the red of cranberry bogs in New Jersey, Cape Cod (Massachusetts), Michigan, or Oregon, taking color photographs or making paintings.

Maybe you are an artist or would like to become one. Many artists have devoted much of their lives to portraying wetland landscapes and the innumerable kinds of wildlife that frequent them. When visiting wetlands, you can travel light; with just a sketch pad and pencil try to capture the lines of wind-bent cattails or tules, or a skein of flying geese, or the breast-wave V of a swimming duck or coot. Light lines can sketch the wisps of cirrus clouds, with darker lines for the flat bottoms of puffy cumulus ones. You may want two pencils, for instance a 2H for lighter lines and a 2B for darker ones, and a pocket knife or small pencil-sharpener. Shade your drawing with your pencils, darkening in the shadows of a willow trunk and its foliage. Along with these *contour shadows*, you can sketch the *cast shadows* of the willow on the bank beneath, plus its reflection in the water. Thus pencils can delineate shapes and indicate areas of lights and darks ("values" in artists' terminology) to help show three-dimensional forms.

For landscape painting on tour, use a pad of watercolor paper. It is a pad whose edges are taped together; sheets are slit off one at a time as you finish each picture—or abandon it in disgust. Have a palette for mixing paints and some acrylic colors in tubes. A couple of brushes, two plastic jars for water, and a package of paper towels complete your equipment—more than a pencil sketcher's but much less than what painters using oil paints carry. Organize it all into a backpack for hiking or saddlebag for biking. For auto touring, a cardboard carton with homemade, glued-in partitions may be just fine. By the way, you may want to include a little bottle of insect repellent. Mosquito-swatting inhibits artistic technique!

Maybe you will prefer to catch the intriguing beauty of wetlands with a camera. Good! But realize that the careful observation required of sketchers and painters can help you become a better photographer than those who only "glimpse and click."

In your travels you will surely at times seek lakes and seashores and follow rivers and be lured by mountains. But I urge you not to neglect *wetlands*. They have much to offer you with their subtle combinations of topography, soil, water, plant life, and animals—all with consummate beauty.

A Wetland Checklist

Marshes   Notes

Freshwater Marshes
_____ *Prairie Potholes*
_____ *Riverine Marshes*
_____ *Wet Meadows*

Brackish Marshes
_____ *Estuarine*
_____ *Inland*

Saltwater Marshes   **Notes**

———— *Seashore*
———— *Inland* (*Playa* and others)

Swamps

Shrubswamps

———— *Alder Shrubswamps*
———— *Buttonbush Shrubswamps*
———— *Highbush Blueberry Shrubswamps*
———— *Viburnum Shrubswamps*
———— *Willow Shrubswamps*

Scrub-Shrub Swamps

———— *Bogs* (some)
———— *Muskeg* (some)
———— *Pocosins*

Treeswamps

———— *Bald-cypress Swamps*
———— *Bottomland Hardwood Swamps*
———— *Mangrove Swamps*
———— *Muskeg* (some)
———— *Red Maple Floodplain Swamps*
———— *Red Maple Seepage Swamps*

Bogs and Fens

———— *Cranberry Bogs*
———— *Leatherleaf Bogs*
———— *Sphagnum* (*Peat*) *Bogs*
———— *Fens*

NOTE: You can add many more types of wetlands as you become able to recognize various environmental conditions—climate, topography, soil, water—and the kinds of plants that respond to such conditions and indicate a wetland's presence.

8 STREAMS

To the west of the house where I grew up was a little valley. The brook in it played games with me when I was alone. I liked to run and so did it, though in different, fascinating ways. Still too cold to slosh around in it in spring, I'd often throw pieces of twig as long as my hand in the water. They were boats of course, ones with imagined cargoes that *had* to get to Boston by 5 o'clock—"Boston" being the budding clump of marsh-marigolds a ways downstream. The trip was a series of adventures with whirlpools, harbors jammed with previous boats who had become stuck, and pirating roots where a streamside shrub had been undercut by the current. I did have a stick to poke with, but there were rules about its use for nudging my boat back into midcurrent on its way to "Boston." Today I still throw an occasional twig into a brook; and on tour I marvel at the skill of tugboat captains maneuvering barges across currents on mighty rivers like the Mississippi.

Current! That's what makes a brook or a mighty river. Water in downhill motion. One good travel game is "adverb hunting," and streams are natural haunts for adverbs. Remember Robert Southey's poem about how the water comes down at Lodore (*The Cataract of Lodore*)? Adverbs, you remember tell "how," modifying the action in verbs. How does the current *flow*? Swiftly, silently, swirlingly, slowly, stealthily, sluicingly, subtly. You may find adjectives easier, modifying the noun *current*. Fast, dashing, slow, lazy, hurrying, lingering, undercutting, depositing, circling, eddying. Or perhaps best, look for verbs. Verbs have action—and a stream always has action. If it doesn't have a current, it isn't a

streameameameameameameameameameameameameameameameameameame*dam*

                                              e

                                              e

                                              e

                                         eameameam . . .

    Play the word game. Each traveler has a paper and pencil; see who can make the longest list of words describing a stream. To collect appropriate words, you must of course *look* at the stream, and *listen* to the stream, and maybe smell the stream and taste it. Perhaps you remember Robert Frost's poem, *A Brook in the City*, wherein he says, "I ask as one who knew the brook, its strength/And impulse, having dipped a finger length/And made it leap my knuckle, having tossed/A flower to try its currents where they crossed." Yes, *feel* the stream. Indeed observation of a brook or river is what comes first; the writing, photographing, painting, telling of it, those are secondary, to be indulged in only if you so wish. You do not have to report on "current" events.

    There is a bit of poet in each of us, even if it has not found expression yet—and a bit of scientist too, even if we do not see ourselves as methodical searchers for truth and faithful recorders of findings. Therefore our travels can be much more meaningful if we follow in scientists' footsteps and read what they have discovered—about currents for instance.

    To scientists a *mature stream* is one whose currents cut sideways into its banks and thus create a *floodplain*. In your travels you can see many. They range in size from the Amazon and Mississippi down to temporary trickles on an almost-level parking lot. Levelness is important. Currents flow more slowly when their grade is flatter, faster when it is steep. (A *youthful stream* is one tumbling down a hill rather than twisting across a flatland.) Mature streams make interesting landforms to watch for while touring.

Bluffs can often be seen bordering a floodplain where a stream has cut into its *hinterland*. When a tributary stream pours down between bluffs bringing the soil it has eroded from the hinterland, it loses energy as it reaches the flatter land and therefore has to deposit much of the load it is carrying. The deposit makes an *alluvial fan* spreading out at the foot of the bluffs. *River terraces* are flat areas between the bluffs and the present floodplain; their *scarp* is the steep bank toward the river where it has cut into an older, higher floodplain of which the terrace is a remnant.

A mature stream wiggles. It uses its energy to cut sideways into its banks and thus snake across its floodplain. Each swing of a channel is a *meander*. The current on the outside of a curve is faster and has more energy for cutting into the bank; on the inside of a meander the current is slower, has less energy, and therefore must deposit some of the sediment it is carrying. Thus the stream moves sideways. The outside, undercut bank is sometimes called a *nipped bank*; on the inside of a curve, a *point-bar deposit* forms a *slipoff slope* where the slower current with less energy must deposit some of its load of sediment. The land between two meanders may be a narrow *meander neck*. The currents gnaw at it and in time often cut a new channel through it to the next meander. Then the short-cut leaves the old channel more or less abandoned as an *oxbow lake*; in time it may become a marsh. We learn to recognize these landforms as we look for them, and they tell us about the processes by which currents worked to create them.

But floodplains have *floods*! Turbulent waters collected from many tributaries on the hinterland may spread over the banks and all across the *floodway* between bluffs and/or terraces. Channel currents flow fastest where there is least friction with banks and bottom. When waters spill over a bank they lose a little energy and therefore have to dump a little of their load of sediment atop the bank; that creates a *natural levee*, a narrow ridge higher than the floodplain beyond. ("Levee" is from the French *lever*, meaning to raise.)

Sometimes a current will cut through a levee and make a *breach*. Then to protect developments on the floodplain, sand bags may be used to plug the hole. To prevent breaching, an *artificial levee* may be built, sometimes for many miles as along the Mississippi and other rivers with highly developed floodplains. *Riprap* of stones may be placed along a channel to try to keep the currents from cutting a bank, or *gabions*, wire baskets filled with stones, may be similarly used. It is the nature of a river to be a ruler of its floodplain. Naturalists who learn to read a riverine landscape can help others to understand wise use of floodways and help prevent loss of property and life in floods.

The area between a levee and the valley bluffs is often called *back country*. A river entering it from hinterland may have trouble joining the main river because of the intervening levee; so it runs down the valley more or less parallel to the main stream until it can become confluent. Such a river is called a *yazoo stream*, named after the Yazoo River, a tributary to the Mississippi. You don't have to go to Missouri to see one, however; you might find a little one in your own town. (I found one in a dirt parking lot.)

Back-country flatlands are not completely flat. Old levees and remnants of river terraces give a little relief. Abandoned oxbows and other channel fragments may be dry or filled with water forming *backwaters* and *bayous* (a term derived from the name in the Choctaw Indian language). These are great haunts for birds and other wildlife of floodplain forests and swamps.

When a stream carries a heavy load of sediment and then must slow down as it enters a pond, lake, or sea, it deposits some of its burden as a *delta* (named after the triangular shape of the Greek letter Δ). A stream's rather sudden depositing of a delta often blocks its own channel; then the stream must turn sideways, often to both sides, to explore for a lower course around the obstruction. It thus becomes a *braided stream* of many intertwining channels.

Similarly when a stream from high land slows down upon entering flatter terrain in dry country, it deposits its load as a *piedmont fan* (alluvial fan) and braids its channel over and around it. In deserts, streams may run only on rare occasions, usually sinking rapidly into the sands when they do.

One way to watch the currents of a mature stream is to find a curve of a meandering brook or small river and pick a grassy bank with a firm brink to sit on. Let your lower legs hang down over the undercut of the nipped bank (assuming the stream is not currently in flood!). Look across to the other side at its slipoff slope, a deposit of mud, sand, or gravel. Your undercut bank is on the outside of the stream's curve where the current is fast enough to have energy for eroding its bank. Across on the inside of the curve, the slower current with less energy must deposit sediment, making a good place to go wading on a hot day. Think twice before jumping in off the nipped bank; the channel may be deep there. It may be a good place, though, to drop a hook for fish lazing in the cooler depth under the bank.

If you wish to catch a trout, you will want to visit a really cool stream, or a *youthful stream.* Travel to the hinterland where the waters come tumbling down a steeper gradient, where they run in a *V-shaped valley* in the hills, constrained so that they cannot meander sideways with cut banks and slipoff slopes. Both banks may have been cut by spring floods or summer thunderpours, but most of the time the waters cut downward rather than sideways. The youthful vigor is obvious as the water dashes down over stony *riffles* between its quieter pools. Bubbles mark the places where trapped air has the oxygen on which trout depend. Where high banks, trees, or bushes shade the water, or where the water is quietly deep, the life-giving oxygen can linger to be breathed in through the fishes' gills; but where the sun shines on an open, quieter stretch, the warmer water will lose some of its dissolved gases. In this warmer spot, however, where slower currents have deposited sand, you may admire the dark shadow-spots on the bottom made by a water strider whose four hind legs dimple the surface tension enough to throw shadows on the sand bottom. (Being an adult insect, it of course has *six* legs. Are you scientist enough to wonder why there are not six big dimple-shadows?)

The fast currents of youthful streams make downhill runs over rough beds. Their energy applied to downcutting removes loose materials and the more easily eroded bedrock. Then the rock particles picked up are hurled as abrasive tools at any obstacle. A *pothole* in streambed rock is formed where a *grinder* stone is swirled around by an *eddy* in a hollow. As the hollow is ground deeper, more grinders accumulate and increase the sculpturing. A few thousand years can scoop out a fair bathtub! But watch your step when trout fishing; you might step in over the top of your waders.

Where a stream tumbles over a *lip* of hard rock or a dam, the waterfall forms a *plunge pool* at its base, overdeepening its bed. If the fall is high over steep rocks it is called a *cataract,* its power perhaps not equaled by its beauty.

Subterranean streams in limestone country have their special beauty as waters flow through the soluble rocks making *caverns,* potholes, and plunge pools decorated with dripping *stalactites* and drippedon *stalagmites.* Indeed, wherever you search for running water you will find beauty.

There are two ways to tour streams, along them and between them. Many a voyager has canoed or rafted from river source to mouth along the same river, enjoying a relatively free ride with the current. Inevitably an uphill battle, some may have relished the challenge of navigating from mouth to source. Downriver or up, either way leaves one better informed about how streams flow. If your health permits, emulate the adventurers. Pick your river thoughtfully; study maps; gather and winnow advice from people more experienced; select your craft carefully, considering its needs as well as yours; be suitably clothed and provisioned. Then . . . *Bon voyage, M'sieur! ou Madam!*

But a river tour can travel *beside* it as well as *on* it. Consider the day-off delight of following a "fishermen's trail," that ill-kept, fortuitous, almost-path that follows the streambank as closely as possible, dodging bushes, ignoring seepy spots, and revealing its makers by an occasional bit of fishing paraphernalia hung on a snatching branch. If you are a line-wetter, 'nuff said. If not, enjoy the imagined freedom of an uncaught fish, the streamside delicacy of ferns, and the patterns made by whirligig beetles and water striders on the tensioned surface of backwaters. All that and much, much more.

To roam farther astream, perhaps by road with harnessed horsepower, study road maps and plan a trip up or down—or up *and* down—a river, following the valley roads. This is impossible for the Amazon, more practical for the Mississippi, and maybe quite feasible for a stream that flows through your city, town, or village. A multitude of lesser rivers await your curiosity and appreciation. As you travel along one, watch the ways in which people have sought to harness the stream's natural flow, as with mill dams. Count them, including any now defunct. Date them if you can. Let history with its struggles, victories, and defeats come alive in your imagination. Were there fords and ferries first before the bridge-builders came? What price do we pay today for our culture's hard-won infrastructure of roads, dams, bridges, locks, levees, dredged channels, and reservoirs, which we often take for granted?

Always be cautious about disturbing water resources, a lesson I learned one very hot July day years ago when a friend and I drove across drylands from Wyoming into Utah. By midafternoon, sweaty and tired, we crested a mountain pass. Then our descending road followed the beginnings of a brook. A brook! It widened and gurgled to us. It was irresistible. We pulled off the road and likewise our clothes. Hot sweat gave way to the cool wetness of the stream. . . . We lingered, submerged in happy relaxation. We watched in wonder a water ouzel, also called a "dipper," that strange little bird of mountain streams that can walk under water in search of its aquatic food. Then refreshed, we reluctantly dressed to drive on down the winding road. Around the very first curve we were confronted by a sign: *No Swimming! Logan Water Supply.*

And on tour, never wash your camp dishes in a stream. Take a pail of water from the stream for washing; then scatter dirty dishwater on land where it can be purified by air and the soil's microorganisms rather than have it pollute the water. Ditto for car washing.

Ski touring through the woods on ungroomed trails may give you the opportunity to explore along a winter brook. Follow a little stream covered by whiteness except, here and there, where its black water winks at you through a snow-lidded hole. These are good places to pause and listen. Can you in the winter's quietness hear *two* streams? One gurgles cold beneath your skis with a tantalizingly irregular cadence; the other thrums warm in your ears with the measured rhythm of your own heartbeat.

Wherever and however you tour, take a little time to ponder the ways so-called civilizations—however civil in their human relations—have treated their rivers. Mistreated watersheds with silted streams doomed Mesopotamia many centuries ago. Later, Romans built amazing aqueducts to capture streams; but some scientists say their lead pipes gradually poisoned the Romans, leading to Rome's fall to the barbarians. As you follow a stream or cross a divide from one watershed to the next, let your mind travel to the twenty-first century. How will our streams be faring then?

As you tour streams, you (or somebody in your party) might like to use a checklist of the terms used in this chapter, much as one uses a checklist for birds:

Mature Streams

_____ Back Country

_____ Bayou

_____ Braided Channel

_____ Delta

_____ Disappearing Stream

_____ Eddy Current

_____ Flood

_____ Floodplain

_____ Gabion

_____ Levee, Artificial (dike)

_____ Levee, Natural

_____ Meander

_____ Meander Neck

_____ Mud Flat

_____ Nipped (undercut) Bank

_____ Point-bar Deposit

_____ Riprap

_____ Sand (or gravel) Bar

_____ Slipoff Slope

_____ Terrace

_____ Undercut (nipped) Bank

_____ Yazoo Stream

Youthful Streams

_____ Alluvial Fan

_____ Bubbles

_____ Cataract

_____ Cavern

_____ Eddy Current

_____ Fishermen's Path

_____ Grinder

_____ Lip (or dam)

_____ Plunge Pool

_____ Pothole

_____ Riffle

_____ Stalactite

_____ Stalagmite

_____ Subterranean Stream

_____ V-shaped Valley

_____ Waterfall

9 LAKES

One morning on my first trip to the north woods of Maine, at age 6, my father took me to a stand of old paper birches, often called white birches. They were beautiful. Gleaming against a background of dark spruces, their shining trunks were reflected in a lake, my first northern lake. In the afternoon we went for a refreshing dip and I had another first, an encounter with a water snake, *Natrix*, the swimmer. And when I came ashore, to my momentary horror, I found leeches attached to my legs. Dad pulled them off and told me not to be bothered; they were just bloodsuckers, a harmless price for a refreshing swim.

Since then I've pulled our rig off the road beside many an inviting lake. After a couple of hours of summer driving, biking, or hiking, shaking off footwear and going wading can be one of life's greatest pleasures.

In her book *Reading the Landscape*, May T. Watts described the delights of approaching a lake shore in a canoe with one's eyes closed, listening to the sounds as the boat glides, swishes, and scrapes through the various zones of plant life. I like to stand near the water's edge and gaze broadly without letting my eyes linger on any details, then close my eyes for a moment or two and tell myself what I have observed; then I glance briefly again to see some of what I have missed. Next I look to note a good barefoot approach to the water, one free of poison-ivy, prickle-bushes of sundry kinds, and broken bottles, the all-too-frequent deposits of environmentally insensitive people. Then I wade in to whatever depth my pants permit, or on a hot, quick-drying day even farther.

Now my temperature receptors tell me of the lake, that it's refreshingly, perhaps even tingly, cool—even a bit numbing if fed by a mountain stream, snow's meltwater, or underground springs. I splash a bit of lake on my face, which is salt-sweaty, dusty, or just plain hot. Brrr-ah! Then I just stand still with eyes closed, resting them, while hearing, smell, and touch tell about the lake.

Wetness, cool or warm. Perhaps the lapping come-and-go of little waves sends messages to your pressure-sensitive skin. Or in calm water you feel the liquid's substance as you gently wobble a foot back and forth. Underfoot sand can be delightfully toe tickling and massaging, a welcome change from the pressures of the accelerator, the bike pedal, or the rocky trail. Squishy mud—you can subside into it a little, much as you would relax onto a soft bed. If you are quiet and patient for some minutes, you may feel a minnow nibbling harmlessly at your ankle or calf.

Now, listen. At first your ears may bring only highway roar from behind you. If so, cup your hands behind them to gather sounds from out across the lake. Only the hum of mosquitoes? If you are patient, you may be able to hear the frizzly vibrations of dragonfly wings and a click as one catches a mosquito, or perhaps the similar sound as a phoebe or other flycatcher or warbler collects an insect for dinner. A lake is a good place to hear birds, insects, and other makers of nature's music. Perhaps you can take some youngsters on a nature tour to a lake and attune them better to nature's "good vibes."

Wind is a marvelous musician, playing on many instruments. Standing at the edge of a lake, you may hear the rote of wind-driven waves on the shore; or the rustle of cattails, bulrushes, or tules; or the rustling of a light breeze jostling myriad needles of pine or spruce. If the zephyr dies, listen to the quietness. Perhaps it's a prelude to a hot afternoon's squall, first bringing the heavy patter of raindrops before the rush-roar of storm wind and its accompanying tympani of thunder. (Time then to take shelter, out of the water and away from any tall tree that might draw lightning.)

We can close our eyes, but we have no "earlids" to close out sound as well as sight. If you try, though, you can block them out and concentrate on lakeside smells. Odors from land usually predominate, ranging from the petroleum-derived smells of a hard-topped parking lot to the fragrance of a lake-margin mint crushed under foot. Where shallows permit a lush fringe of sedge and rush, you may discern the redolence of marsh gases, mostly methane; it speaks of the prodigious activity of microorganisms helping to recycle the underwater accumulations of organic matter. Just above the water's edge, a windrow of algae and other aquatic plants washed up and rotting may yield its essences to your inquiring nose. But you may wish for "noselids" if a dead fish lies amid the jetsam!

To stand at the water's edge is only a beginning. To wade can be prelude to swimming, to snorkeling, to scuba diving if the water is deep and clear, and to boating, fishing, wildlife photography, and to cloud watching, star gazing, and singing across the water—love songs perhaps. Lakes do have water snakes and leeches, not necessarily evil and always possessing their own kinds of beauty. But lakes have much, much more to offer as we pause in our touring to increase our sensitivity to nature's manifold gifts. Lakes are like life. They hold more wonders than we can ever know.

Every lake is in some ways different from all the others, as I learned as a graduate student researching the vegetation of Cape Cod pond margins. Each has its own geological environment, water supply, plants and animals, and of course *history*. As you tour you can ask yourself, How does this lake happen to be here? Why has this depression of Earth's surface formed, one able to hold water, and where does the water come from?

Half of Canada is lake country and the northern tier of the United States also is blessed with many lakes and ponds. (There is no clear distinction for most of us between ponds and lakes; often one person's "pond" is another person's "lake.") For this multitude of basins we can thank the great Pleistocene ice sheet. It disrupted previous drainages by blocking them with ice, rocks, and soils, and by weighting down the land, reversing the direction of flow of some rivers and damming others, thus making *glacial lakes*.

Many of the huge lakes of glacial times have long since gone, but their remains are still worth visiting even though lacking water. You can admire the expanses of very flat lands with their fertile *lacustrine soils* that settled to their beds. The excellent farmland of northern Ohio west of the present Lake Erie reveals the bed of Glacial Lake Maumee. In Michigan, Glacial Lake Saginaw also left excellent agricultural land. Countless other low, flat farmlands owe their fine silty loams to long-gone lakes of glacial age.

When lakes receive water from upland streams, they slow them down by friction with the lake water. Losing energy, a stream starts to drop some of its load of sediments, the heavier stones first, then gravels and sands, while the finest particles, silts and clays, stay in suspension longest and move out into the lake beyond the stream's delta. The Connecticut River Valley once held Glacial Lake Springfield. Today the City of Springfield sits on the former delta of Glacial River Chicopee, giant forerunner of the present little Chicopee River, memorialized by the city fathers when they set aside the Delta Hills Preserve.

Some 10,000 years ago lakes made beaches much as they do today, often on a vast scale as impounded glacial meltwaters worked over and sorted the sediments that streams brought them. Water-deposited materials are almost always sorted into layers of coarser and finer depending upon the energy of the currents. If your route takes you to Minnesota's Red River of the North, look for a highway sign in Polk County west of Mentor that points out a long low ridge. Here, local historians want it known, is a beach some 9000 years old marking the eastern edge of Glacial Lake Agassiz, whose extent in those days was greater than that of all the present Great Lakes combined! Lake Winnipeg in Manitoba is a modern remnant of it.

Or perhaps you are going to Salt Lake City in Utah? Of course you want to see Great Salt Lake; but do look also to see the old beach lines of Glacial Lake Bonneville. It covered 20,000 square miles of northwestern Utah to a maximum depth of 1000 feet! Great Salt Lake is all that remains. Because the glacial lake had different stages, some higher and some lower at different times, you can look across the valley at the mountainsides and see the remarkably horizontal beach lines at different levels. The City of Salt Lake is built on a delta formed when the lake was at the "Provo level."

Many glacial lakes presumably just dried up as climate changed. Not so Glacial Lake Missoula! Many geologists believe that it burst through whatever restrained it in a tremendous flood to the northwest. How else to explain the weird landscape of the Channeled Scablands of eastern Washington State?

Today's Great Lakes grew as the last Pleistocene ice sheet melted back leaving depressed basins to catch melting ice, snow, and rain. The bottom of Lake Superior is at places over 700 feet below sea level. Tilting of beaches formed in late glacial times indicates tipping of the land as the weight of ice diminished.

The Finger Lakes of central New York today lie long and thin in valleys deeply scoured below sea level by southward-moving ice; and even with some 10,000 years of postglacial filling, the beds of Seneca Lake and Cayuga Lake are still below sea level. Scandinavia and Switzerland are among other areas where *finger lakes* occur.

Kettle hole lakes are also a postglacial phenomenon. Where icebergs broke off into a glacial-front lake, they were often subsequently buried by great amounts of outwashing sediments from the ice sheet, for glaciers pick up and carry vast amounts of pulverized rock as boulders, cobbles, gravels, sands, silts, and clays. When depositing waters receded and left exposed land, the icebergs that had been insulated by the overlying soils melted and let the land above them slump in. The resulting depressions now catch surface runoff and are hosts to groundwater. Don't look for the outlet of a kettle hole lake; unlike valleys made by rivers, there is no overflowing channel. *Pothole ponds*, described in the Wetlands chapter, were similarly formed; the term pothole pond is used especially in the plains states and provinces.

Mountain glaciers too have been parents to lakes. Mountain snows accumulating and solidifying use their great weight to gouge into peaks and carve U-shaped valleys. (Note the steepness of the upper sides of a U compared with those of a V, as in the valleys of youthful streams.) High on a glaciated mountain an amphitheater-shaped gouge called a *cirque* or *cwm* may hold a gem of a lake called a *tarn*, first named by ancient Norse people. Often nearly round, it is, as seen in many lights, a striking blue-green color. Much of its special beauty comes from the reflection of the peak that cradles it. You can find tarns in Glacier National Park, in the Canadian Rockies, and in other high, glaciated mountain regions. You may want to make sure you have your camera or paints with you. Farther down alpine valleys you can sometimes find a finger lake. Such lakes may have been formed by the terminal moraine (deposit) of a valley glacier, or perhaps more recently by damming caused by an avalanche or rock slide hurtling down from the overly steep wall of the U-shaped valley.

Earthquakes too can on occasion create lakes by disrupting a river's flow. In 1959, a quake loosened more than 30 million cubic yards of rock from one side of the gorge wall of the Madison River in Montana. Some twenty-five campers lost their lives as the mass swept across the canyon and 400 feet up the far wall. The resulting dam created Earthquake Lake in the Madison.

On rare occasions volcanoes make lakes, as when a lava flow crosses a valley and dams a river. The southern Cascade Range in Oregon has a long volcanic history. Many of its lakes are dry, however, because the lava is porous. Crater Lake, though, has abundant water some 2000 feet deep in the throat of an extinct volcano, ancient Mt. Mazama; the volcano erupted in late Pleistocene times, blew its top, and thus prepared the hollow for this gem of a lake.

In regions where limestone is a predominant surface rock and the climate is humid, *sink hole lakes* may be common, as in the lake district of central Florida. Long ago in Miocene times that part of Florida was under the ocean. Over millions of years the shells of marine animals accumulated on the floor and eventually became limestone rock that was uplifted making Florida's backbone, but a very soluble one and therefore weak! In such topography, called *karst*, water easily penetrates the ground and forms underground rivers as it dissolves the limestone. The rivers carve out caverns. When the roof of a cavern collapses and the ground subsides, a sink hole lake is formed. Camp beside one some day; you can eat locally grown oranges and watch herons come to roost in the evening.

Some mature rivers make their own lakes while meandering sideways—*oxbow lakes*, as described in the chapter on Streams. Most oxbow lakes, being remnants of channels, are relatively narrow. Much broader lakes on rivers—reservoirs—have been made by dams. In the rather dry prairie and plains states west of the Mississippi, almost all lakes are manmade. The great Missouri River watershed has forty-six major dams storing water useful for irrigation, recreation, and flood control. Many blessings have their drawbacks, though. While supporters of lakes irrigate their crops and recreation enthusiasts enjoy flatwater fishing, boating (and iceboating), the flowwater fishermen complain of drowned streams and bottomland farmers see their most fertile soils submerged. When dammed rivers are used primarily to generate power, a lake is kept as full as possible. When it serves for flood control, it may be drawn down to provide storage for excess water, and the drawdown may be a drawback for power producers and consumers. To control lake levels to please everybody can be very difficult.

Among nature's lake creations are some now-you-see-them-now-you-don't types, more technically called *intermittent lakes*. In arid areas such as the Great Basin of Utah and Nevada, eastern Oregon and Washington, and the Pacific Southwest, mountains catch moisture and, being short of vegetation and humus to retain it, let much of it flow down at once into the usually dry intermontane basins. There the water forms the temporary lakes known as *playas*. Under desert sun, some of these last scarcely longer than the mirages that torment desert travelers; others may linger long enough to enable specialized desert animals and plants to complete the active portions of their life cycles.

In southern California and other regions with a Mediterranean-like climate and more predictable winter rains, small temporary lakes called *vernal pools* fill up in late fall and winter and then dry up after spring, the vernal season. Enjoy them while you can, with their watersheds painted with wildflowers and grasses still green before the sun sears them to gold.

So lakes come and go, sometimes in a year and sometimes in 10,000. Whenever and wherever, they fill in some of the land's low spots with water, wonderful water. As you come and go on your tours, may you have special regard for lakes, remembering that each one is special.

10   SEASHORES

On days spent on the shore, my grandchildren enjoy a periwinkle fight—friendly competition akin to throwing small green apples at each other back at the farm. Different environments offer different missiles for young people. Probably the periwinkles, secure in their snail shells, have no major objections to being hurled about just so long as they land back in the rocky intertidal zone where they can resume their grazing on algae with the return flood of the tide.

What do *you* choose to do at the seashore? Swim? Soak up the sun's rays? Periwinkle-watch or people-watch? When you visit a shore, you may find either blessed solitude or convivial companionship. Try at different times for some of both to suit your moods.

A crowded beach with barely room to spread a bath towel lets you study human nature. But even on a teeming beach you can find primal nature close at hand. Strips of sand between adjacent bath towels and under beach chairs give opportunities for prone naturalists to come face to face with Mother Earth. Dry sand sifts sibilantly through the fingers. Pouring a handful in one place forms a conical hill—the constant angle of repose reminiscent of sandbox volcanoes. Blowing on it hard realigns the lighter particles to form miniature dunes with slightly different slopes on the windward and leeward sides. Wind from sturdy lungs can sometimes sort out grains of different minerals, especially when sands have been derived from a variety of rocks such as those scattered by a continental ice sheet long ago, as in the northern United States, Canada, and northern Europe. Pink patches on a beach may be formed by grains of ground-up garnet, black ones of hornblende, bits worth a close look.

Perhaps you have brought field glasses to the beach for watching offshore ducks or wave-edge sandpipers and plovers; but the beach may be too crowded for bird watching; and people watching is more discreetly done without binoculars. You can use them, however, to get a closer look at sand grains. Look through them backwards, with one ocular lens close to a few sand particles and with its objective lens next to your eye. When you don't have a hand lens with you, field glasses thus make a good substitute.

During the hottest part of a summer day, usually between noon and 3 o'clock, a swim can make a delightful break in a day's travel. Of course always be careful where you swim. Beware of the undertows where water runs back deep under incoming surf. Alongshore currents can be swift. Seaweeds such as kelps can entangle swimmers, and so can eelgrass. Rocks can be very slippery. Never dive off rocks without knowing the depth of the water. Watch out for stinging red jellyfish and, in warmer waters, sharks. Water by its nature is refreshing, but it can be hazardous, too.

A cooling onshore breeze may develop in midafternoon as the land heats and draws ocean air inland. If you sunbathe after a swim, don't forget to put on sunscreen lotion; even on cloudy days the sun's rays can give a bad burn. Don't go to sleep and, oblivious, overexpose yourself to solar radiation. Don't count on horse flies or beach fleas to keep you awake, though they may help. They are admirable creatures when seen through your hand lens or reversed binoculars, amazingly adapted to beach living without getting sunburned. If you have a sketch pad with you—and are tired of drawing beach people's well-revealed figures—try to make a heroic-sized sketch of the fly that crawls across your paperback book. Toward evening on the beach, you may wish to substitute mosquito repellent for sunscreen lotion.

If you prefer some solitude at a beach in summer, usually your best chance for being alone is early morning, perhaps seeing the sun rise over the Atlantic or watching the dune shadows shorten on the Oregon coast. Where permitted, try a sleeping-bag night on or near the beach, with sand beneath you sculpted to fit your body's contours; flat sand is hard as rock. If you jog, try barefoot comparisons of upper-beach dry sand and the packed surface of wet sand near the water; the dryer sand is inefficient for forward progress; the packed, more jarring to knee joints and spine, requires more springy ankle action from your calf muscles. If waves tumble and slosh up the beach, forget distance running and try to improve your sandpipering skills. No need to probe for sand worms, amphipods, and other little invertebrates for bird breakfasts; concentrate on footwork by trying to keep close to the oncoming edge of each approaching wave and then follow its retreat until the next wave challenges you. Try playing this game with Neptune while running backward; compare your scorecard footprints with the graceful swash marks of the waves, best seen when the tide is receding. Beach running before the heat of the day can awaken mind as well as body.

Seldom do I like to paint at midday. Shadows are too short; the light appears flat. To be sure, early morning on the beach will have only little shadows in the hollows of yesterday's footprints, with longer shadows of driftwood and strand plants above normal high tide; but low-angled sunlight gives hues not seen at midday. Sea and sky often exhibit a mother-of-pearl tint mirrored in the momentary wetness of the last swash before a wave rejoins its fellows or completely subsides into the sand. You may enjoy the subtle violet colors of early morning, perhaps to paint or photograph, or to record just in your mind the memory-print to be recalled in bed some winter night while waiting for sleep.

You may want to plan a tour that includes a variety of beaches, for beaches are not all alike. In England, people often call beaches "the sands." A good name—it describes the texture of the rock particles of which the beaches are composed, bits larger than silt and smaller than gravel. But where parent rocks are hard, tidal currents strong, and the coast geologically youthful, as in Canada's maritime provinces and Maine, a beach may be made of cobblestones, flattened shingle pebbles, or gravel. Not a real beach? Define it as you will, it is a somewhat sloping expanse of bits of rock along the shore, worked over by water and wind and with only minimal if any rooted vegetation.

A *cobble beach* does not invite you to lie on it: too bumpy and steep. Bits of gravel and sand that may have resulted from the ocean banging the stones together have been carried away by waves and currents. Rather than lingering to rest, you might be tempted to take one or two cobbles home for decoration, so beautifully rounded and smooth are they. As with all collecting though, be thoughtful. At Acadia National Park in Maine, a natural sea wall of cobbles was in danger of disappearing until the rangers put up a sign asking people to leave the stones where nature's storm waves had put them.

A *shingle beach* is truly an oddity. The little stones are thin, flat, and mostly rounded, often more like well-worn coins than shingles. If not too thin they are excellent for skipping over the water when thrown underhand with a flick of the wrist. As the stones bounce out away from shore, you can wonder how soon the energy of shore waves will equal your arm's thrust and thereby bring the skipped stones back to lie with their fellows on the beach. Sometimes these thin bits of sedimentary or metamorphic rock bed down in an amazing fashion, tightly packed with all their long axes parallel and almost vertical as though nature were shuffling a pack of cards.

When you find a shingle beach, try to be there with an incoming tide, a not-too-strong onshore wind, and moderate waves, so you can listen to the jingling music of the waves jostling stones. Their sound is very different from the thump and bump of cobblestones when waves are big enough to bang them together, and different also from the sibilant swish of sands.

For every hundred yards of cobblestone and shingle beaches there are hundreds of miles of *sand beaches*, much more familiar to most of us. From southern Maine and New Hampshire, they stretch all along the eastern seaboard and the Gulf of Mexico; on the West Coast are more varied but also beautiful beaches. As a youngster vacationing on Martha's Vineyard in Massachusetts, I enjoyed digging down to the water table while making sand castles with moats. I was awed and scared by the surfs of the South Beach during storms; but I didn't really fall in love with sand beaches until years later when writing a senior thesis on "The Vegetation of Plum Island in Winter," an island north of Boston.

Only then did I really trouble to learn about the vibrant edge between land and sea, to study the interplay of waves and winds as they toss sand grains back and forth between them. The north-south-oriented beach at that latitude is far different in winter than in summer, narrower and steeper as winter storms bring their greater energies to bear upon it. Wearing warm and wetproof garb, you can enjoy a winter storm when a nor'east wind picks up wet sand and plasters it on the wind'ard side of your face while it hurls tons of frothing water at your feet. When the storm moves off to sea, a high-pressure air mass from the icy continent begins to blow from the northwest; the tattered rainclouds show patches of cobalt blue sky, and the dune sands resume their drifting up the gently sloped windward sides of dunes, to deposit on the steeper leeward sides.

Then you may be tempted to snuggle against a sandy bank, to eat your lunch in its lee, watching the storm waves rolling in, their white tops blowing back to sea. If so, be prepared for the "rain" of settling sand as the wind loses energy in the dune's lee and has to dump its load of triturated rock. The hood of your jacket can keep the sand out of your hair, but how about your sandwich? Perhaps you will postpone eating or else perch atop the dune, preferring the full force of the wind to its gift of grit. From that exalted place you can watch the patterns of drifting sand skitter up the windward surface of the dune and disappear over the leeward. And looking out to sea you can watch for sea ducks, eiders and scoters perhaps, bobbing in the troughs of the combers.

Shore dunes are born of beaches. The ocean cuts away bluffs and cliffs, dissolving, grinding, and sorting their substances into cobbles, gravels, sands, silts, and clays. These it deposits according to the waters' energies at various places, coarsest materials on the more tumultuous shores, the finest in placid places such as salt marshes behind protecting barrier beaches. Rivers too supply sediments for the sea to sort and deposit on beaches, most notably beaches of sand. Dunes build up when shore vegetation slows down winds that have whipped up beach sands. The shapes and orientations of dunes depend upon strengths and directions of prevailing winds and storm winds.

How about taking a dune-and-beach tour around the United States to inspect them? You can start at Wells Beach and Ogunquit,

Maine, and talk with people about the problems of keeping the stormy North Atlantic out of one's yard. Drift southward to Massachusetts and have lunch on a Plum Island dune where the Merrimac River has brought down its contribution of sand, or visit Ipswich Beach across the creek where tides flow and ebb from the Newburyport marshes, so famous for birders. Skip around rocky Cape Ann and Boston Harbor with its recreational beaches and islands, and proceed to Boston's South Shore and the beginning of almost continuous sand spits and barrier island beaches all the way to southern Texas.

Cape Cod dunes give you a chance to compare those at Barnstable, where the shore trends east-west, with those on the outer Cape with its north-south shoreline. Some of Barnstable's beautiful dunes form shapes reminiscent of the barchan dunes of deserts. The better stabilized slopes have a gray-green cover of woolly beach-heather (not a true heather) and bushes of bayberry and beach plum; dune hollows have cranberries. On the Outer Cape at The Cape Cod National Seashore you can study the progressive building of spits by alongshore currents and some of the highest dunes in the East, built up and more or less protected by the American beach grass *Ammophila* (Latin for "sand lover"). Bluffs along the Outer Beach have been eroding away at about 3 feet a year, supplying material for spits and dunes to the north and south.

Cape Cod, as beautiful as it is at all seasons, has no corner on the scenic market. Visit ancient, windswept holly trees at Fire Island National Seashore on Long Island, New York, and other trees in the *maritime forests* protected in the dune hollows. Note too the attractions of other New York and New Jersey beaches where millions of people live near or visit the ocean. Refreshingly different are Assateaque and Chincoteague Islands off the shore of Virginia and the southern tip of Maryland, protected by Assateague Island National Seashore and Chincoteague National Wildlife Refuge.

The Outer Banks of North Carolina have survived fierce buffetings by the North Atlantic. The Cape Hatteras National Seashore and Pea Island National Wildlife Refuge preserve some of the East Coast's highest dunes, with the help of the dune-forming sea oats *(Uniola)*. Remote Ocracoke Island is especially valued by naturalists.

Florida's southern beaches have grown from the Miocene

limestones domed up above sea level and from the warm-water corals and shells of shellfish and snails of more recent times. Much of the coast has barrier beaches protecting the Inland Waterway. Everglades National Park preserves the saw-grass environment with its islandlike *hammocks* of subtropical woody plants, and the park has a Wilderness Waterway for small-boat access to the exotic habitats and primitive campsites. The park's shores are largely mangrove swamps.

The chain of islands known as the Florida Keys has miles and miles of Caribbean beaches fringed by palm trees and sea-grapes. Many of the Keys are traversed by the Overseas Highway between Miami and Key West. John Pennekamp Coral Reef State Park pioneered with the establishment of an underwater nature trail to help people see a coral shore from a fish-eye view.

Florida's west-coast beaches have some of the best shell collecting known, rivaling the beaches of the Indian Ocean. Sanibel Island is particularly noted for its shells—some residents think *too* well known. Pine Island National Wildlife Refuge is perhaps a better place for shelling by the public.

If you were a wild Canada goose, you might well want to winter at St. Mark's National Wildlife Refuge on the coast south of Tallahassee; or maybe you would just like to go to see the geese congregate in that hundred square miles of woodland, ponds, and marshes. Farther west you can enjoy the beautiful beaches of Santa Rosa, a 50-mile barrier beach on the Gulf of Mexico.

The birdfoot delta of the mighty, muddy Mississippi River is best explored by boat, much of it being inaccessible by road. Lafayette, Louisiana, is a recommended place to start exploring its vast Atchafalaya Basin swamps between it and New Orleans. Coastal Avery Island is a flavorful salt-and-pepper place. Set up as a bird sanctuary—by a millionaire who grew peppers used in Creole cooking—it also includes a geological salt dome being mined for salt, reminding you that what is now a low-lying shore in a humid climate was once an arid area where salt lakes evaporated. Land sure has its ups and downs!

The Texas coast has no high dunes to boast of, but its barrier islands have many, many miles of sand tossed back and forth by wind and water. In winter the Aransas National Wildlife Refuge hosts the endangered whooping crane on its vast marshes, sheltered by its barrier beaches. South of Corpus Christi the Padre Island National Seashore with well over a hundred miles of barrier beaches separates the Gulf of Mexico from the Laguna Madre. Here you can get a bigger feel of ocean-edge wilderness than anywhere else on the East and Gulf Coasts, if you can hike beyond the tourist accommodations at each end. Of course you can watch birds typical of sea, beach, dune, and marsh. But during migrations a startling wealth of land birds drops in on Padre Island thickets before or after their passage across the Gulf.

Western beaches of the United States have evolved on a different kind of coast, one with a rampartlike geological structure. This coast stretches from the bluff-backed white sandy beaches north of San Diego to the dark basaltic sands under the cliffed headlands of Oregon and Washington. And the Pacific! Much of the year the prevailing westerly winds with their long fetch across the vast Pacific keep ocean rollers, tier on tier, piling in on the shore. No wonder surfing is primarily a West Coast sport. And you will find no better place to watch a line of pelicans fishing as they follow the uprising air along a trough of the waves.

North of San Francisco you can see a typically broad, flat California beach at beautiful Point Reyes National Seashore and learn about the seismic geology of this unstable west edge of the continent. Farther north, Trinidad Beach Drive on Route 101 north of Arcata provides for 20 miles a notable mix of ocean beaches, marshes, and lagoons for watching shore processes and wildlife.

And the Oregon coast! Nowhere else around the conterminous United States can you find so much coast unspoiled by development and still open to the public. From Gold Beach at the south to Astoria at the north, coastal Route 101 hugs the shore, always inviting you to stop and enjoy the many scenic pulloffs, rest spots, picnic areas, and over thirty state parks. You can search the beaches for agates at Humbug Mountain State Park, at Newport, and other beaches, looking for ones exposed by winter storms. You can go down into sea caves where the Pacific surges in, and by the dim light watch the sea lions there. Or you can climb the almost mountainous dunes replenished endlessly by the ocean-sorted sands, sands drifting landward burying forests.

Plan time to visit the ocean strip of Olympic National Park on the Olympic Peninsula in Washington State. Remote beaches between craggy headlands express the wildness of nature, where land and sea meet without human intrusion. Perhaps go to La Push, the western-most town of the Lower Forty-eight. Hike out from the Quillayute Indian fishing village along the shore. Climb up onto a driftwood trunk of Douglas fir or sitka spruce, a giant thing higher than your head—like a dune-top in Massachusetts, an exalted place for both observation and contemplation. Of all the many shores you have visited on your tour, was any more beautiful than this? You have no answer. Nor should you. Each in its own way is beautiful.

Tidal *mudflats* are too seldom recommended for tourists unless a chamber of commerce pushes clams or geoducks dug in their habitat rather than devoured in a restaurant. Mudflats should be more appreciated. Mud is a wonder-filled mix of silt, clay, and water, and usually is very fertile. Often it is deposited near the mouth of an estuary or edge of a salt marsh whence comes the enriching detritus of decaying organisms, for example the common cordgrasses *(Spartina)*.

Fertility of course promotes life. Sometimes a green carpet of algae—okay: "scum" if you'd rather—paints the somber-colored mud at low tide; it may be threads of *Enteromorpha* ("intestine-shaped") or an expanse of *Cladophora,* the sea lettuce. Shorebirds probe the mud for collectible delectables. Minnows begin to swim up the tidal channels as the moon impels the ocean to thrust landward yet again. Mud-hidden worms respond to the flooding by extruding fabulously fringed tentacles from their holes to happily gather in another meal. How can you not enjoy this so-fertile environment?

Approaching tidal mudflats from land suggests either shorts and sneakers or pants and rubber boots. A broad-brimmed hat (with jaw string) gives some protection from the sun and, as you bend over inquisitively, shades shallow water while you peer into it to look for snails or whatever. You don't need to walk far in wet mud; life is all around you though often hard to see. Scratching in the mud with a stick or bent wire coathanger may reveal some clams—or clam worms, one poetically called *Nereis,* the sea nymph. Biologists often see beauty in worms; they have taken the trouble to look. Be sure to return the coathanger to its rightful shape and duties rather than abandon it on the flats, which may already have too much metal and plastic debris.

An excellent way to enjoy mudflats and salt marshes is by canoe. I like to tour with a small, light canoe atop our auto. It is ideal for floating up a tidal channel along with the minnows, scarcely paddling and scaring almost none of the herons and other wildlife. With a meal or snack and a water jug, you can wait for the outflowing for your return trip. Try it. And remember the wisdom of hat, sunglasses, sunscreen, and life preservers. Maybe take supplies for sketching, tape recording, and/or photographing. But don't always work, if recording observations seems like work. Maybe pack a book and pillow.

Rocky shores where long cliffs confront the ocean or craggy headlands jut out to sea are widely promoted by tourist bureaus, as well they should be. Whether sun-scalded and encrusted with guano deposits of seabird colonies, like the west coast of Chile, or fog-misted by ocean moisture, like the Big Sur coast south of San Francisco, rocky coasts have endless beauty. But, again, be careful. Some rocks are unexpectedly slippery; others crumble when stepped on.

Ah, those coves of the Olympic Peninsula or Gaspé Peninsula are indeed so alluring. But beware of the peril of beachcombing in their delightful coves; the high headlands around them may be difficult or impossible for you to scale. Watch for incoming tide that might trap you when it reaches the points of the promentories. You could have a long wait to escape until the next ebbing tide, assuming the high tide does not drown you!

Clambering along rocks below the line of highest tides should usually be done bent over with one hand on or close to the rocks, for balancing support if needed. All around the world's oceans blue-green algae, which are individually invisible to the unaided eye, form a dark band just below high-tide line. They coat the rocks and make them exceedingly slippery, unexpectedly and dangerously so.

But what fun it is to explore the tide pools! For those of us who for one reason or another cannot snorkel or scuba dive, the next best exploration surely must be the search for sea anemones in their tide pools or for the little treelike kelps called "sea palms," their rubbery fronds dancing in the surf of the U.S. West Coast.

Observation is of course basic to all nature study. Observation should not be limited to *looking*. Conscious *listening* can be rewarding at the edge of the ocean. Surf crashes on rocks a wave at a time with distinct loudness, pitch, timbre, and rhythm along with a continuous overall tumult of sounds. If rocks slope seaward, you can probably hear the gurgle of the retreating backwash. If waves are pounding on the flattish pebbles of a shingle beach, listen for the tinkling of each subsiding wave. Rounded cobblestones of an exposed sea beach rumble as the water tumbles them. On sandy beaches, the up-running front of an almost-spent wave makes a frothy-swishy sound, while in a storm the combers' thunder can be heard from miles away.

Gulls crying. Sea lions barking. A bell buoy clanging. A fog horn blowing. The wild flapping of yards and yards of canvas as a close-to-shore schooner comes about into the wind, then slips off heeling on another tack. Listen!

11 SEAS AND OCEANS

My imaginings as a boy no doubt grew mostly from books I read. One I vividly remember portrayed the boy Columbus watching with longing the sailing ships leaving the docks of Genoa for distant lands. As a child I did not live by the ocean, so my vessel of exploration was of necessity an old apple tree by the upper meadow. When under full sail with lee scuppers under, it went nowhere; but in the travels of my mind, *I* did. You may wish to go beyond those hauntingly beautiful sea tales and *really* travel the oceans of our "Water Planet," as Jean Jacques Cousteau has so aptly and affectionately called Earth. A first trip? Or one more after many?

Most tourists today contemplate our oceans from an altitude of 30,000 or more feet while jetting through the upper atmosphere. Even at that exalted height, the grandeur of the sea is apparent; but to be on the lilting level of the sea is quite another adventure.

If perchance you own a seaworthy vessel, I have little to offer you for advice, Cap'n. Just don't try to take your first voyage from Boston to Bar Harbor, navigating along the foggy Maine coast with an oil company road map of New England as some have done. Detailed marine charts are only the beginning of all you need in preparation for coastal sailing, prelude to touring Earth's oceans.

Travel agencies can direct you to companies with cruise ships. I get advertisements regularly from some and am sorely tempted to embark. One agency is sure I'll someday buy a round-trip cruise on its luxury Antarctic cruise to see whales, penguins, and castellated icebergs, or to the Indian Ocean with its romantic ports. Also tantalizing are the offerings of special-interest organizations promoting their own tours. A college alumni group tries to lure me on a Mediterranean odyssey. A horticultural society sends a brochure of visits to the Cape of Good Hope and its botanic gardens. A photographic club challenges me to take my camera to sea with its members. Senior-citizen groups combine camaraderie and education with the special care that older folk often appreciate.

An ocean voyage by boat is slow compared to most modern travel. Take advantage of the pace. Relax. Even be a bit bored at first—maybe. Being one of the few passengers on a freighter has some advantages over my long-ago sailings on ocean liners. One can be less involved with the question of whom it is proper to be associated with. When I was just 12, my mother was quite shocked by my attraction to a young lady on our voyage from New York to California via the Panama Canal. While pretty little Frances was noteworthy enough to be remembered this long, my most vivid memory is of a glance out through the porthole of our below-the-waterline cabin during a storm off the coast of Mexico; at that instant a giant sea turtle, unbelievably large and otherworldly, swam gracefully by.

On boarding a ship find your berth, stow your belongings so they will not tumble around, and start to explore the vessel as it sits quietly in the harbor. Have confidence that it will carry you along safely on the exciting edge between sky and sea. Be inquisitive about the nature of the boat itself. Think of good questions to ask officers and crew later when they are not quite so busy. Do not be surprised if they speak little or no English; sailors go to sea from many lands.

As the ship gets under way, with hausers tossed off the bollards or the anchor weighed, admire the land you are leaving, its docks, buildings, trees, and skyline all shrinking away into blue-gray blur.

As land recedes, there is more sky to watch. More sky and more water. When out of sight of land, these vast spreads of nature comprise the setting of ocean's dramas. Your vessel shrinks correspondingly, becoming a precious speck. You too can feel very small. That can be a good feeling. Enjoy the immensity.

Your feelings, though, may include some motion sickness. You want to enjoy your voyage and prove to be a "good sailor." Probably you will be. But if you have a history of motion sickness and have been helped by medicine, you may wish to take a recommended dose before you become much involved with *mal de mer*.

In rough weather, the once-quiet vessel becomes a quite different environment from what it was in the harbor and must be ridden somewhat like a horse or camel. The wind-and-water forces of nature influencing the ship now involve *you*, and willy-nilly you must respond, preferably rationally, using boat-knowledge including the following basics.

Explore the deck as it relates to sea and sky—unless in a storm you are ordered off of it; on shipboard, captain's orders must always be followed. The view of the horizon from a side railing apparently goes up and down if the craft is *rolling* from side to side, and the hull is mostly parallel to the crests and hollows of the waves. The horizon's appearance from a side rail is quite different if your vessel is *pitching*—bowing down into the waves and then lifting skyward. Practice adjusting your whole body to the rhythm of the deck's dance. Slowly extend a down-deck leg and shorten an up-deck one, and thus to be at one with the boat—and thence with the waves and the wave-inducing winds. "*Bon santé de mere*": Good sea-health to you.

Getting your "sea legs" requires more than just holding onto the railing. Watch the sailors' rolling walk going from bow to stern as the ship rolls; notice how they lean forward or backward as the boat pitches. Try it. Your first exaggerated motions will become gentle, unconscious accommodations to the subtleties of the sea's surface. If allowed on deck when the wind is really strong, perhaps even in a gale or storm, your body must lean over into the wind—or take the consequences!

But perhaps all your conscious efforts to adjust to the waves have not fully satisfied your semicircular canals and somewhat confused stomach. Your brain still sends messages of uncertainty about whether your digestive cargo is safely stowed in your hold. Perhaps it is wise to be near the railing just in case you and your previous meal are forced to part company. If so, be sure to consider the wind direction relative to the boat's course. If the air is light, the apparent wind may be made mostly by the boat's forward motion. In that case, favor the stern rail if it is accessible to you. The stern often offers beautiful views of following gulls to take your mind off digestive rebellion. If, however, the wind is blowing vigorously on one side of the ship, the windward side, you should seek the leeward rail in your distress. If in a cabin, stay close to a toilet (called the "head" on English-speaking vessels).

What seas and oceans you travel will of course influence the kinds of skies you will admire. The apparent height of the sun from glorious sunrise to glorious sunset will vary with your latitude, which you can usually learn from the captain or mate. The constellations on clear nights, with no competition from city lights or airports, will also vary with your distance from the equator. A good star book and/or star chart increases the enchantment of nights at sea. Binoculars make the stars and planets seem closer and more colorful and help reveal the dark "seas" (*mares*) of the moon when it brightens the sky and fades the stars. Field glasses are best used when the sea is calm, because the boat's motion on rougher seas makes the stars a quivering jumble.

Of course the season of the year will determine what segment of our star sphere is visible at night. Meanwhile people on the other side of the Earth, the antipodes, are sunning themselves by our nearest, brightest star. The Earth's axis creates our changing seasons and overhead star-scenes. Studying stars can make us feel very small. By giving us a perspective on distant galaxies it can also steady us. I wonder what psalms David might have written had he been a sailor rather than a shepherd.

As a teenager, I was a counselor at a sailing camp Down East on the Maine coast. The director used to say, "When on the water, always keep your catswhiskers out!"—in other words stay alert to your environment. At sea, you should keep a "weather eye" on your environment, especially upwind whence a storm might come. Watch the clouds to be apprised of what may be the next act of the ocean's drama. And also watch the water.

In equatorial waters, watch the towering cumulus clouds that so often bring midday tropical downpours, momentarily cooling the air before adding steaminess to the ubiquitous heat. When cruising in the belt of calms known as The Horse Latitudes on either side of the equatorial zone, clouds may be rare indeed. In the days of sailing ships, horses in transit to the New World would sometimes die of thirst before ocean currents drifted the vessels to a zone where winds brought renewed motion. Be glad if your craft is powered by fossil fuel; you are not at the mercy of long delays in a deadly calm.

In archipelagos—as in the South Pacific, Caribbean, and Mediterranean seas—you may often be treated to blue skies everywhere but with cumulus clouds rising resplendent over warm islands, often ones still below the horizon. These clouds have long served as landmarkers for ancient seafarers. In higher latitudes, clouds may enshroud your vessel for days as cool fog, which can sometimes suddenly reveal close at hand a looming iceberg.

Knowing the major types of clouds by name will aid your marine sky watching: the wispy high *cirrus*, accumulated puffs of *cumulus*, and the layered *stratus*. Studying books on climatology and meteorology will afford greater appreciation of marine weather. Your voyage should provide ample time in a deck chair or bunk to savour the sea tales of those who have kept a weather eye on the clouds.

And the water! No other expanse of nature can appear flatter than a calm ocean. No mountain can rise above you more threateningly than a monster wave. Between these extremes, nature orchestrates an infinitely complex repertoire of ripples, waves, swells, and tsunamis. Physicists can give dimensions of troughs and waves and calculations of their energies. Photographers can still waves' fleeting images on film and paper. Painters can strive to catch visual impressions of water. Poets and other writers can try to pen thoughts revealing what waves say to them. Now what about you, a tourist who perhaps is none of the above?

Take a quick glance for an instant impression of what the water looks like stretching from ship to horizon, distant shore, or other limit of visibility such as edge of fog bank, curtain of rain from a squall cloud, or crests of storm waves. Then look more closely at the subpatterns of the water that compose its overall appearance. The constant motion of waves will be disconcerting at first—and subsequently too! Acknowledge it. Accept it. Enjoy it even if its ever changingness thwarts your attempts to visualize and hold onto its repetitive patterns. Keep looking, again and again. Your observations can improve with time and effort.

Most of the waves you watch are windmade. They have used wind energy to build up their forms and to travel from a calm lee shore or other calm place. That distance is called their *fetch*. A long fetch with plenty of wind tends to make bigger waves than does a short fetch, though winds can peter out and leave a calm. A change of wind can start a new set of waves in a new direction, often superimposed on persisting waves still motivated by the energies of the former wind, hence some of the often-seen triangular patterns in water. Tumultuous storm winds smashing across the crests of billows will coexist with defiant little winds from totally different directions in the troughs and under the lee of whitecaps. Roaring confusion! Big patterns embracing smaller patterns. Exciting. Ineffable.

I have never experienced the "Roaring Forties" or the "Howling Fifties," those latitudes where planetary winds are forever blowing easterly south of Cape Horn and the Cape of Good Hope with almost no landmasses to stop them. Such storms! If you tour down that way and arrive safely in port, do send me at least a post card to tell of your safe arrival.

Gazing at calmer waters furrowed by your vessel, your visual analysis of waves near the boat must contend not only with wind-induced waves but also with those generated by the boat. If you can stand safely on the bow, or better still lie on a bowsprit projecting from it, admire the bow-wave at the boat's cutwater. If the speed makes white foam, sailors say the ship "has a bone in her mouth." From there the ship's water-displacing energy sends V-waves astern to contend with wind-waves. Watch their fascinating interactions. They are easier to photograph than draw or paint. Studying a photo that stops the motion can make the patterns more understandable and easier to draw.

Stand on an afterdeck and look astern at water boiling together as it replaces itself after your craft's disruptive passage. Watch the sea gulls as they use the turbulent air astern for gliding on their own voyages (from where to where?). And when tired of watching the total seascape and its infinite parts, return to the cabin to read some of the world's best literature, books born of nautical experiences. Read of whales and the men who have perilously sought them. Read of boats crafted of reeds bound with hemp that have crossed the Indian Ocean, of oxhide boats that have met the challenges of the North Atlantic, of wooden ships and ones of steel. And whatever boat *you* tour on, think of it as precious, and be glad it has seas and oceans to sail across on our Water Planet as it goes on its cruise through infinite space.

12 WILDLIFE

"Do you see it? Do you hear it? Do you believe it?" Those were the first words a bird ever said to me. When I was about 4, my mother repeatedly used those phrases to introduce me to the song of a red-eyed vireo high in the oaks behind the garage. Ever since then in spring and summer the red-eyes have been saying that to me, repeatedly, insistently, even in the extreme heat of a midsummer day while other eastern woodland birds are snoozing. Thus Mother alerted me to bird songs.

Millions of species of birds and other animals inhabit this planet with us. Many are like vireos, colored like the leaves amid which they live their hidden lives. The more alert we are, the more we shall see and hear, although few speak to us in "English" as does the red-eyed vireo. While touring, we are of course on the move, whether wheeling across a continent or creeping around the yard to see what the ants and doodlebugs are doing. Motion often scares wildlife away. On any tour, pauses help us to know and appreciate animals better than if we are always rushing to get somewhere else. Take time to discover what is close at hand.

Even minipauses help us see animals. Perhaps you are strolling through a meadow in late summer. As you go you listen to the "orthopteran symphony," the multimingled songs of innumerable grasshoppers and crickets. A circle of sound surrounds you. Turn around 360 degrees. Listen. How these insects have multiplied in one season! The high trill-buzz sings sweetly to you of sun on meadows. (At least I hope you have good associations with these insect songs. If you are a Great Plains farmer whose investment of seed and labor has been devoured by such straight-winged insects, these grasshoppery sounds may be distressing.)

Sit down or sprawl amid the grasses, if the meadow has dried enough from the summer sun. Take a longer pause. Now instead of taking the broad, 360-degree survey of the meadow from above, just focus your attention on the grasses low in front of you. Inspect them. Watch them. If you are not a well-trained observer yet, you may not see much, just a miniature jungle of stems. What is there to see? Wait. Note the thicknesses and directions of the grass stems and the angles the leaves form with the stems. Think of their color, still green perhaps, or turning yellow or orange, or bleached. Motionless are these grasses of summer midday heat. But wait.

What is that slight movement? A stem bends a trifle from the shifting of a brown grasshopper whom you have outwaited. It renews its chewing on a leaf. Soon you hear a chirp by your shoe and see a black cricket fiddling. A little spider resumes work on a fishing net. And if you are quietly patient and lucky, as I have been sometimes, you may have a visit from a meadow vole; it accepts you as an unthreatening part of its environment. You may even be able to watch it gather seeds or make its miniature haystacks of cut-up grass.

Responsibilities elsewhere may bring you to your feet, or perhaps a desire to see what animals live in the hedgerow at the field's edge before you hike back to town or camp, or get your rig rolling on the highway again. As you stretch your limbs, unbend your back and flex your neck and fingers and thus prepare to move on; but pause one moment more to again take the broad view of the meadow. This second look will help you remember long afterward this grassy home for a million million little animals. They at first seem insignificant; but when you pause on your tour to let them show themselves, they become more important.

At 55 miles per hour on an interstate highway ("double-nickel on the superslab" in truckers' lingo), the only animals you may notice may be dead skunks, opossums, squirrels, jack rabbits, or armadillos (depending upon where you are), unless you have been alerted to other possibilities. If you are driving, keep your eyes *and* your attention on the road and traffic. A little bird watching, though, can prevent boredom and inattention. Restrict your attention to a cone of vision down the road ahead, just wide enough to watch for any hazards along the shoulders. Watch out for a deer crossing the road, and especially for any following directly after it! Your cone of vision broadens as it goes away from you to include more sky and landscape farther down the road, where you may spot interesting birds and mammals.

On the gravel along the shoulder, a pair of doves may be feeding on weed seeds, or a crow may be pecking at a road-kill of bird or other animal. (These DORs or "dead on roads" as zoologists call them, can be collected for research if not too mangled.) A snake may be seen sunning itself and absorbing road heat. On the verge, the mowed grass strip, a robin may be looking-listening-feeling(?) for earthworms, sparrows may be feeding on weed seeds, and starlings probing for the larvae of beetles.

A fence along the highway invites many perching birds. At 55 miles per hour you can identify several species by their size, shape, and posture (based on study of field guides consulted at rest stops). Some have "banner marks" aiding identification, for example white outer tail feathers on meadowlarks and wing bars or wing patches on some blackbirds.

A fence is always designed to mark an edge, a boundary between two environments: public highway and private property, pasture and cultivated field, meadow and woods. Most wildlife likes edges. An edge provides a border zone that gives an animal choices, for example a chance for a bird to feed on the multitude of summer crickets in a field or to seek the midday coolness of an adjacent woods; or for a rabbit to come out to nibble clover or to dash back for safety—if he senses a hawk's shadow—into the shrubbery at the wood margin.

When my cat goes stalking, he usually follows edges of habitats, for that is where he is most apt to have successful hunting. A fox's tracks in winter show where it too has been looking along edges for food. So you too, when looking for wildlife, will do best if your eyes scan environmental edges, fences for instance. That is true whether you are rolling at double-nickel or just going for a stroll from the motel or village inn.

Another edge worth watching is the treeline where perching birds can be seen against the sky. Tips of branches have characteristic shapes for different tree species. When you become practiced at recognizing tree tips, a bird's shape looks quite different and more or less noticeable even when perched motionless. Experienced ornithologists amaze beginners by the rapidity with which they spot birds.

Those red-eyed vireos who are so common in the "middle" of deciduous woods frequent the canopy of the forest, in the sunlight at the *top edge* of the trees. The hermit thrushes, which we associate with deep, dark forests, sing in the early morning and evening twilight from the tops of tall trees, where the beauty of their view must be almost equal to the glory of their music. So when you are in the middle of woods and cannot see their edges, listen for wildlife in the treetops. Not just birds either. At appropriate seasons in appropriate places you may hear squirrels scrambling to harvest acorns or other nuts or, in other continents, monkeys leaping and swinging in rainforest lianas, or a koala bear adjusting its sleeping position in a gum tree crotch.

In so-called "open country," neither built up nor clogged with trees, you do have opportunities to see some wildlife in the *middle* of their grassland habitats. The large mammals who are fleet of foot do not count on trees and shrubs for protective cover; they favor an unbroken view in which to watch for danger and then use their speed to try to outrun predators. The true antelopes are one example. In the Great Plains of North America, the so-called "antelopes" are more accurately called pronghorns. How they can scamper on their thin legs! Watch for their slower grazing movement in the broad spread of the short-grass plains, which may appear inanimately still, the only motion being the passing of midafternoon cloud shadows and windblown seeds of goatsbeard drifting by.

The little rodents of open grasslands called gophers, ground squirrels, and prairie dogs are definitely dependent on the edge between above-ground and below-ground environments. So too are the woodchucks who live in the mowed grasslands along highways, side roads, and fencerows, and their relatives the marmots whom you see emerging from or diving into their rockpile homes in the mountains. The rodent tribe has so many members and has adapted to so many different habitats that you can probably find them somewhere on your tour. I recommend traveling with a field guide to mammals as well as ones for birds and flowers. Many people give scarce thought to our fellow mammals, not understanding Saint Francis of Assisi speaking of Brother Wolf and Brother Rat.

A great advantage of open environments, whether spacious grasslands, deserts, shrublands, or wide bodies of water, is their expanse of sky. Birds are undoubtedly the kind of wildlife most enjoyed by most people. Skilled bird watchers are also sky watchers. For some kinds of birds, the more sky the better. The vultures and those hawks with broad wings adapted for soaring are fun to watch as they circle in wide skies. Take time to keep your eyes on one until it goes out of sight, a disappearing speck perhaps miles away. Near bodies of water you may be lucky enough to see an osprey, also called a fish hawk, circling, hovering, and diving for a fish to be carried off head-forward in its talons. A twittering of swallows may remind you to look up to watch their flittering progress through the air. In open country, you can often follow the swallows' flight to their nests in a river bank, barn, or hollow tree, depending upon the species.

During migrations, swallows, blackbirds, and many kinds of waterfowl seem sometimes to fill the sky in broad bands of winged motion, enthralling to see as they pass from horizon to horizon. The birds follow age-old routes called flyways. Perhaps you can plan a tour, as others have done, to coincide with the flights of winged travelers. Northward spring migrations of the colorful New World warblers flitting from tree to tree and bush to bush are more exciting to observe than their return trips in the autumn, when molted adults now accompanied by nondescript young are less conspicuous and more confusing to identify.

On the other hand, southbound migrations of shorebirds from midsummer to autumn are fun to follow along coastal beaches. Without an airplane you will fail to keep up with any one flock of sand-pipers, yellowlegs, or plovers, but you too can trend southward as the millions keep flowing to their winter homes. While enjoying the birds of ocean beaches, you can keep an eye on the vast flocks of migrating swallows that drift southward in late summer over the edges of salt marshes, no doubt reducing the populations of mosquitoes and green-head flies. So wave to the swallows; they will not scare as easily as the little "peep" sandpiper flocks settling to feed on the ocean beaches.

Many hawks also follow coasts, but greater numbers use fly-ways along ridges flanking river valleys. Prevailing winds in clear weather meet the mountainsides and create updrafts above them, thus making "bird elevators." A topographic map and advice from one of the many hawk-watching groups can enable you to plan a hawk-fol-lowing tour. Not only will you enjoy beautiful country in spring or au-tumn, but you can, *if* the appropriate winds develop, thrill to the sight of hundreds or even thousands of hawks spiraling upward and onward in whole "kettles" riding the rising air currents. Find a peak with panoramic views for the best hawk watching. Have a field guide to birds to help you identify some. As with people at a party, it's nice to know some names in case you might meet them again—or want to look them up.

While on your hilltop watching for hawks, you may notice the large numbers of insects that tend to accumulate on mountaintops in favorable weather. If you have brought lunch with you, yellow-jacket wasps or their relatives may swarm to get their share, particularly if you have a jam or jelly sandwich. In dry weather especially, they may be thirsty and attracted also to your moist sweet lips. Ah wildlife! I find it best in such situations to share my riches with the wasps, setting a juicy crumb aside to attract them. If that doesn't work, I wrap up my lunch and philosophize that it will taste even better later. Then I be-come absorbed in noting the rich gathering of beetles, flies, dragon-flies, and unidentified you-name-its that the elevation has attracted.

Concentration of animals at hilltops, along shores, or in herds are apt to attract our attention. When you are touring by car, insects may be most noticeable when they squash in great numbers on your windshield. Some warm evenings in spring or early summer, driving down into a little valley, you may suddenly hit a flight of mayflies. If traveling into the sunset, you will be wise to pull off the road in a safe place to wash your windshield; driving into the light especially makes bug-blots impair vision, even dangerously as darkness approaches. In my car I keep a bottle of WWW, windshield wash water, and a plastic-covered sponge for such occasions. Headlights get a cleaning too; they need it. (If the road has been dusty, I polish rear lights also, for safety.)

Such a pause impedes progress on a trip. But really what is progress? Only forward motion toward a destination? The stopping time may be well invested if it enables you to watch a live mayfly in its floppy flight or see it perched with upright triangular wings and gracefully upturned abdomen decorated with two long cerci. If you have wisely turned off your motor during this interlude, you may be treated to the evensong of a thrush. If you have a tape recorder with you, try to pick up the bird's music. You might end the recording with the sound of your motor starting, reminder of the day you hit those "nasty mayflies."

Another evening you may walk to a stream in a little valley to see if the mayflies have hatched and the fish are jumping for them. If you like to fish, you may want to plan your vacations around the seasons when you can rendezvous with the glimmers and splashes of sport fish, the lines and hooks, the knives and pans. (I've long been bothered by the name U.S. *Fish* & Wildlife Service. Fish *are* wildlife! When the old U.S. Biological Survey was reorganized in the 1930s, fishery interests held out for including the word *Fish* distinctly, thereby causing continuing confusion by implying that fish are not truly wildlife. This book does not perpetuate that illogic by having one chapter on wildlife and another on fish.)

In your travels, do give attention to fish, whether leaping, sulking in cool pools, spawning on gravel beds, schooling in tidal creeks, or taking flying leaps onto your deck from warm ocean waters. I've never seen a truly ugly fish—grotesque perhaps, but never ugly. When 9 years old and visiting Italy, I was served my first *whole* fish. Its cold eye staring up at me from my plate unnerved me for a bit and led me to wonder whether it might still be alive. It did not look as though it wanted to be eaten. But it was beautiful. With parental prodding, I managed to eat some of it.

A tour can be enriched by a visit to a fish hatchery. Children, whether of fish-fancying parents or not, will be delighted at the big fish usually on exhibition. A fishing adult will be interested in how the hatchery is managed, the water flow and its temperature, the fish food, and precautions against diseases in the abnormal concentrations of fish. Nonfishers may enjoy a glimpse of fish-eating birds such as osprey, heron, and kingfisher; they live the good life on such a glut of fish, but dangerously, usually not for long around fish hatcheries.

As you leave a fish hatchery to continue your tour, you may turn over in your mind this matter of our society's apparent need for "put-and-take" game management. We raise large quantities of fish and pheasants to *put* in environments where sports people with rod and gun can *take* them. This is not only good sport from the fisher's point of view but also good business for those who profit from outdoor recreation. Urban concentrations of people have destroyed so much wildlife habitat, both land and water, that put-and-take is necessary to supply hunters and fishers with game, which often could not support the added "puttings" were it not for the "takings." This complicated matter of wildlife management near cities is worth much thought. Get more facts. Ask questions as you tour. Get information from objectively knowledgeable people.

In France there is, as of this writing, a shortage of frogs. Their populations are shrinking because of the high demand for their delicious legs. As you tour, give thought to frogs, and to their relatives the toads and salamanders. They are some of the most interesting wildlife when you get to know them. Do not be oblivious to animals amphibious. They have tricks for using both land and water at various stages of their lives. I am a particular fan of their music during mating seasons. The trill of an American toad has a subtle simplicity that I listen for each spring. Fowler's toad has a belligerent, twangy way of singing of love. On spring evenings, make a trip to the edge of some wetland to hear the peepings, trillings, gruntings, and banjo strummings of an amphibian chorus. If you want to hear an almost deafening symphony, go to the Deep South and hear the chorus frogs in the bald-cypress swamps.

I knew a wonderful man who used to take toad tours around town. He knew all their haunts and would borrow individual toads from them to show to children in the city schools. One very wet spring evening, I accompanied him to the amazing one-night nuptials of spadefoot toads. If you live too far from Louisiana to travel to hear chorus frogs, perhaps you can tour around your town to find the whereabouts and what-they-are-doings of your local toads and frogs. Or take a tour around your own garden and be on friendly terms with your local toad. Its color probably matches the soil, and it patrols your garden eating pesty bugs while you're asleep.

Long tour or short tour, you can see wildlife if you look and listen for it. If snow is deep, you will have to look longer and listen more persistently. In the city, you will have to be content with those animals who have proved they can put up with and profit by association with humankind. But even urban pigeons—and cockroaches, of lineage far more ancient than ours—are worthy of our admiring attention, even if only while trying to reduce their populations to numbers we can live with. Especially while traveling, give thought to wildlife. Your trip will be enriched by it.

And if possible, introduce someone to the song of the red-eyed vireo, that "Do you see it? Do you hear it? Do you believe it?" that still questions me from the treetops of its deciduous woodland habitat.

III

PEOPLE'S
PATTERNS

13 FARMS

Some landscapes are wild, some tame. Farms are designed to be tame: they are lands which are supposed to do what they are told, to be obedient to farmers' wishes. But getting obedience from nature can be difficult. As you travel, you can see farmlands in many stages of obedience and disobedience. Farming is always a struggle.

Productively managed soil is the basis of much of what we call civilization. My first experiences with managing soil, at age 12, came when my father asked, "Would you like to have your own garden this year?" Would I! Dad plowed it and helped me to buy manure, lime, and vegetable seeds, and to set straight rows and sow them. He did *not* help me weed. That was when I learned how nature likes to have its own way.

While you tour you can keep an eye open for farmers' successes in getting nature to serve them. Nature's servants include sun, air, water, soil, and bees. Don't forget bees. All these have been basic to farming ever since our long-ago ancestors first scratched the soil, sowed a handful of seeds, weeded around the upsprouting plants, and guarded them from wild animals—and probably from prehistoric dogs who would try to bury bones in these first attempts at gardens.

Humankind has come a long way since these earliest agriculturalists experimented with controlling nature. Look around at agricultural landscapes as you travel. They can reveal what farmers are getting *from* nature and what they are doing *to* nature. Farmers have made new designs on the countryside.

Each of nature's climates has its own patterns, and within each climate, its microclimates, topography, and local soils make subpatterns. For each, different peoples have their own traditional ways of trying to make soil productive; and in many places modern methods are dramatically changing the complexion of Earth's face.

If on your tour you jet long distances, you may start in potato country and land amid lands of terraced rice; or take off from wheatlands and alight near pineapple fields; or leave blueberry barrens and arrive in sugar cane country. But your tour may be on a much smaller scale, say a short walk or a ride by bike, car, or bus to the nearest gardens and farms. Except in cities, deserts, forests, and steep mountains, farms are usually plentifully awaiting your inspection.

Close to cities only the best soils are still in farms. Economic pressures of nonagricultural development often put farmers out of business. Unfortunately only a very small fraction of the fertile, easily worked soils are still farmed in urbanized and urbanizing areas. The remaining ones are worthy of your special attention. They are usually "truck farms" owned by people with a long tradition of caring for and about the land they till. The soil is mostly fertile, level, lowland loam. Around the older cities it used to be enriched by cartloads of manure hauled out from the horse-car barns on return trips from trucking vegetables to city markets.

In near-city truck farms, the farmers' houses are often small compared to the neighboring buildings. The yards too are small and usually neat, with little space for recreation. Almost all the land is needed to grow cash crops. In the eastern United States, look for colorful flower beds, grape arbors, small fig trees, and maybe still some old Lombardy poplars suggesting that the farm family has southern or central European origins. In the West, see if you can spot indicators of oriental influences along with Hispanic and Amerindian cultural contributions.

106

When touring in Europe, you often still find homes clustered within rather distinct village boundaries beyond which villagers have their small plots of gardens or farms. Some have been owned by the same families for centuries. The resulting patchwork patterns often have great esthetic appeal for tourists from the States. Although the land's beauty undoubtedly appeals to the owners too, their devotion to growing crops stems largely from the importance to their families' economies. Look for various kinds of walls and fences between properties and for little tool houses built so that implements do not have to be carried out from town, often while walking or cycling.

By comparison, the Black Forest region of Bavaria in southern West Germany has many larger farms. There the landscape pattern results partly from the inheritance system: the youngest son, rather than the oldest, inherits the farm. Tourists often rave about the beauty of Der Schwartzwald (The Black Forest). If you have not been there, I hope you can go; and if you have had that pleasure already, like me you may long to go there again. Those youngest sons, for years working with their fathers and in turn being fathers, have been good custodians of the rolling hills where pastures and fields of hay and potatoes are backdropped by the dark spruces that lend the region its name.

In the steeper mountains of nearby Switzerland and Austria, pasture lands predominate with some grains and other tilled crops in the narrow, U-shaped valleys. Villages are often on the triangular alluvial fans of gravels deposited by mountain torrents where they meet the leveler lands of valley bottoms. These gravels supply good water for the village homes and shops. The farmers go up the slopes to their herds or out onto the fertile valley terraces and bottoms for their cattle and tilled crops. In the villages, tiny gardens use every inch of space intensively for flowers and vegetables. For instance, a masonry wall may be resplendent with flowers in niches or on top of walls in planters. Any level place is at a premium for planting in the Alps.

Farming in any alpine valley has two major problems: erosion and sedimentation. It is difficult to hold the soil in place on slopes whenever the native vegetation is removed by cultivating, overgrazing by cows or sheep, or overbrowsing by goats. Goats are now prohibited on many Swiss mountains. Terracing to make level strips for planting is laborious, and the retaining walls are hard to maintain. Wherever in your travels you see terraces you can marvel at the investment of human energy that produced them, almost all of them before machinery could take some of the strain off human backs. The battle against soil erosion on steep slopes is an age-old one, increasingly being fought by people in many parts of the world.

Sedimentation results when soil washed from slopes must be deposited when the current carrying it slows down on leveler land. You can sometimes see large areas of fertile valley soils buried by sterile gravels brought down by streams from melting snow and glacial ice. If your touring takes you to the Alps, Himalayas, Andes, Rockies, or other lofty mountains, watch for patterns of fertile loams and sterile piedmont gravels. A farmer's family can live on well-cared-for loams for generations. Only one or two generations may be able to survive financially by selling gravel for highway roadbeds and for concrete construction; gravels cannot be considered a renewable resource.

How different are the farming patterns of flatlands! Of course climate is always a dominating influence, in different ways in different places. In southern Florida dark muck soils, developed over centuries under native grasses in the Everglades, have been exploited for vast fields of sugar cane, carrots, celery, and other crops. With the sawgrass and its associated plants removed by gigantic machines and the water table lowered by ditching, the soils can yield crop bonanzas. But when the cane is burned over to facilitate harvesting, valuable organic matter goes up in clouds of smoke, lost. And when the subtropical sun broils down on exposed muck, the soil shrinks and crumbles, again losing precious organic matter. Some of these fields are flooded in summer to protect their organic matter from sun-caused deterioration.

In climates much colder in winter and dry in summer except for spotty thunderstorms, for example North Dakota, wheat can be grown in summer, so-called "spring wheat" planted in spring (as compared to "winter wheat" planted in autumn in warmer climates). There may not be enough moisture, however, to grow a crop every year. Here the landscape has vast patterns of alternating stripes of dark loams lying fallow and of crops in some stage of development from little green shoots to waving golden grain and then cut stubble.

In such windswept landscapes, the farmhouses lie low to the ground. Some may be partially shaded by a grove of prairie cottonwoods planted years ago by foresighted and optimistic pioneer farmers. Some may have one or more windbreaks of Siberian elm, cottonwood, boxelder, and perhaps Scots pine, along with shrubs that can withstand the drying winds. Long windbreaks of similar trees and shrubs may stretch for a mile or more along one field. During the 1930s, plans were made for such a "shelterbelt" from the Gulf of Mexico to Canada, trying to remake the farming climate of the Great Plains. Many farms did not maintain their segments of this grand plan. Some windbreaks have even been destroyed to make bigger fields for bigger machines. More erosion by wind is sure to result.

Watch for barns in the farming landscape. They stand as evidence of farmers' struggles with nature's climatic adversities. Old barns are fast disappearing from the American farmscape. Many an old-timer built his barn and lived in it with his family and livestock while he built his house. Fire and disrepair have been the symptoms of changed fortunes and changing times. Modern transport has decreased the importance of storing produce on the family farm; instead it is shipped off to industrial processing plants or to markets. Formerly lofts were stuffed with sun-cured hay. Occasionally this hay remained damp enough for microorganisms to thrive in it, generating enough heat for "spontaneous" combustion; the resulting fire, almost impossible to quell with buckets of water, spelled tragedy for the barn and the farm family. In time, neighbors might help with a barn raising, but often the farm would be abandoned.

Lightning too took its toll: a snap, crackle, and pop would suddenly no longer have his barn. Modern hay-balers compress hay into cubes or huge cylindrical bales that can shed water and therefore be stored outdoors. Who, then, needs a barn? Some still do.

Dairy farmers in cool climates still need barns. Some are glad to have visitors to admire their cows and learn a little about dairying. The odors in the barns convey warm feelings of vitality to anybody who appreciates the cycle of grazing and cowflop fertility in pastures or the munching of multipatterned milch cows in their stable stanchions at milking time.

More prevalent in many regions than old barns with haylofts are tall, cylindrical silos holding nutritiously fermenting silage of chopped corn and alfalfa for cattle feed. Even silos may in time give way to the bulldozed trenches for trench silage or the aboveground storage of fodder and other farm products under huge plastic tarpaulins held down by discarded tires. Landscape artists may be disappointed by such trends.

Old multisided hop barns are disappearing from upstate New York. Apparently one can now flavor beer without storing hops in hop barns. Round barns, ones built "with no corners in which the devil can hide," also seem out of fashion, although there is considerable evidence that the devil is still around. In the Connecticut River Valley of New England you can still see tobacco barns; some have sides with vertical boards that pivot so they can be tipped out in summer to ventilate the tobacco leaves drying inside.

Touring in upstate New England you can see barns attached to the farmhouses, again as an adaptation to climate. In weather deemed bad, at least blizzard-difficult, trips back and forth between the barn and main house—through the connected kitchen, woodshed, and carriage shed—are much more convenient than struggles across the yard. One disadvantage of such connected construction has been the problem of saving the house if the barn catches fire. The destructive forces of nature, lightning, and spontaneous combustion of hay have been supplemented at times by human failings to control kerosene lamps, exhausts of internal combustion engines, and burning tobacco. And add electric wiring: We had a goat who ate the wires to the radio that had been installed to make the cows more content.

In warmer and often drier climates, stables are important elements in farm landscapes. Usually only one-story high, they include one or more stalls for horses, mules, donkeys, or goats, and sometimes other animals, plus rooms or open bays for storing grain, hay, and salt. A harness room, also called tack room, is an important segment of a stable.

While on tour you can profitably give attention to architecture of other farm buildings. A small family farm will likely have a chicken coop and fenced hen yard. By contrast, a large poultry business may have a three-story poultry house that looks like a factory. Thousands of laying hens or broilers are tended by automatic feeders and waterers; in the basement a bulldozer may push straight through to harvest the chicken manure.

Older farms often had a horse barn separate from the cow

barn. A pig sty had its own little shelter. A blacksmith shop might stand by itself, ready for maintaining farm machines and for shoeing horses and oxen. A well house kept water clean and cool, and in summer made a good place to linger before returning to a hot kitchen.

Yes, outbuildings have contributed much to the productive daily life of farm families as well as to the picturesque design of rural landscapes. Children on tour, especially those from cities and suburbs, may enjoy seeing how many different kinds of farm buildings they can spot. During the game they can learn about lifestyles unknown to many children today.

For many years, indeed centuries, one outbuilding has been very important. It has been dignified by many names including outhouse, latrine, privy, and one-holer, two-holer, or three-holer depending upon its furniture. I like the eighteenth-century name for it, "the necessary." Its location was downwind from the main house.

All of which should prove that farm scenes are worth more than a passing glance if you are at all intrigued by how people and nature get along together, with climate always in ultimate control.

14   RANGELANDS

How much pasture does a pony need? How much land was needed for the 40 million or so bison that America used to support? In both cases an answer depends upon how much grass the climate and soil can grow. Climate, soil, grass, and animals are all worthy of our attention when nature touring. So let's go to grasslands where animals range.

We say an animal *ranges* when it wanders over an area looking for food and water and, when mature, a mate. And when we think of cowboys and cowgirls and their ponies tending cattle, we speak of cattle rangelands. That is where the cows and calves and heifers and bulls spend most of their time looking for grass and grazing. There are shepherds and grassy sheep ranges too, and people who tend camels and llamas and alpacas, and lands where goatherds care for goats that browse on woody vegetation. People also speak of poultry ranges where fowl are fenced. Roaming the world we can find many kinds of rangelands. This chapter, though, focuses on grasslands for cattle.

Grasses grow naturally where trees cannot, because of climate. That is a useful statement even though you can think of many exceptions, for example the grassy plains of Africa with their scattered acacia trees, and other savannas. So to travel to rangelands you must find a climate with enough water for grasses but not enough for forest trees. In the United States that means areas mostly west of the hundredth meridian of longitude (that is, 100 degrees west of the prime meridian in Greenwich, England). That invisible line passes through Texas, Oklahoma, Kansas, Nebraska, the Dakotas, and Manitoba. It marks the division between the moister East and the drier West. To the west of the hundredth meridian, you see grass and cowponies and wide-ranging cattle under a wide-spreading sky.

Many cattle ranges are like kitchen ranges in one respect: they are either hot or cold much of the time. Of course you can dial *warm* on an electric stove; and Pacific grasslands are somewhat moderated by air from the Pacific Ocean; but, broadly stated, most rangelands are hot in summer and cold in winter. They lie under cloudless skies giving plenty of sun for grasses, cattle, and horses, but usually not much rain. Snow? Sometimes no, sometimes yes. If you tour western Texas in winter, be prepared for a "norther," a blizzard worthy of Maine but with stronger winds. Going to Kansas in summer? Wear a broad-brimmed cowboy hat; you will need its shade. Even so far north as Manitoba summer temperatures can reach 100 degrees Fahrenheit.

The great plains of North America, Eurasia, Africa, South America, and Australia exhibit *continentality*: They have climates far removed from the moderating marine influences of ocean waters. They are not good places for trees to grow, except for a brave few such as cottonwoods and Siberian elms. Annual rainfall averages less than 20 inches. Where rainfall is truly scant in deserts, the only grasses that can survive are widely scattered *bunch grasses* and *annual grasses* whose seeds lie sleeping until some year a thundershower may bless them with its holy water. Where a little more moisture is available, *short grasses* cover the land thinly. More moisture yet supports areas of somewhat taller *mid-grasses*. Areas with sufficient water for *tall grasses* are called "prairies" in North America. They hold wind-waved sway along the borders of treelands. As climates change—as climates do over centuries or even decades—prairies advance into the woodlands in drier periods; in moister times, they retreat as trees invade them.

I usually tour with maps of topography, climates, and vegetation. Sometimes I take small photographs of maps on 2-by-2-inch slides; these can be carried on a nature tour with an inexpensive hand lens rather than a projector for viewing. I once made a set of such vegetation maps for a student bicycling across the continent. They are easy to pack and consult en route. Having maps with such data sharpens your eyes for ways the physical environment shapes the lives of plants and people in different areas.

There is no problem recognizing rangelands when you are in the middle of them; but to be sensitive to the subtle transition zones between vegetation types, maps of natural resources help you see much more detail, supplying little pictures within the big picture. Human land use often follows nature's little patterns, as well it should.

So what do *you* see where the cattle roam their ranges "and the skies are not cloudy all day"? Whether walking or speeding on wheels, you see *sky*. Mostly blue sky in summer, often with a few cumulus clouds, and sometimes with a gray-bellied cell of clouds that might develop into a towering black-belly producing one of the thundershowers typical of midcontinental climates. Winter brings more layered clouds and more or less snow. The condition of range vegetation for ranchers' cattle and crops depends on what the sky provides of sun and moisture—the latter being the limiting factor most of the time. People who make a living from the land, or try to, keep an eye on the sky as surely as do sailors on the sea.

The wind that sweeps across the range you will not see, but you will surely sense it almost every day. It moves unhindered by tree friction for miles and miles and miles. It waves the shimmering prairie grasses and ripples across the short grasses of the great plains. It conjures up spiraling dust devils that swirl up bare soil into roving funnels. Sometimes it orients the stance of cattle and may bring them some relief from flies. At times it whips up and blowtorches dread prairie fires and bush fires. It hums through utility wires and whistles or howls around corners and windows of the space-dwarfed ranch buildings. One of the most difficult aspects of life for pioneer women from the forested regions was the ever-present sense of wind, one of nature's apparently alien forces to be contended with. But wind turns the windmills to pump water from underground aquifers for human consumption, for cattle tanks, and for irrigation, making life possible for people and their animals.

Rangelands often have some shrubs along with grasses. Sagebrush is perhaps the best known in America, but many other bushes may dot the ranges of cattle, sheep, alpaca, llamas, or whatever stock are being herded where you travel. Some shrubs, for example creosote bushes, are widely scattered in desert ranges; bunch and annual grasses are sparse indeed there, and thin cattle have to range widely for slim pickings. In the Sonoran Desert of southwestern United States, the creosote bushes give a characteristic smell to the environment, perhaps distasteful at first to touring strangers but pleasant to those who linger long enough to learn the delights of desert life.

Where moisture is more plentiful but not enough for trees, a shrubland with more continuous cover of bushes may share the soil with grasses, for instance on the foothills of mountains that capture some of the moisture from passing winds or which create updrafts triggering an occasional thundershower. Rabbitbrush is locally common in the western United States; this yellow-flowered cousin of the sagebrush is a member of the great worldwide Composite Family of plants (*Compositae*).

Some ranchers have declared war on shrubs. On dry rangelands the bushes do take up space and use water which could support more palatable fodder for livestock. In arid areas, some shrubs called "well plants" (*phreatophytes*) send their roots amazingly deep into the ground after a single rare rainstorm and thus can tap a low watertable below the reach of most desert plants. Other shrubs have wide-spreading roots near the surface that secrete chemicals inhibiting the growth of other plants which might compete for the scant water. Typically such shrubs create what has been called "leopard-spotted vegetation," individual bushes being widely spaced.

Ranchers sometimes snag out shrubs by dragging a chain between two parallel tractors, or pull huge spiked drums across the shrubbery to break it down, or spray selective herbicides to kill the woody plants and spare the grasses; these methods are more or less effective in promoting better grazing. Brush control is one form of range management. Sometimes the excessive shrubbery has been a result of former overgrazing, with weakened sod unable to resist invading shrubs and herbs like the tumbleweed known as Russian Thistle, especially during dry phases of climatic cycles.

You can form your own opinions about the merits of various

115

kinds of land management. I remember the excellent exhibit of the Landmark Visitor Center in northern Scotland. You walk along a twisting, up-and-down corridor representing the Highlands; along its walls are pictures and signs describing grouse moors, peat bogs, sheep pastures, reforestation plantations, and hydropower developments. At the corridor's end is a bare little room with one sign over the exit. It says something like: *You have just been given 1000 acres of highlands. How will you use them?*

Suppose *you* were responsible for managing the rangelands you are visiting, in the Scottish highlands, Wyoming great plains, Argentine pampas, Australian outback, or wherever? Would you advocate removing *all* the shrubs, or a percentage of all kinds, or just certain species? Would you perhaps leave all the bushes and limit your grazing to the grasses naturally available? Would you set aside one natural area of grassland and shrubbery—an exclosure from which you would fence out your stock—to see what nature would do unattended? If so, how large a patch should it be, and should it be on your better soils or on those least desirable for raising grass for your domestic animals? How much consideration would you give to the native fauna, jack rabbits, pronghorns ("antelope"), bison, or whatever life your area might naturally support?

As a tourist unfamiliar with rangelands, you will not jump to quick answers to these questions. If you lived in a rancher's boots for a year—or, better, through a wet-dry-wet climatic cycle of several years—you would have a deeper understanding of people/land relationships. Yet you would still be humbly doubtful about some aspects of your rangeland management, still a seeker of more facts and greater understanding. There is always so much to know.

Consider for instance the complicated problem of "prairie dogs," gophers, and their relatives living in rangeland burrows. As you travel you may spot them sitting by their little mounds of earth or frisking about when not eating the grasses and forbs (non-grassy herbs) nearby; or they may remain hidden, retired in their burrows, maybe pulling the soil back to close their homes against enemies, heat, or cold. Ranchers often feel the need to poison these cute little rodents who compete with livestock for forage. Other animals, though, may eat the poison. The food webs of "who eats whom" can thus be disrupted. A prairie rodent population explosion may even be due to ranchers' attempts to control other animal "nuisances." For example, rodent predators such as coyotes may have previously been poisoned because they killed lambs or other young stock.

Another problem of rangelands develops when people decide to change from a grazing livelihood to farming. Perhaps plowing up native grasses and planting crops promises more income. As you travel from a more humid area to a drier one, watch for the transition from farms to ranches (or conversely from ranches to farms when touring to a more humid region). The changes may be subtle: Big cultivated fields of moisture-loving corn gradually change to wide expanses of wheat, then to small patches of wheat amid grazing lands, and finally to ranches whose only cultivated land may be a tiny garden partly shaded by the house or a cottonwood, and watered with dishwater. Again, climate is in control of land use and human lives.

But climate changes. A few wetter years can tempt a rancher to convert grasslands to tillage and plant wheat. But if a new, drier spell comes the wheat may fail, producing no grain and abandoning soil to the winds, creating dust storms and wind erosion of topsoil developed over centuries. This can be tragic; banks foreclose on the landowner, and tradespeople who depend upon his business may fail too. But far worse, short-term error in land management can bring irreversible disaster to the rangeland environment. A century may pass before grasses and forbs can recolonize the eroded soil and create topsoil to replace what has blown away. A desert may result.

I well remember as a schoolboy near Boston one late spring day in the mid-1930s, looking up and seeing a *brown* sky! It was colored by soil from the "dust bowl" in the southern Great Plains. I was seeing the soil of Nebraska, Kansas, Oklahoma, and Texas up there over my head. That image returned to me years later when I saw brown sky over the Tasman Sea east of drought-stricken southern Australia. I hope that in your travels *you* never see brown sky. Millions of people today depending on overpopulated grasslands are in a no-win situation—until their numbers are reduced in one way or another, to proportions in balance with their climate, vegetation, and animals.

People patterns are less conspicuous on rangelands than on farmlands. Ranch houses are ground-hugging in the windy environments and widely scattered in the vast spaces. You can see some cultivated crops—most notably an occasional conspicuously green field of irrigated alfalfa—but most of the vegetation that puts meat on a steer and money in the bank is grass, usually native grasses distributed according to nature's patterns and thus unmanaged. You may see a windmill that pumps water into the stock tank. In the ordinarily dry weather, a plume of dust in the distance may indicate a rancher in a pickup truck whisking along a dirt road or taking off across country to look for cattle or to mend fence.

Fences are a more omnipresent feature of rangelands except where there are still occasional tracts of *open range* where livestock can roam unrestricted. Fences follow roads and occasionally branch off across country, but away from a road you may have to walk or ride your horse a long way before you come across another fence! In strange country, better to follow one fence than to leave it and get lost looking for another. Besides, you may well see more wildlife along the fence; in the American Great Plains, listen to the meadowlarks, bobolinks, lark buntings, and, near any swales, red-winged blackbirds singing from their favorite posts.

Fenceposts speak of privately held land, a concept foreign to American Indians before Europeans came to take grasslands for themselves. Posts and the wire strung between them speak of the history of rangeland use. Posts did not come easily to the American plains where the only trees might be cottonwoods and hackberries along a distant watercourse; and in South and Western Australia, in the endless-seeming expanses of the Nullarbor Plain, only a shrubby gum tree *might* be available. ("Nullarbor" means "no tree," a most descriptive name for that part of the Australian Outback.)

When homesteaders came to eastern Kansas and Oklahoma after the Civil War, they encountered a beautiful stretch of midgrass prairie with little bluestem to the horizon and far beyond. They wanted to plow it for crops but couldn't because of the underlying limestones rich in flint, an obdurate rock if ever there was one. Today these Flint Hills hold some of the best remnants of the original midgrass prairie, saved by the rock substrate that lets grass roots go deep but excludes the plow. I knew I'd reached the Flint Hills the first time when I saw stone fenceposts along the highway.

On that same tour I visited the Nebraska Sand Hills, another beautiful grassland of some 24,000 square miles (though none visibly square on the gently contoured hills). Miles of fence flanked Highway 83, some posts steel, some wood; now and again wooden posts carried wires away from the road across the rolling hills of little bluestem and its fellow grasses wearing their purple-red and golden autumn colors. At one place I was taking pictures, a black stallion appeared over a rise, watched me perhaps disdainfully, restricted as I was between two highway fences, snorted, and kicked up a storm of fine sand as he wheeled around and disappeared, able no doubt to gallop for miles before coming to the next fence.

In the western Texas panhandle, flat as a pancake, pioneers venturing across the treeless shortgrass plain lacked any landmarks by which, if necessary, they could retrace their way. So, as they went, they drove stakes into the ground as markers. To this day the region is called by the Spanish name, *Llano Estacado*, the Staked Plain. But new people patterns have been added. Watch for highways radiating from Amarillo and Lubbock and the right-angle network of local roads to the widely scattered ranches, some with meager plantings of low trees and shrubs as windbreaks. Fenceposts? Watch for scissor-tailed flycatchers on them.

Cattle ranges in the United States are not all on the prairies and high plains east of the Rocky Mountains. They can also be found on the Colorado Plateau, in the Great Basin of Utah and Nevada, and the Palouse of eastern Washington. Pacific bunchgrass ranges of California's Central Valley can still be found along the foothills of the Sierra and on the Coast Ranges, but they have been diminished by irrigated agriculture and extensive urban and suburban development.

Very different are the grasslands of south-central Florida. The Kississimi Prairie, probably the best known, lies between Orlando and Lake Okeechobee. The grassy flats interspersed with oaks and palmettos are a good place to look for sandhill cranes. Cattle raising increased in Florida as stock breeders raised animals better adapted to the humid heat than were the original longhorns of Texas introduced by Spaniards. Patterns of land use are increasingly influenced by genetic research creating plants and animals better adapted to what would otherwise be economically marginal areas for crops and herds.

One great reason for travel is to provide comparisons with the way things are at home. Since we in America have almost entirely fenced the open ranges, we have *en*closed our stock. In Great Britain there is emphasis on *ex*closures. In England I saw wild-running ponies in the New Forest (incidentally *not* new, dating back to 1066 and the Norman conquerers!). Elsewhere in Britain many areas were fenced to keep stock out of agricultural areas and reforestation projects. The Swiss use fences to keep sheep off the upper slopes of the Alps where former grazing has denuded slopes and promoted avalanches. What works in one part of the world may not in another, where both environments and patterns of human culture may be very different.

Today there is much turmoil in the tropics and subtropics. Overgrazing of the Sahel south of the Sahara Desert and elsewhere in Africa and India has promoted desertification and brought misery to millions. In the Amazon Basin, reducing the tropical forests to grasslands for disease-resistant cattle (for beef export) is certain to create ecological problems. But here's a happy thought: We can perhaps learn from experience, and traveling with our eyes open can make us more experienced. To try to understand relationships between nature's patterns and people's patterns is, to my mind, what nature touring is all about.

15   FORESTS

A tour in your yard or down a street may reveal a maple. One tree is hardly a forest, nor a woodland, orchard, or grove. But if you have followed its yearly cycle of budding, leafing, flowering, and fruiting, you have come a long way in your understanding of forests.

On our Planet Earth, nature tends to grow trees wherever a year produces 30 or more inches of rainfall plus enough warmth to allow leaves to make food for the roots, stems, leaves, flowers, and fruits. The fruits develop, protect, and distribute seeds to replace trees, which, like all living things, must perish. This neat process of replenishment has helped trees sustain us humans to the present, with food, shelter, fiber, medicine, and many amenities such as shade, filtered water, protected soil, flood control, flowers, perfumes, flavors, and, to be more specific, music of jostling aspen leaves.

If you are a gardener strolling around your yard, you may have mixed emotions about the impressive number of maple seedlings sprouting in your flowerbeds. They do not belong there. If allowed to grow, they will spoil the pattern of your garden. Plants in the wrong place are weeds to be eradicated. You know they belong in your compost pile, to rot and help make new soil for your garden. You know how to manage this incipient "forest."

Now please buy an imaginary ticket for a quick flight of the imagination around our "Water Planet." Watch as we fly for the patterns and distribution of forests. In *high latitudes* of the northern hemisphere, you see spread across the north of America and Eurasia dark spruce-fir forests; their needle-leaved evergreen trees have evolved short branches that bend rather than break under the weight of winter snows. Fingers of spruce-fir forests extend southward along tops of mountain ranges, which have colder climates than their valleys, and in places along coasts where cold ocean currents make favorable climates.

In *upper middle latitudes*, forests have mostly broad-leaved trees such as maples, oaks, and hickories. In summer they look a lighter green and in autumn a mixture of reds and yellows before shedding their leaves for the grays of winter.

Now we jet down into the *lower middle latitudes*. We note mostly areas with drier climates, or at least ones where the greater heat and evaporation leave less water for trees—less than that 30 inches of annual rainfall. Many swampy valleys, though, have forests of broad-leaved trees and, in some places, bald-cypress, and have in general far more species than do the forests of higher latitudes. Also darker pine forests can be seen, especially on sandier soils. Where these forests are on desert fringes, the trees are scattered and stunted, more like shrubs than trees, forming scrub woodlands such as the pinyon-juniper woodlands of the American Southwest.

Flying over the *low latitudes* of the equator, you look down on the tropical rainforests of broad-leaved evergreen trees. Up in the cold stratosphere, in your pressurized cabin, it is hard to imagine the hot and steamy forests far beneath you, and the torrid deserts devoid of trees.

If you are planning a real, more down-to-earth-tour, you will do well to seek forests. They are cooler in summer and warmer in winter than adjacent open spaces, at least in those middle-latitude climates with such seasons. In the low-latitude tropics also, forests have more moderated, uniform climates than do open areas. Many recrea-

122

tional parks boast of their trees. People who live in dry regions are particularly attracted to wooded areas for holidays. Perhaps you have enjoyed campgrounds in one of the many U.S. National Forests or in national or state parks, with shade, a cool stream, wildflowers, and wild animals. I have been grateful many times that trees have been protected in these recreation areas.

One of the best tours I ever had was with American foresters going to Germany, Austria, and Switzerland to study forest recreation in the Alps. European foresters showed us cable cars, ski runs, and the most beautifully built and maintained mountain trails that I have ever seen. But what impressed me most were the efforts to replace those forests that had been destroyed on the upper slopes during the previous 500 years. Their burning and overgrazing had brought grief to the villages in the valleys because of erosion, sedimentation, landslides, and avalanches. New trees were needed to anchor the steep slopes. I saw in the Swiss town of Andermatt a whole community of adults and children who joined in replanting the mountain pastures with little trees grown in valley nurseries.

During the writing of this chapter, television brought news of disastrous floods near Zurich, Switzerland. Sadly I though back to the deforested Swiss mountains where trees long ago had drunk deeply of the rains and melting snows. How important are forests! Forests held absorbed water and helped it trickle in where dead roots left little tunnels in the soil; forests with their fallen leaves and twigs held the developing soil in place century after century; forests held the deep mountain snows and prevented avalanches; forests prevented floods. And I thought of the little trees, about a foot tall, which people had been planting, such little trees with such a big job to do replacing the ancient forests. I must go back to Andermatt to see how much they have grown in a quarter of a century. If you get there first, please let me know.

In the early 1940s, on a tour of duty for Uncle Sam, I planted little evergreen trees on abandoned pastures on the upper slopes of the Susquehanna River watershed, in New York State near Cooperstown. Some 40 years later I revisited those fields, but they were pine forests now, with some of the spruces and larches we had planted, plus nature-sown maples coming in as understory. In those new forests the pattern of the evergreens revealed that young men had planted thousands in curving rows along the contours of the hillsides. I like to think that those trees helped during the Susquehanna's severe floods, and that they will live to do so again and again.

But those New York hills are not the high mountains of Switzerland. "My" trees grew fast. They dropped many needles making absorbent duff and humus on the forest floor. But those little trees high above Andermatt, Switzerland, would be lucky to barely survive the alpine winds, the mountain cold, the frost-heaving of the thin, stony soil, and the shock of daily freezes and thaws. Surely it would take 150 to 200 years for those small trees to grow as tall as my New York pines—if ever they could.

When you travel, look for little trees as well as big trees. Think about how they grow. Little trees may be old and big trees may be young. When I was a boy on my first trip to Switzerland, I bought a wooden alto recorder made of Brazilian rosewood, a tropical hardwood with hardly any evidence of the seasonal wood-grain rings typical of middle-latitude trees. The smoothness of a recorder's wind flue is important for its tone. Mine makes soul-satisfying sounds. I could not afford to purchase a violin made of the native alpine spruce. Trees grown at high altitude are the best for making the vibratory boxes of stringed instruments; their seasonal rings are paper-thin because of their very slow growth in the harsh alpine climate; the resulting density of the wood gives remarkable resonance.

By contrast foresters, by using genetic breeding, have developed plantations of poplars and pines that grow 6 feet or more in height in a season. Their light wood, fibers useful for fabricating paper and building materials and for fuel, can be harvested in much briefer growing cycles.

This economically valuable technology, made possible by science, poses problems for long-run land management, however. It tends to promote monocultures, forests of one kind of tree. This lack of diversity diminishes the number of wildlife species; it tends to put imbalancing strains on soil fertility; and the trees stand vulnerable to rapid spread of insect pests and fungal diseases, thus encouraging wholesale use of chemicals to combat them. Many people also find uniform plantations uninteresting esthetically. (One ecological advantage of the new hybrid trees is their use to reclaim land made barren by mining.)

So watch for plantations of trees when you travel, especially on the flatlands of the southern United States, in the national forests of our western states, and on the vast holdings of paper and lumber companies elsewhere, often where clear-cut areas have been replanted. You can form your own opinions about their plus and minus values.

Souvenirs of wood can be valuable for those interested in regional crafts. I like to collect wood carvings from tree species growing locally where I tour. If you can find the artisan and talk with him or her, so much the better. I remember a happy day when a Passamaquoddy Indian showed me how to split the wood of black ash trees to make a packbasket.

Factories, designed to mass produce things, are worth visiting when touring. They may not be creating handmade works of art like Indian baskets, but they can demonstrate the ingenuity of designers of machinery to fashion products out of nature's raw materials. The factory workers too have their skills, some of them remarkable. I remember watching a head sawyer in a great West Coast lumber mill as he directed the rotation and cutting of gigantic, hydraulically debarked logs of Douglas fir. A factory tour guide explained, "The skill of that head sawyer determines the financial success of this whole company."

A craft shop in Fiji made decision making difficult for me. I was inspecting the wood carvings. I was short on travel money, but I *wanted* one! The carved parrot? The figure of the madonnalike girl? The bas-relief of the Fiji cottage and coconut palm? The names of the native woods meant nothing to me, but the craftsmanship was impressive. Being nautically minded, I finally bought a model of an outrigger canoe. Then I broke down and bought the parrot, the maiden, and the bas-relief—"to show the school kids back in Brooksville."

Most of our three-day stop-over on the island of Viti Levu was spent with a most cooperative, *slow*, hired driver. In his air-conditioned car he took us to photograph coral shores, sugar cane fields, a refinery; we saw native Fiji crafts, a tropical marketplace, and finally his home and family, their pets and garden. Near the end of our Fiji visit, I spotted a plantation of weird-looking pines; a sign nearby announced the Fiji Pine Commission's Nabou Station. It was too late to stop and ask questions, but back home in Maine I often thought back to those strange trees. Those pines are only one of the many reasons why I want to return to beautiful Fiji with its hospitable people.

My concern with tropical forests is not limited to the Fiji archipelago. When friends of mine finished Peace Corps duties in Peru, they returned to the east coast via thousands of miles of the Amazon's southern tributaries and the great river itself. On their return, they shared it with us on photographic slides. Recently Jean Jacques Cousteau's research teams have taken a similar trip, gathering data about the largest tropical forests on Earth, forests fast disappearing because of "development."

Scientific exploration and evaluation should precede exploitation of any natural resource, forests included. Economic pressures for development, however, are so great that neither scientists nor artists have time to record what exists in many places before they are destroyed. Brazilian forests are, unfortunately, a notable example of this problem. In the 1950s when I was working to preserve natural areas for schools in the United States, I approached botanists at Harvard University asking for aid. "We can't help," I would be told. "We *must* research the tropical forests in South America before they are all gone." I understood.

Some of those forests have as many as 300 species of trees per acre! And some of those trees may well have undiscovered properties of infinite import to humanity. A new birth-control drug? A cancer treatment? Who knows? And forests are more than just trees; they are homes for many other plants and wild animals of untold value.

When dense tropical shade trees 100 to 200 feet tall are cut, the red laterite soils are exposed to the tropical sun. In a few years such soils often become unmanageable, like brick. We need to give more thought to short-term commercial gain weighed against long-term environmental loss. That loss may include a worldwide lack of oxygen in our atmosphere because of the removal of the photosynthesizing forests.

In northern Australia as in the Amazon, forests are home for aborigines. When foreigners convert forests to other uses, the impact is similar to what would happen to city dwellers if foreigners took down their apartment and office buildings in order to develop *their* kind of cultural environment, whatever it might be.

In the Aboriginal Traditional Art Gallery in Perth, I had the pleasurable fortune to meet three aboriginal artists from Arnheim Land in northern Australia. They let me watch them painting exquisite designs of the animals with whom they share their forest homes. The bark they painted on, their paints, their stone palettes, and their brushes, as well as their themes and their expressed feelings toward them, came straight from nature with stone-age integrity.

I would like to visit those aboriginal artists in their home in Arnheim Land, to live and learn from them for a while. But I would be too much an intruder. A very few trained and sensitive anthropologists and biologists should have that privilege. Not seekers for oil, coal, or metals. Nor tourists. We should let them live their traditional lives in privacy, as long as they so wish. May it be as long as they and their forests can withstand our more aggressive "civilization."

Monterey pine, native of California, grows wonderfully in some other parts of the world, places with Mediterranean-type climates, with hot, dry summers and cool, moist winters. South Africa, New Zealand, and Australia have extensive timber plantations of Monterey pine, typically monocultures that take the place of native plants. New Zealand is a classic example of islands where native species have vanished because of introductions of foreign plants and animals. In former times, people saw only advantages and none of the disadvantages of new plant introductions; and many foreign species arrived unbeknownst to people, often as stowaways. Nowadays there is greater understanding of the ecological problems that can result. If you are touring in New Zealand, you may be able to find an elder Maori citizen who can describe some of the changes in the nature of that beautiful country during his or her lifetime.

Meanwhile in Australia the rainforests continue to fall as people require more timber for construction and paper. The growing population wants to free itself of dependence on southeastern Asia for wood products. To replace the old-growth forests, the Monterey pine is being planted, its growth much faster than that of native eucalypts.

Forests and the human race are inextricably intertwined. When we pull out the thread of forests, the fabric of humanity unravels also. That happened centuries ago, in western China, the Near East, and northern Africa, where today we find deserts. The same is happening

127

now near the end of the twentieth century. Nomads and small farmers are perishing in the Sahel Region south of the African Sahara. Their trees have gone, destroyed by changing climate and the desperate grasping for wood by too many impoverished people. African cities are jammed with refugees. On the southern slopes of the Himalayas, the forest-denuded slopes of the great mountains pour down catastrophic floods. Efforts at reforestation are brave but puny in the face of population pressures. The inhabitants would be grateful to have even one maple growing by their door—but they might have to cut it down for fuel to keep from freezing some winter night. And then?

16 QUARRIES AND MINES

Quarries and mines have a way of lasting a long time. What is excavated has economic value. Usually the hole they leave does not, but it
may have other values. I've enjoyed painting watercolors of quarries.
They are a bit like the barns that beginners paint because of the relatively simple outlines and planes. In well-vegetated New England they
create diversity amid summer's greenery. Their slopes, changed from
season to season by frost action, present intriguing angles to the horizontal flat where trucks and loaders leave their lizardy tracks. A
working quarry may have the right-angle shapes of blue-gray sheet
metal sheds. Diagonal conveyor belts stretch up and spew sands and
gravels from their giraffe mouths while standing on spindly legs cross-
braced by triangular struts. A vertical batching tower prepares the
mixes for the concrete trucks loading beneath it. At the right season,
you may with luck find a colony of bank swallows in a recently cut
vertical bank.

In New England, we call these delightful landscapes "gravel borrows," as though what is removed would be returned some day to let nature reclaim it. But the borrows stay empty, except perhaps for trash that thoughtless people dump. Nature, however, has a way of setting things in order again, given time.

In the humid eastern United States, nature works quite fast. In wet seasons, shallow "pans" of water appear in a borrow pit's almost flat bottom. Rushes soon make a decorating fringe. A sandpiper drops by for a visit, then soon leaves taking its reflection with it to adorn some other puddle—on the coast of South America? Meanwhile cattail seeds have found a muddy pool edge and pussy willow seeds also have fluff-flown to a damp spot. In time redwings may be nesting there. By then aspen seedlings will have colonized some of the gravelly slopes and flats; when autumn rains come, they will flutter their golden fans on topmost twigs against gray skies.

In the early days of auto-touring before campgrounds for recreational vehicles were conceived, we often camped in abandoned gravel quarries. Today it is wiser to circle our covered wagons at a regular campground. In arid parts of the American West, we have often camped surrounded by the bare sands, gravels, and rocks that are naturally exposed where vegetation cannot cover them. We always hope to find the welcome shade of a cottonwood, that brave tree of arid zones. It mitigates the heat and glare from stone by holding off the sun's rays and cools the air by evaporating water from its leaves. Never thought of a tree as a friend before? You certainly will the first time you camp under a desert cottonwood on a hot summer day.

Cottonwoods are close relatives of the aspens. As you tour, you find them surviving in dry places where most trees cannot, often along a dry streambed. Cottonwoods and aspens belong in the genus *Populus* along with the poplars. You can recognize them by their somewhat triangular leaves; they have flattened leaf-stems that are fluttered sideways by even a slight breeze. Quaking aspens, *Populus tremuloides*, have especially fluttery foliage. Listen as they clap their leaf-hands at the play of a little breeze. Let them lure you into taking a cottonwood tour.

Cottonwoods and their relatives are some of the commonest plants you see around quarries and mines. They often pioneer on bared soil and "spoilbanks" at mines. During most kinds of mining, excess rock accumulates and has to be put somewhere. It may be "overburden" removed for open-pit mining so as to get down to a layer of mineral or coal, or it may be the ore rock from which the mineral is removed. In either case the disturbed rock has more volume than the original solid rock, due to the air spaces between fragments. Heavy, hard to move, and usually considered worthless, the cheapest choice is to leave it at the mine's edge or to shove it a short way aside to give work room. For some reason, miners call this material "spoil"; hence "spoilbank" where it forms a bank. Miners have almost always just left the sterile stuff in heaps, apparently without much thought for landscape values.

Sometimes you can spot spoil heaps from far off. They may loom like mountains across the countryside. Sometimes they tower over mining towns, as in Wales. Sometimes they are almost hidden in narrow, V-shaped valleys where they encroach on a stream's floodway and increase the severity of floods downstream. The piled, broken rocks sometimes contain poisonous materials—for example, the sulfur compounds from coal mine spoilbanks; the acids leaching from them can kill fish and other aquatic life in nearby streams. Almost always spoilbanks cause problems of some sort.

But when you travel, you don't want to go seeking sick landscapes. Instead go looking for cottonwoods and aspens! You can find them planted by nature around the edges of many mining areas, growing from the cottony, wind-scattered seeds. As the seedlings mature, they often send out suckers from their roots and thus form little colonies of genetically identical trees. For long years, patient tree geneticists have been working to create hybrid cottonwoods and make clones of them. Now they have nurseries of superior ones, ready to plant and speed the revegetation of spoilbanks. Find a nursery where hybrid cottonwoods are grown and you can ask how they are reproduced and to what areas they are shipped. Then follow their distribution on your cottonwood tour. You may find yourself at a mine.

Mining experiments with so-called "oil shale" in the western United States give ecologists special concern. Attempts are made to crush the shale rock and squeeze commercially profitable hydrocarbons from it for fuel. One major problem is the amount of water needed by the process, water already required for agricultural irrigation down stream. Another problem is the enormous amount of dark, infertile, groundup rock left over, called "spent shale." Any large-scale operation would fill canyons with the stuff, maybe even spreading it over valley flats of fertile soil and encroaching on needed floodways. Botanists have been experimenting with various native and introduced grasses that might stabilize, hide, and heal any new mountains of pulverized rock. Some progress has been made; water, though, is always a problem when trying to reclaim land in dry regions.

A botanist once showed me a pretty little weed, a colonizer of the spent shale crept in over the dark powdered stone. It was copper mallow, a relative of hollyhocks, marsh mallow (not the confection), and hibiscus. That native plant may be one of nature's ways of restoring order to land that humans have damaged. May it thrive.

I have made visiting mine sites a major focus of my touring because of my concern for the balance of energy consumption with maintenance of livable landscapes. As with gravel borrows, you can see beauty in great piles of bare rock with various angles, textures, and colors. In humid forested regions they remind me pleasurably of arid areas of the West that I love to visit, spacious and colorful landscapes with landforms laid bare because of the absence of vegetation. Mines in arid areas, however, speak to me more of beneficial employment for people in places with few ways to make a living. But even in the desert, mines can look messy. Their apparent messiness comes from their disruption of nature's patterns that, no matter how obscure they may at first appear, seem to express ultimate orderliness.

Today I am writing outdoors as I so often do, using a clipboard with a clip at the top and elastic at the bottom to keep the breeze from blowing my paper. The clip is metal. I wonder what mine it came from. Maybe the Mesabi Iron Range in northeastern Minnesota? That clip represents to me the thousands of metallic objects that serve our culture so well. I often dream of a tour that I would really like to make some day. The tour starts at a Mesabi mine with its heavy machinery, goes by ore truck full of iron-ore pellets to Duluth to watch a crane load the ore into an ore vessel, and then crosses the Great Lakes to Cleveland or Erie. From there I ride a train to a steel mill in Pittsburgh, thence to a factory somewhere making metal clips for clipboards, and then in another truck to a store where, with metal money, you can buy a clipboard with a metal clip.

To follow almost any modern trade route like a modern Marco Polo can provide fun and education no classroom can provide. Or if you have an anthropological or archeological bent, attempt to hike the routes that pre-Columbian Indians from the northern Great Lakes took to exchange their mined copper with distant tribes. Or perhaps volunteer to help with a professional dig at a Bronze Age site.

Today, though, the scale at which we disrupt nature while grasping for below-ground resources for our "necessities" and "creature comforts" is *not* pre-Columbian. Our mining roughs up the land at an awesome rate. Surface mining of coal is safer for workers than deep mining with its vertical shafts and horizontal drifts gnawing into the rock; deep miners must flirt with black-lung disease along with mine fires and mine collapse. There has been a great increase of open-pit mining (strip mining) since the oil-import problems of the 1970s. But large tracts of the American Midwest, the Great Plains, and many other areas will never look the same after their coal has been removed; gigantic machines now rip away at the "overburden" of soil and rock, which nature placed on top of ancient swamps whose vegetation formed the coal. Fortunately because of the newer federal and state mining laws and enlightened thinking, some mining companies have made conspicuous efforts to "restore" mined landscapes, sometimes with the help of cottonwoods.

One such case is in southern Ohio. There, great gouges and ridged spoilbanks have been regraded to gentle contours at great expense, reloamed with topsoil, reseeded with grasses and legumes, replanted with shrubs and trees, and refurbished with recreational ponds and campgrounds. In some ways at least, an attempt has been made to rehabilitate the land. And millions of tons of coal have been recovered for an America hungry for energy. But to a naturalist that land reclamation in some ways is lacking.

When taking any tour focusing on changing land use, you will do well to start by inspecting a relatively natural area of the kind being modified. Even the hunt to find such a place may be an intriguing journey. Perhaps you can visit a tract set aside by The Nature Conservancy, some other conservation organization or government agency, or a university. You may even be able to find a little patch of Ohio forest almost untouched by human hands, maybe one used for research. When there, note the height of the trees, the depth of the topsoil, and the diversity of plants and animals. *Then* go to see the reclaimed mining areas.

In fairness to mining companies and the ecologists who advise their land managers, look with imagination at reclaimed land. Ponder what it will be like in 10, 20, 50, or even 100 years. Nature has had much longer to do her intricate miracles with land. Quick covering by machine-sown grasses and legumes is a great help in minimizing erosion. Hybrid poplars, pines, and locust trees together with a few species of carefully selected shrubs soon provide food and cover for some kinds of wildlife, and they help begin the slow accumulation of duff to make humus in the redeveloping topsoil. Nature *is* being given a helping hand while trying to recover.

But the reclaimed land of course lacks nature's diversity and subtle complexity. For example, one type of strip mining produces a "high wall" where it stops excavating, a cliff of rock. One law has stipulated that no high wall should remain after reclamation. When a company complies with expensive regrading, it of necessity prevents any niche plants from growing there, or a pair of peregrine falcons from nesting on the new cliff. Peregrines are one of the most exciting of endangered species, and ornithologists are making great efforts to reestablish them on suitable cliffs.

When strip-mined land in the Great Plains is reseeded with grasses and legumes, it would be difficult and probably not worth a company's expense to reintroduce the many species of forbs that gave such variety to the landscape. In more arid areas, water supplies suffice for only token areas of reestablished vegetation after mining. The little demonstrations of reclaimed land look lovely, but water is lacking for revegetation on a scale commensurate with the mining.

So manmade diggings will continue to leave gouges in the natural landscape. We cannot dig holes without disrupting nature's patterns. Not that we should not dig, or that we should not try to rehabilitate where we have dug, using all the art and science we can. We should. But we should also try to use less energy and use less nonrenewable materials. We should dig on a smaller scale and at a slower rate. We should be more creative in forming the revised landscapes. As you tour to see mining areas, perhaps *you* can think of new ways to make mined land more useful and more beautiful, and not just with cottonwoods.

17 TRAILS

As many country children know, going to and from secret places poses the problem of keeping secret trails secret so that competitive siblings or friends cannot find you. A beaten-down track through tall grass, snapped branches on bushes, or a line of compressed, trodden soil might reveal your hiding place. When is a trail not a trail? When it is a secret.

Some of my earliest experiences with secret trails found frequent use in my later work as an outdoor leader, especially with young people learning no-trace camping on an island on the Maine coast. An entrance to a trail can be hidden with a well-foliaged low branch on a tree, which functions as a closed door but is flexible enough to be swung aside for entry. A secret trail can be started behind a large boulder that must be clambered over for access. Where trees or boulders are lacking, stepping stones in an abnormal pattern at the start of a trail enable one to make an inconspicuous hopping entry into it without beating down the grass or forest duff to make a telltale trodden path. And there are many other tricks to concealing a trail head.

Most trails, however, are inviting. "Come follow me to a beautiful view," they say. "Come to the water's edge and see the yellow pond-lilies." "This way to the pine-grove picnic tables."

Knowing the types of trails is important when you want to make one. Should it be direct—the shortest possible to get people somewhere? Should it be temptingly tortuous, to give folks a whole series of interesting experiences on the way to somewhere? Or had it best be a loop trail, one ending where it begins? And if you are about to travel a trail made by others, it is wise to know what kind it is; then you will know best how to take it. Running? Hiking? Walking? Strolling? Creeping? Maybe with some rappelling and chimneying up the cliffs? And how long will it take: 10 minutes, an hour or two, until sundown, the weekend, a week, a month, or even the whole summer?

Some trails are like a good fried egg; it doesn't last long, but it nourishes you later. When you begin to travel a route, assume that for some reason it will be a memorable journey, whether short or long. To fix it in your memory, stand at the beginning point, the so-called trail head, and note the time and weather conditions. These quick time-and-weather observations put you in touch with some of nature's basic realities. For any larger trail, look at its entrance, its "doorway." Something on each side of the path must look different from the path itself; otherwise how recognize the trail? The portal may be only up-standing dried grasses flanking a narrow line of trodden grass; it may be formed of bordering bushes or marked by a tree trunk on one side and a signpost on the other.

The trail head is a good place to be sure you are suitably shod. Also check your compass directions—just by a glance at the sun, moon, or stars if they are visible—and note the lay of the land in relation to its direction of slope and the presence of valleys and heights, if visible. In familiar territory, such inspection is not so ridiculous as it sounds; it refreshes your *consciousness of place*. When entering new terrain, it keeps you from getting lost.

Make a habit of turning around now and again as you tramp a trail to see what it looks like when facing the other direction. Not only does this provide an opportunity to note landmarks and how they will appear if you wish to retrace your steps, it also gives you a view of the back side of objects such as trees, rocks, and hills, and it permits you to see things in a different kind of light, if the day is sunny or the night moonlit. Front-lighting, side-lighting, and back-lighting give objects and scenes quite different aspects. Walking across a prairie into a sunset, it is another experience to turn around and see a grove of bur oaks shimmering the silvery undersides of their leaves. Had you kept looking ahead you might have missed that memorable moment.

When you reach the trail end, turn around for one last look at the way you came, to enter it in your memory, and pause to think of the experience you have just had. Maybe you have traveled a loop trail or retraced your steps; maybe it is a different portal. You may want to take a glance at whatever prospect the end of the path presents. Perhaps you see your car at the trail-head pulloff, or the back of the inn where you are staying, or the rear of the garage where your car is being lubricated. The experience of the trail is behind you now. A retrospective pause can let you decide what you may most want to remember.

Some trails you will follow often. The tours of your own yard for instance should be a mixture of the usual and the unexpected. If you are unaware of the ordinary, how can you savor the unusual? Really to know the commonplace, you have to meet it frequently. My neighbor's dog is a creature of habit. He tours my yard almost every morning to get the nose-news at all the same canine signposts, and he leaves messages for other dogs who might not otherwise know that my yard is part of his territory. This systematic dog always goes around my yard in the same direction. When I tour my yard for pleasure rather than science, I make a point of doing it in different ways on different mornings.

If, however, you are scientifically inclined, you may wish to be precisely repetitious in your touring. Interested in wildlife? You may like to make a regular census along the same route, be it a mountain track, an abandoned railroad bed, or the sidewalk around your block. Noting the birds or other wildlife systematically will help you learn things you would otherwise never know.

Every year in New England people report their first spring robin; few, however, can tell you when the last one left in the autumn. That observation can be made only if you faithfully keep daily records of robin sightings. On any one day you will not know whether you will see a robin again on any succeeding day; only by looking back at your systematic records can you tell when you last sighted one. (Even then, with scientific uncertainty, you may wonder if a robin is hiding somewhere just out of sight!)

If your interests are more botanical than ornithological, you can plan a census route along which you make seasonal notes about what the plants are doing. I have a friend in southern California who makes quite regular trips down the hill from her ranch house to the rural mailbox, a seemingly minor journey. The letters she writes are full of you-are-here descriptions: the changing aspects of the vegetation, the summer heat drying out the vernal pools. Reports of buttercups, miner's lettuce, and mustard lead us through her summer to October browns and November grays, when autumn rains regreen the grasslands and refill the pools. Her trek down the trail to the mailbox is not just to get there and get back quickly.

Some people can listen to a lecture without taking any notes and still remember almost all of it. I've had students who would sit and watch me lecturing for 50 minutes without taking a note, or would knit during my lecture, and then get an A on examinations. But *I* have to take notes at lectures, and I profit from doing so when hiking a trail. They supplement my purposeful looking, and notes are especially important when I'm following a census route.

My note-taking equipment is usually minimal. I prefer a No. 2 writing pencil. It has dark enough graphite to show up well yet is not too smudgy and will not blur if rained upon. A pocket knife keeps it pointed. I like a brightly colored pencil, easy to find if I drop it. Light green sheets of 8½- by 11-inch paper, less glary in sunshine than white papers, are held on my clipboard by a metal clip at the top and a stout elastic at the bottom to keep them from blowing. I date each sheet and file it when I return. The clipboard has an over-the-shoulder string tied to the clip and to a hole drilled at the bottom. Some scientists prefer a notebook, often a pocket-sized one. I find, though, that data from previous trips are safer at home than carried on succeeding trips, often to be rained upon, lost in powder snow, or dropped in the mud. If you use a notebook, tear out and file the filled pages or else make file copies of them. A tape recorder is useful *if* you ever have time to play it back.

A camera makes an excellent companion on a trail. Suitably exposed, its emulsions can remember more than we can perceive. You can find some hints on its use in the chapter titled "Recording Your Observations." A tape recorder can help you remember natural sounds along the trail, the noise of your footsteps, and your comments and musings. To make the most of any record, you will have to budget time to use it, whether for scientific reference, source material for illustration, or for pure enjoyment.

Some trails we think of as primarily historical, for example the Lewis and Clark Trail named after the explorers who traveled from the Mississippi to Oregon; the Santa Fe Trail of the herders; the Oregon Trail followed by pioneers; the Natchez Trace between Natchez, Mississippi, and Nashville, Tennessee, used by the "Kentuck" boatmen as they hiked back after delivering their flatboats to Louisiana; and El Camino Real of the Spanish missionaries in California. As we immerse ourselves in the past and visualize the experiences of old-timers, we realize how important to them was the nature of the lands they moved through. Today we can follow in their footsteps—by auto or boat if not by foot—sometimes on guided tours, noting the landmarks described by them and rejoicing that some of the native vegetation and wildlife where they ventured still lives for us to see.

One day while pulling my trailer over Trail Ridge Road in Rocky Mountain National Park, I was caught in a snowstorm at the summit. I remembered that this beautifully graded modern highway followed the route taken over the mountains by Indian women and their children while the braves took an even higher and more difficult route. I hiked through the snowstorm up a park trail. Amidst the alpine tundra, I realized anew how brave the Indians must have been, and how knowledgeable of terrain, weather, plants, and animals.

America still lacks the many farmland footpaths between villages that are such a delight in Europe, but we have a growing number of excellent trails for hiking and biking, horseback riding and packing, canoeing, rafting, ski touring, and snowmobiling. The Appalachian Trail between Maine and Georgia is the longest and best known in the East. In Vermont, the Long Trail, over 250 miles plus branch trails, runs the length of the state over the crests of the Green Mountains. In the West, the Sierra Club has led in the building of trails and has educated people to their wise use.

140

Numerous outdoor-oriented organizations are glad to have you join the many trips they lead. In addition to the Sierra Club, many others devoted to hiking, rock climbing, caving, canoeing, and other outdoor sports can inform you of trails—for example, the Appalachian Mountain Club—as can natural history societies such as the Audubon Society and the wildflower societies. Libraries, museums, and nature centers can provide information about them.

Do not overlook the many opportunities for enjoying nature from trails along water. Some of the most popular canoe country is in the Boundary Waters Canoe Area of the U.S. Superior National Forest; it has a Visitor Center outside Ely, Minnesota. Many canoeists enjoy the Niobrara River in Nebraska, the Allagash Waterway and St. John's River in northern Maine, the Rogue in Oregon, and the Klamath in California. There are so many wonderful rivers! You will of course think of the great rivers like the Colorado, but remember there are delightful small ones, like the Wading River through the New Jersey Pine Barrens. Maybe you live in a city with a little stream that can be canoed; but be ready to remove the junk in it first if need be. The intangible rewards are great.

We often hear the term "nature trail." I'm glad to know that such trails are now to be found at many parks, sanctuaries, nature centers, and some schools, camps, and campgrounds. A nature trail is a trail that is easy to follow; it will have signs along it to help people see and hear natural phenomena, and sometimes there will be organized opportunities to touch, smell, and even in rare instances to taste natural objects. Nature trails have given a great boost to recreation and environmental education, for school children, campers, local adults, and tourists. When you tour to a new environment, a well-labeled nature trail makes a delightful introduction to its natural history.

There is one problem with nature trails: they are not always well labeled. A beautifully crafted sign telling you to listen for the song of the red-eyed vireo is not helpful if it's winter and you are following the tracks of a snowshoe hare! Neither are out-of-season labels for wildflowers that have gone to seed and disappeared underground for the winter. Some labels are too wordy; you will probably not want to read them. Some are too faded to read.

When a nature trail is not well labeled, it is because some hardworking, dedicated naturalist—professional or amateur—just did not have enough time to keep the trail up to date. When hiking a nature trail at a park or nature center, study it. If it is in good condition, praise somebody. If it is in poor condition, volunteer to improve it. Perhaps some old labels should be removed, to be discarded or reconditioned. Suggest some new labels. If their design is approved by whoever is in charge, make and install them. As seasons change, alter some of the labels. Quickly repair or replace any vandalized ones. If you can, get others involved in helping you. And how about making a *new* nature trail? Every local school should have at least one.

Ideally we should consider all routes we travel to be nature trails, unlabeled ones. Even indoors we are surrounded by artifacts made from natural materials and the infiltrations of natural things. Sometimes my students and I would take a "nature creep" down the basement corridor of the old dorm where I had my laboratories, going some 70 feet in perhaps a half-hour. There was so much to see and talk about. For instance, the institutional green paint—probably containing casein from milk made by a cow in a distant Vermont pasture, where sun beat down on timothy grass, a native of Europe. And we would find dust with pollen grains of wind-loving plants; and bits of fibers from student sweaters made of wool—maybe from sheep on ranches in Australia, the Pyrenees, or Utah—or of synthetics derived from flatland pines of the South.

Short tour or long tour, indoors or out, on land or water, may all your trails be nature-revealing ones.

18 BICYCLING WAYS

On a smooth road skirting a maple swamp in the Northeast, quietly pedaling along on a summer evening, you can hear the brief and a bit nasal call of a veery, which used to be called Wilson's thrush. You stop beside the road and put one foot down, sitting comfortably on your bike seat, waiting. Nothing. After a bit you shift, putting the other foot down, waiting. Then you hear it, those mystical, downward spiraling notes of the veery's song, again and again. So what if it's a few miles back to the house. You are home in almost no time. If you had walked, you might not have had time to get to the veery's swamp. Had you driven, you might have stopped your car at several places along the swamp road but have missed the veery's notes each time. Your cycling permitted you to listen while rolling. Indeed a bicycle can be a birder's best bet for many birding trips.

A bicycle route of your own design can provide good counting of bird populations. Your route may actually be a portion of a large city. It may have heavy vehicular traffic, but you can squeeze through it faster than autos. Be careful to avoid slotted manhole covers, broken bottles, and car doors suddenly opened in front of you; and of course stay clear of moving cars and trucks. On a street map, mark out a tour of open spaces such as parks, cemeteries, railroad yards, vacant lots, and waterfronts. Select the safest, slow-speed streets and alleys. Plan for a particular time of day for regular counting. Early morning is often best because of the greater bird activity then; birds are more visible and/or audible making it easier to spot them and get the most accurate counts. Early morning also has less traffic before commuting starts, at least in the longer days of spring and summer. Plan your direction of travel to minimize having sun in your eyes when it is low in the sky.

Your route may be through a suburb, perhaps an older one where plantings of trees and shrubs have matured and now attract many birds, or perhaps a newer one with considerable bare soil and young lawns. If you can lay out a bicycle census route visiting both kinds of suburbs, you can make interesting comparative studies of bird populations and of other natural phenomena also. When you think about it, you realize there are many kinds of suburbs to cycle around and study.

Your route may be in a village, one more or less typical of your part of the country. Perhaps it is a mill town on a river, a farming center at a country crossroads, a resort at mountain, lake, or shore, or a fishing village. Seasonal bird lists, notes of roadside flowering plants, observations of what common insects are doing, and other matters that a cycling naturalist will see can be of interest to villagers when written up for the local newspaper. Also they can be useful to a local science teacher in the high school. Teachers at the elementary school level may also be delighted with such information to incorporate in their curricula. Some students may start making their own bicycle censuses, letting you sleep late mornings!

Your route may encompass a whole township of open countryside. The roads may almost all be gravel, muddy or dusty depending on how the seasons dictate, not so smooth for bicycling as hardtopped ones. But with less traffic and more beautiful country, your cycling joys can be as great as elsewhere. The area of your township that you cover will depend on many factors, including your ambition, health, strength, and the diversity of your area's terrain and wildlife habitats. If it is a flat farming area with some 90 percent of the land in corn or wheat, a small sample regularly taken can tell you much. With hills and valleys, water bodies, fields, and woods, you may wish to run your route through many or all of them to get as long a list as possible of birds, flowers, or whatever; or you may decide to specialize on just one environment, visiting it more often. For instance, a regular bike trip to one pond at several seasons can provide an excellent census, though for safety you should keep your cycle at home in any snowy or icy weather.

For an extended bicycle tour over a night, a week, or longer, you may want to seek indoor accommodations at motels, inns, bed and breakfasts, and/or at friends' places. You can pedal more easily carrying less gear than if you camp, and you will not have to spend so much time shopping for food, cooking, and cleaning up. You may have more comfortable facilities for reading, writing, and drawing during evenings and inclement weather. Of course, unless you have many good friends whom you have kept in mind as you planned your tour, and who expect you and will not be inconvenienced by your coming, a noncamping trip will be more expensive day to day than camping. However, you will save some money because you will not have to procure camping equipment—except for a sleeping bag, which saves friends from having to provide bedding. You will probably wish to share expenses with hosts and hostesses or give them a small "house gift," followed after you leave with a "bread-and-butter" note.

A camping tour by bicycle has advantages too, a main one being that you are in the outdoors 24 hours a day. That means many evenings you will probably sit by a campfire, maybe that of other congenial campers, until the stars come out—unless you huddle in your tiny, lightweight tent listening to the rain and eating supper cooked on a little one-burner stove just a safe distance beyond the tent flap. Some nights you will hear owls or coyotes or other nocturnal animals that indoor sleepers usually miss. In good, stable weather, you may choose not to set up the tent; you just spread your ground cloth, a short foam pad, and sleeping bag on the ground, facing east if you wish the rising sun to awaken you, facing west if you want to sleep a bit later. There are the inevitable discomforts that attend camping, including insects, excessive heat, cold, rain and, when cycling, headwinds. But then there are those wonderful tailwind days and bugless nights.

Your cycling equipment must be carefully planned well before your extended tour begins. Any old bicycle will probably not be right for you. I suggest a somewhat sturdy, three-speed cycle rather

145

than a racy, thin-wheeled ten-speed. You may prefer a five-speed as a compromise. Whatever bike you select—after considerable reading, looking around, and asking for advice—get used to it on short runs before you set out on any longer tour. By then you should not only be expert at its maintenance, spoke-changing, and all, you should also be in love with it. You also will have practiced balanced loading of all your gear. Consult books and magazines on cycling and camping for suggestions of essential items. In general you will need certain types of clothing (lightweight, used in layers as needed); a sleeping bag, pad, and ground cloth; toilet and first-aid articles; small flashlight; bike repair kit; and safety hat and flag.

As a nature-oriented tourist, you will probably want a hand lens for inspecting flowers, insects, and minerals, and maybe for removing an occasional thorn. You can use reverse-held binoculars instead, but a hand lens is small, light, and convenient to use. Instead of binoculars for watching birds and stars, I like a monocular, which is smaller, lighter, and almost as useful; for most observing, the stereoscopic effect seen through binoculars is not necessary. A small pocket-sized telescope has served me admirably. To supplement nature's music, you may wish to pack a harmonica or a small wooden recorder, especially if daylight is short and nights long, or if you hit a long spell of rainy weather and are more or less tent-bound.

Books? You may want to pack a small field guide. I suggest carrying only two at the most, because even small books add weight and are hard to handle in bad weather. Select a guide of special interest for that tour, perhaps for wildflowers, trees, birds, mammals, or minerals. For another tour, specialize on another topic if you wish to broaden your natural history knowledge. You may want a nonnature paperback for relaxation, one you can part with when you have finished it, to be replaced with one picked up as you travel. Rather than taking books along, you can depend on town libraries and those at nature centers to help you learn about the region you are touring in and about its natural history. To do so, budget time for such places and realize that they may be considerable cycling distance from where you can bed down for the night. Sometimes a librarian or staff at a nature center can suggest a camping place nearer than ones advertised in touring guides.

Whatever you decide *not* to take, be sure to have No. 2 pencils, a pocket knife for sharpening them, and a small notebook with a cover that can be folded underneath the back for good support. A clipboard can be too cumbersome for any but short tours. When you see a bird, flower, or "ziggle-sided whatever" that you want to identify later, make a sketch of it in your notebook and add any written notes about color, habitat, or other information that the sketch can't record, together with date and place. Also use your notebook for recording each photograph you take, to aid in labeling it later. Pack your notebook in a plastic bag; a breadwrapper will do. See the chapter titled "Recording Your Observations" for more ideas on making notes, including using a small camera. Another plastic bag can hold a little address book, postcards, and stamps.

In one sense a "bikeway" is any route you want to bike. In common English usage, though, a *bikeway* is a route that has been officially designated as a relatively safe and in other ways desirable way to bicycle. Standard bikeway signs usually mark it. Sometimes a recommended bikeway is unmarked along the route but is shown on a map. Unless you have good reasons to do otherwise—perhaps a naturalist's special interests—it is wise to follow bikeways where they are available.

Bike paths are even better. They have been established, indeed often constructed, to provide the safest and most convenient routes for cyclists, with all other vehicles excluded. You still can have an accident on one by tangling carelessly with another cyclist or by being preoccupied with the surrounding nature rather than with the narrowness of the bike path; so while bike paths can give you some of the most carefree cycling, don't relax too much while wheeling along them!

The following organizations will be happy to give you information about bicycling, including tours:

AMERICAN YOUTH HOSTELS, INC.; National Headquarters at 1332 I Street N.W., Suite 800, Washington DC, 20005.

INTERNATIONAL BICYCLE TOURING SOCIETY, 2115 Paseo Dorado, La Jolla, CA 92037.

SIERRA CLUB, 530 Bush Street, San Francisco, CA 94108 (plus numerous regional offices).

WHEELMEN, Box 467 RD #2, Clayton, IN 46118.

Locally you can ask for information about the many trails, too numerous to list here, that have already been made to bring us in close contact with nature. Inquire at sporting-equipment shops, listed in the Yellow Pages of a telephone book, about trails not only for biking but also for canoeing, hiking, horseback riding, scuba diving, skiing, and snowmobiling.

Access to cycling should be for everyone. See what you can do in your own community to promote more and safer bicycling along with nature study. People of all ages can profit from the healthy exercise and from being brought closer to their natural surroundings. The aged and handicapped can benefit from pedaling three-wheelers; they should be helped to realize that they are bona fide cyclists and welcome to take part in your community's shorter nature tours. Bicycle shops and dealers will be glad to help you promote marked and/or mapped bikeways and bike paths. You may find that helping others to go nature touring on bicycles is even more fun than doing it yourself.

19 ROADS

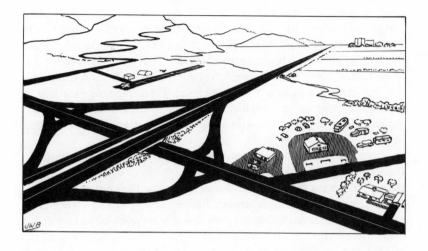

The roads you travel are far more complex than trails or bike paths. They use more natural resources in construction and have greater influences on the countryside through which they pass. Nature-sensitive eyes see any road as part of nature: the natural materials of which it has been made; the immediate condition of the road as sun, wind, rain, and snow affect it; the plants that try to creep in over its shoulders; and the animals that venture across it and fly over it.

Thus a person versed in *nature history* appreciates the *nature* of the road itself. But how about its *history*? Every item and every aspect of nature has a story of its past. To read the landscape as you tour, you look at the patterns made by nature and people, the design of the environment as you find it today. It is never dull reading when you analyze it at any particular time. But what you glimpse is but one frame in nature's motion picture reel. To be able to envision the past and imagine the future brings far more delight. So it is with today's amazing nexus of roads, and therefore the following brief natural history of roads may add enjoyment to your inspection of landscapes across which your roads will run.

Before the invention of wheels there were trails. Then along came roads to help the wheels roll. Probably before wheels were invented, a section of round tree trunk was put under a log to roll it. Later a few poles lashed together were put across such a roller as a platform on which to push something; but then another roller had to be put under the front of the platform as the first one passed toward the rear when the platform moved forward. Then the back roller had to be carried forward and placed at the front as the front one likewise was left behind; and so on. What a chore! Then somebody thought of having the roller on an axle suspended beneath the platform so it could maintain its position. A breakthrough. "Hey, let's see if the ox can pull it!"

The roller, though, was heavy. It had lots of friction with the ground, sinking into soft places and having to climb with difficulty over bumps. Then came the bright idea of using just the ends of the roller, fastened to each other by a strong, straight pole—an axle. Wheels! At oxen speed, the solid, still-heavy, wooden wheels wobbled as they rolled over uneven ground. One day a bright person felled a hollow tree, cut off two thin sections, invented spokes to hold the axle in the center of these rims, and lo! a much lighter wheel.

So far as I know, pre-Columbian Native Americans didn't have wheels. They pulled their belongings on sleds or sledges or dragged them on a frame lashed to two travois poles. The pioneers from Europe used hollow sycamore logs for making wheel rims, oak wood for spokes, and elm for hubs because its fibers run every which way giving strength in any wheel position. Knowledge of iron also came from Europe and contributed iron rims to make wheels last longer. Road-building skills also came across the Atlantic to make easier rolling for the marvelous wheels of the European settlers.

The Romans masterfully engineered long, thin, smooth places along which to drive chariots and wagons full of grain and other articles of their developing commerce. They called a road a *via*. When you travel in Europe today you can still walk and drive by such Roman roads, so well have they lasted with their cobblestone paving. Less durable were other early European roads made of logs laid parallel across wet places. It was probably French Canadian loggers who first called such roads "corduroy roads" because of their resemblance to the ridge-

and-groove fabric of that name (derived from the French *corde du roi*, fabric of the king), which they used for their work pants and jackets. Logs, especially when covered with soil, can last a long tme in acid bogwater that prevents fungi from rotting them. Logs of red-cedar, white-cedar, redwood, bald-cypress, and locust are among the most durable kinds; you can still sometimes find corduroy sections as you ramble along old logging and farm roads.

Just as wheels have evolved from rough natural materials to technologically processed steel, aluminum, and plastic components intricately assembled and capped with rubber tires, so have roads evolved from soil, cobblestone, and wood paving to superior surfaces on which we roll as we tour. We recognize roads as very important parts of the infrastructure of our highly mobile culture. As we travel, it is fascinating to look at roads and try to understand how engineers have endeavored to design them so that they adapt intelligently to nature's patterns, especially in relation to soil and running water.

A country child who perhaps has never traveled far may understand roads better than many city children who have ridden across the continent. Mud season in the country may have required a boy's labor to help pull wagons, cars, and even tractors out of deep ruts. He may have sweated heavily in digging and cleaning out roadside ditches to keep the dirt road properly drained. He may have chain-hauled a scraper made of a squared log along roads to smooth them, trying to maintain a high *crown* for the road, usually along the middle so that water raining on it would run across the road into the ditches rather than along the road making ruts. He might have helped his father build a logging road into a woodlot, the two of them deciding where to fell trees for making the best grade with the least work. A modern country boy may have laid his share of corduroy road and chucked many a stone into mudholes. In America, a farm boy might later become a capable road contractor or highway engineer. His sister may have helped her mother try to keep road dust out of the farmhouse when a car drove by or when an afternoon wind swirled dirt into the house, or she might be out driving that tractor with the road scraper.

A so-called dirt road is sometimes termed a *graded road*. That important crown must be maintained by grading. On a curve the high portion may be on the outside to counteract the centrifugal force of cars cornering, as on a race track. Tires have a tendency to squish soil sideways, thereby leaving ruts that must be filled by scraping, and also by depositing soil in ditches that must be maintained by redigging.

Sometimes dirt roads are better called gravel roads. Some "gravel" is a mixture of whatever soil is available, with more or less gravel-sized pebbles along with the smaller sand, silt, and/or clay particles. Sometimes larger stones come in the gravel; this is gravel "with bone in it." Such mixed road-building material is called "run of the bank," because it contains the same components as the bank in the borrow pit where it was dug, whatever nature's running water or glacier deposited there. Other gravel may have been selectively screened by machinery at a gravel pit to give a certain particle size. Sometimes the gravel is crushed stone. As you tour, you can look for road cuts and other exposed banks to see what kind of soils they contain and consider whether they might make good roadbuilding material. Whoever engineered whatever road you are traveling had to find a source of material that was suitable and close enough to be hauled economically.

Sometimes before a road can be constructed, there must be a destructive stage of removing vegetation and topsoil. That is when many naturalists and environmentalists become apprehensive, because we think we recognize the value of wetlands and other environments that some engineers may not. Where a road *must* traverse a deep deposit of organic matter—as in bogs, fens, swamps, and marshes—all the peaty material must be excavated down to firm mineral soil or rock. If it is not dug out, any roadbed constructed on it will subside, sometimes dangerously and certainly expensively. In calculating costs of any proposed alternate routes, engineers must have test holes dug to try to find out the depth of such organic deposits.

Whenever possible, a roadbed should be built up considerably higher than the surrounding land; it is then better drained. Good drainage is especially important in cold regions such as northern New England and Michigan because it can reduce the heaving and subsiding caused by frost action. Water held by fine particles of soil freezes and expands, then thaws and shrinks; so gravels are usually better than "fines" for building roads, usually with coarser material beneath and finer above. In cold and windy climates such as the northern Great Plains, snow tends to blow off a high roadbed rather than accumulate on it.

In some parts of the United States, gravel is in short supply. It has been dug for many years to make the world's greatest highway system and to provide concrete for our city buildings and sidewalks. With reduced supply, the cost increases for building new roads and resurfacing existing ones. High petroleum costs are also a factor because asphalt is used to mix with screened or crushed gravel for resurfacing.

While touring along roads, watch for sources of gravel. In the northern states and Canadian provinces you find gravel in glacial deposits. In the mountainous West, great piedmont fans of gravel slope down to the valleys and plains of intermontane basins. Many western streams with gravel bars where trout and salmon spawn have suffered first from gold mining, which scoured through the gravels, and then from dredging of gravel for building roads along them, across them, or near them. Such dredging supplied gravel at relatively low immediate cost; but the environmental cost, both short- and long-term, has sometimes been great. In some areas along the Gulf of Mexico, the supply of sea-shells used in place of gravel for roadbuilding has now been nearly exhausted.

In all but absolutely rainless deserts, which are very rare, roads relate to *watersheds,* areas which shed water when it rains and/or when snow melts. A *divide* is the crest of high land that separates one watershed from the next, as along the top of a ridge. In humid areas, a watershed may have a permanent stream in its valley, or an intermittent one flowing at some seasons but dry at others. The stream may have smaller tributaries, each with its own little valley in its watershed, which is therefore a sub-watershed of the first. That little stream may have its still-smaller tributaries, and so on almost infinitely with sub-sub-sub-watersheds. Examples: a stone, which has intermittent trickles down its various sides when it rains; your face, where rain or tears at some time flowed down the two watersheds separated by that very personal divide, your nose. One of the most intriguing and valuable ways for a nature-oriented person to travel is with a keen eye for watersheds.

Here is a simple, basic classification of roads as they relate to watersheds. You may follow *ridge roads* along divides, *valley roads* up and down along streams (permanent or intermittent), or *pass roads* over passes, which are relatively low spots where they cross divides from one watershed to another. However, any one road may be composed of stretches of all three kinds. You can recognize them when you look for those little sub-watersheds along with the major ones to which your road obviously relates. Nature *is* complex; and when people build roads they inevitably add to that complexity.

Here is a travel game dealing with roads and watersheds. Use paper and pencil to make a sketch map of the following imaginary tour in hypothetical Sweet Valley. To start, make a north arrow pointing to the top of your paper, and make a line across the bottom of the paper to represent Amy River running westward. Suppose you and I are traveling west along Sweet Valley's Main Street. It parallels Amy River on its north side and is obviously a valley road. We go over a little bridge over Ben River, a tributary entering Amy River from the north. Then we immediately turn right onto North Street and follow it north out of town. We are now in the Ben River watershed but are still in the Amy River watershed of which it is a part; and we are going up hill as surely as Ben River runs downhill. North Street is heading for a pass in the Mining Range. (You can draw a ridge of saw-toothed mountains across the top of your paper.)

Now we come to east-flowing Claire Brook. It runs under North Street through a culvert, maybe an ancient stone one, or maybe a concrete one; we can't see it from up here on the road. On Claire Brook's north side, by that pasture, there's the Claire family's old barn with the little house beside it. The main ridgepole of the house runs east and west, so the house faces south looking down across the pasture to the brook. The roof has two watersheds, the south-facing slope with the gutter leading to the rain barrel at the corner, and the north-facing one we can't see. Do you see the two dormer windows in the roof? The one on the right is little Jimmy's bedroom. Last year he climbed out the window and scrambled up atop the dormer with his soap bubble mixture. Well, he spilled it. It ran down the dormer watershed onto the main roof, into the gutter, and into the rain barrel. His ma was mad and had Mr. Claire dump the barrel. It ran foaming into Claire Brook, Ben River, Amy River, and they tell me flying fish are blowing bubbles in the sea.

Now forgetting that bubble business, suppose North Street had been built without a culvert for Claire Brook. In heavy rains that brook would have ponded on the uphill side, dammed by North Street; it might then overflow across North Street with enough eroding power to wash it out and make impassable this main road over the pass in the Mining Mountains. If a culvert had been installed but was too small to carry all the water from Claire Brook watershed, that could also have caused a washout. What would have happened to the town of Sweet Valley if Main Street had been built across Ben River without a little bridge?

So a road not only has its own drainage problems, but it also affects the drainage of whatever watersheds it crosses. Nature cannot be pushed around without reacting. Whenever a contractor dumps loads of gravel to build a road bed, he must install a culvert or bridge at the low spot of any crossed watershed that might overflow the road if impounded by it. As you tour along country lanes, roads, or highways, watch for culverts. They are not just pipes. They are one way people work with nature, having deference for its watersheds. As surely as "boys will be boys," watersheds will shed water. As you drive, you are above the culverts so often you do not see them; but you can notice two stakes or a set of posts with rails, one at each side of the road, which usually indicate a culvert beneath. Watch for them and glance up hill to try to visualize their watersheds. Because rain falls on urban areas as well as on fields and woods, the surface waters of towns and cities are led through grates into catch basins, and thence by pipes under the streets to a river, lake, or sea.

In your travels you may find another device used by road-builders for centuries, a *ford*. A ford allows a stream to drain its watershed *over* a road, not under it. Or should I say that the stream allows the road to go under it? Taking nature's point of view can be revealing.

Crossing a ford by car in a dry season may be no problem. Low water can be splashed through gently. But use caution when traversing a ford during high water of a wet season. Too much splashing may short-circuit your car's electrical system and leave you stalled in the middle. Inconvenient—and in flooding conditions dangerous.

One difficulty with fords is maintaining a safe roadbed and road surface under the stream. Sometimes a ford has a concrete surface that is made to prevent any erosion. But a ford on a country road may be just dirt, or whatever is the natural material of the stream's bed. When a brook runs slowly, it can deposit only fine particles of sand, silt, and/or clay on its bed. A faster current may remove these fine materials and leave only gravel. A still faster flow may wash away the gravel and allow only cobblestones or even boulders to remain. You would not want to drive across on them! If you are going to cross a dirt-road ford, be sure you first ascertain the depth of the water and the condition of the roadbed, which may be difficult to see if fast-moving or muddy water obscures it.

Another difficulty can occur when people's roads and nature's streams share crossings at fords. When water flows fast it has energy for digging. Even during a short hour or two during a freshet, a brook can excavate a deep hole in an otherwise smooth streambed. The friction of the water alone does only a small part of the digging; the water may carry a little stone to a low dimple and keep swirling it around there as a hard, efficient excavating tool. The water removes what the stone grinds off; thus a streambed pot hole is dug. Of course a pot hole can be an axle-breaker.

In arid areas your road may cross a *dry wash,* a valley where a stream flows only at rare intervals during flash floods. The desert conditions prevent vegetation from covering the ground sufficiently to form a deposit of leaves, twigs, and other organic matter that can absorb rain. When a desert shower does come, it is usually a short but torrential downpour from a great black-bellied cloud. The water from this cloudburst suddenly fills the dry washes. The little ones collecting rainwaters from their little watersheds pour them into the watersheds to which they are tributary. Those dry washes, no longer dry, then pay their tribute of water to larger watersheds that in turn contribute their waters to . . . well, it might be the dry wash you are about to drive across.

In arid areas, be respectful of dry washes. Realize that a black-belly capable of causing a dangerous flash flood may have been miles away over a mountain. It may have poured there a half-hour or more before its accumulating waters on your dry wash's large watershed come frothing down to where you are about to cross. Many a car has been swept away by a flash flood. I've seen it happen. And lives have been lost. On some roads in the Southwest of the United States, a road sign may say "Dip" on each side of a dry wash. Beware. But don't just rely on road signs. Keep an eye on nature's signs: black-bellies, even distant ones, that might affect your watershed. Also keep looking up the streambed of a dry wash for a foaming wall of approaching water. And *don't* park your car or set up camp on a dry wash; always do so on higher ground. Be prepared for company during a flash flood; snakes and other little animals may join you for a bit after the flood has flushed them out of their living rooms!

Highways—especially limited-access ones—show you a different aspect of nature than do corduroy logging roads, well-graveled farm roads, or desert tracks. You are often treated to a broader view of terrain. The roadbed may be built up quite high across and along valleys, thus giving you treetop and rooftop views of both natural and human patterns. The highways are less inclined than other roads to zig-zag on switchbacks up and down mountains; they are more likely to blast lower through a pass when climbing over hills, or to tunnel through a mountain, to provide gentler grades.

On a highway you often have a greater sweep of sky to watch. Clouds, sunsets, stars, and sunrises are often beautifully displayed. Contrasts between regions are more clearly shown when they seem to come closer together as you speed from one to another.

We can thoroughly enjoy a stretch of superhighway, but not for too long at a time without taking a stretch. Well-timed rest stops help us unkink and keep us from getting woozy and inattentive to our driving. Pulloffs help keep us adjusted to a pace more befitting our evolutionary background. Nature designed us to walk and run, not ride. Do not get too enamored of travel on highways designed primarily to move lots of people fast over long distances. Appreciate highways for their efficiency, safety, and beauty, but realize that you will meet more of nature's intriguing details on byways.

A noteworthy date in the history of roads may be 1973. In that year a former highway commissioner of Racine County in Wisconsin started a Rustic Roads Board as a "positive step backward" in an effort to safeguard samples of rural landscapes. Now the Wisconsin Department of Transportation (P.O. Box 7913, Madison, WI 53707) can send you a brochure listing thirty-two scenic byways marked along the way with yellow and brown Rustic Road signs.

20 BRIDGES AND CAUSEWAYS

Bridges help people get from one side of something low—a stream, a gully, a canyon—to the other side. Our distant ancestors used a naturally fallen tree or one felled by a stone axe or fire to make a wooden bridge. Robin Hood and Little John used such a bridge and with their stout sticks argued about who was to cross it first.

In some climates, woody vines called lianas could be used to permit a crossing. Plant fibers were braided to form ropes. Stone bridges too were invented by the ancients. At first straight, flat stones were laid across stone pillars, as with the prehistoric "clapper bridges" of southern England. Cantilever bridges with their balanced spans helped ancient Chinese cross narrow valleys. Bridges with stone arches, a most significant invention, apparently first appeared in the Near East. It was the Romans, however, who became masters of stone arches with wedge-shaped key stones placed at the middle of the top of the arch so that the stone sides could lean against each other for mutual support.

Romans made bridges not only for pedestrians, wagons, and chariots but also for water piped across valleys via aqueducts, thus leading captive streams over natural ones. Amazing!

Modern times have brought modern materials. With the coming of the Industrial Revolution, the first iron bridge reputedly was built in Shropshire, England, in 1779. Today steel girders, suspension cables, and concrete unite with quarried stone to build most of our bridges, though in the country we still find small ones of stout wooden timbers making the span between stone or concrete abutments. Up-country covered bridges, roofed to protect the timbers from the weather, are now scarce indeed.

Today in addition to spanning streams and canyons, bridges are needed to cross railroads and roads at different levels, with resulting underpasses and overpasses. When we travel, not only can we watch to see what natural and artificial materials are used in these structures, we also can note the negative impacts and positive influences that bridges make on the landscape and on the plants and animals around them. For example, some bridges enhance the scenery while others appear utilitarian only. Nineteenth-century railroad bridges have a beauty of their own that befits the artificiality of urban scenes, but usually bridges do not blend much with the countryside. Perhaps in your travels you can spot a bridge that so appeals to you that you will stop to photograph it, or even take time to sketch it. If it happens to be a famous bridge, you may find a postcard of it to send home to a friend.

Highway bridges delight pigeons. If you travel an interstate highway, watch for pigeons, called European rock doves by ornithologists. The American street pigeons' ancestors came from Europe, probably as food-providing birds on the slow sailing ships bringing early colonists. Some pigeons probably escaped being eaten or made a getaway from a dovecote in the New World and hung around settlers' cabins and cottages. Later city buildings were much to their liking, being similar to the old stone houses and rock-cliff nesting sites of Europe.

And why do pigeons like overpasses and underpasses? Naturalists know that under bridges the birds find shelter from rain, snow, and wind, perches for roosting, and niches for nesting. Some bridges may help birds get water by making catchments for it. Once I photographed a pigeon drinking from a puddle on a hard-topped road. As you tour, let bridges and pigeons raise questions in your mind. Where it rains only a few times a year, can pigeons live under bridges? Native doves live in the Arizona desert; do they get all their water from seeds, fruits, and dew at night? Perhaps rock doves can do the same. I must go back to Arizona to see for myself; or perhaps you'll write and tell me.

As you tour, pigeon-watching may stimulate you to keep count of how many bridges are host to birds, especially in nesting season. Watch for those other immigrants from Europe, starlings and house sparrows. Who knows, you may become a serious ornithologist investigating the mysteries of bird life. If less scientifically inclined, you may be satisfied with noting the beauty of pigeons, the many browns, whites, pinks, and grays, the grays often more blue than gray. The fanning of a tail, the slap-flapping of wings at takeoff, the set of upheld wings for landing beside a mate on a girder—these can delight.

Bridges create microclimates around them and under them, because of the shape of abutments, the piers supporting the span, the flat surfaces of roadways or pathways, and the slope of ground beside abutments. If you are hiking or cycling, bridge abutments make good resting places. In hot weather, you can catch more breeze on top and a more extensive view than elsewhere. If a shower comes, you can duck under the bridge. If banks have been recently planted with grasses and forbs (for instance clovers), there may be butterflies or other insects to watch. If shrubs have been established, small birds may be nesting in them in spring and summer or gathering seeds in autumn and winter.

If you are traveling by auto, a bridge's shelter may be welcome in a storm or if your car is disabled. But if you are driving a light car, beware of the sudden impact of wind jetting through an underpass or of strong cross-winds on an overpass; the wind is natural, but its concentration results from the engineered structure and its graded surroundings. In cold climates bridges ice over before roads, where underlying soil retains heat.

The banks of bridge abutments must be disturbed during construction. Then the bared soil must be stabilized to prevent erosion. Soil may be paved with concrete or blacktop, spread with gravel, riprapped with stones, or planted with grasses, legumes, and/or shrubs

160

to keep it from washing or blowing away. As you travel, you can note variations of these bank treatments, especially the many different plantings. The plants must be adapted to the amount of slope, soil types, and exposure to sun and wind. Along highways, landscape architects select plants also for their form, color, lightness or darkness (value), texture, and the appearance at different seasons of their foliage, flowers, and fruits. They plan for visual beauty as well as soil stability, and also for the safety of motorists. The plantings help keep drivers alert on otherwise monotonous stretches of road and remind them that underpasses and overpasses often make the roadway narrower with less shoulders.

Causeways, similar to bridges, provide ways to cross wetlands or shallow bodies of water. Soil and stones are dumped to build up a narrow way above the highest expected waters. Because a causeway often acts as a dike obstructing the flow of water from one side to the other, it usually includes one or more little bridges or culverts through which the water can move. In case you are caught out in a tornado, a culvert may be your best refuge.

Causeways delight naturalists because of the easy access they give to wetlands and water bodies where wildlife can be viewed. Causeways also create "edge," that is, the edge between two habitats— in this case water and land. Edges of habitats almost always have a greater variety and larger populations of wildlife than do the middles of habitats. This "edge principle," which also applies to human populations, was described in the chapter titled "Wildlife."

Being elevated, causeways let you look down into tall marsh grasses, reeds, cattails, and shrubswamps so you can watch birds that come up to the top of the vegetation. If you had to slosh down among those plants you would probably scare most of the birds away before you could get a good look at them. However, your good visibility from up on a causeway works both ways: you can see wildlife, but they can readily see you. Fortunately you can take precautions. Wear clothing colored somewhat like the environment to camouflage you. Use earth colors and vegetation colors. Mix and match for minimum conspicuousness. Use broken-up patterns for what biologists call "disruptive coloration" to obscure your contours. Also, when you move, do it slowly to avoid drawing attention and startling any wildlife.

Sitting quietly in one place for a while limits the number of environments you can experience in a given time, but often you can discover much more life in a particular habitat than if you dash off impatiently to some other place. If you have not already practiced quiet observation, you may wish at first to have a book to read, or pencil and paper to write a letter; quiet activities like these help you still yourself until you begin to notice what is going on around you.

Fortunately many wildlife refuges have *wildlife hides* (also called "blinds" or "bird blinds") along their causeways. I particularly remember some in Britain. One at Loch Lewes in Scotland was built so that folks could observe through field glasses and telescopes the nesting across the loch of a pair of ospreys, very rare in Britain. People's approach to the hide was concealed from the hawks by a brush fence made by school children. Another hide was on a merse (salt marsh) in Dumfrieshire, Scotland; it was a tower secretively approached by a path between two high dikes, preventing one from being seen by birds out on the merse on either side. In Devon, England, I found a hide whose roof had just been thatched with reeds by the sanctuary manager's small daughter. Some refuges use portable hides more or less modified from latrines such as are used at construction sites, with observation slits instead of sitting holes and with camouflaging paint.

Hides, causeways, and bridge abutments all provide good places for quiet observation of nature while you are on tour.

21 CANALS

Mud season occurs in spring when the ground tries to thaw after being frozen all winter. Warmer places have their mud seasons too. When rain falls on clay soil, you get mud. Anything with wheels (tricycle, bicycle, car, truck, or ox cart, even tractors) sinks into the mud. As vehicles roll away they leave ruts of course, and ruts soon fill with water. Then is the time to get a garden hoe and apply your elemental knowledge that water runs downhill. The challenge is to see how much rut-water you can drain away to help the soil dry out in the farmyard, driveway, or wherever. Where ruts cross each other, one may be the lower. Then a poke with your tool will let the higher one pour into it. Be a hydraulic engineer. Get muddy.

After mud season brooks run free and warmer. Then is the time to float a toy boat (a twig will do) down some tiny brook, imagining you are traveling on it. Miniscale imaginings are good preludes to actual tourings. Again, be a hydraulic engineer and get to know the nature of the brook by playing with it. Dig a little canal to detour around a riffle; then convert a wooden box into a little lock to let your boat descend *gently* to the lower level downstream from the riffle. Make a wooden, up-sliding door at the upper end of the box and one at the lower end, to raise and lower the water level in your canal's lock.

Canals are flatwater, a bit like long, thin lakes rather than streams. Mostly their currents flow gently, and gently should they be traveled. The pleasures they afford are leisurely, their vibes not those of rafting, whitewater canoeing, and kayaking. Where their waters descend, they are harnessed by dams with locks leveling them for navigation and slowing the pace of travel. When you take a tour on an English canal boat, you can get off at the locks and help manually to open and close the gates.

Today I write this on the bank of the Erie Canal in New York State. It was first built between 1817 and 1825 for commerce between the Great Lakes at Buffalo and the Hudson River at Albany. This morning I talked with a real lock keeper, at Lock 25, a pleasure I had dreamed of many years ago. Some day I want to take my children and grandchildren on a canal trip. "You come too," as Robert Frost said.

Perhaps we'll traverse New York on the Erie Canal. We'll watch gulls, swallows, kingfishers, and herons. We'll enjoy floodplain forests of willows, elms, silver and red maples, swamp white oaks, pin oaks, and sycamores. We'll stroll and jog on the tow paths occasionally, naming wildflowers that are old friends and discovering new ones. We'll watch the perching birds and insects that frequent the bankside shrubberies. And of course we'll chat with lock keepers and others who live by the canal, for people are a very important part of nature.

Perhaps you have already tasted life along canals. Perhaps you have idled along the canals of France with their pollarded willows, neat little farms, long-integrated villages, and vineyards where tasting wine is a part of tasting life. (The scientific name for grapes is *Vitis*, deriving from the Latin *vita*, or "life.") Perhaps you have skated in the Low Countries (if only in your imagination as you read *Hans Brinker and the Silver Skates*) and watched windmills take the wind sweeping in from the North Atlantic to pump water from the polders into the canals. Some day I must go to the Netherlands and watch the trees on the canal banks, the fields of flowering bulbs, the wildflowers, birds, and insects, and struggle with language, sketches, and gestures to learn from the people there about life along the canals.

America too has its enticing canals for travel, at least in the humid eastern states; in the more arid West the canals are more for irrigation than for boating. In Ontario, the Rideau Canal south of Ottawa leads through forests and farmlands; pleasure boats abound in summer. In New York State, the Cayuga and Seneca Barge Canal branches southward from the New York State Barge Canal through the Montezuma Wildlife Refuge in the Finger Lakes District. The Cape Cod Canal between Massachusetts Bay and Buzzards Bay is convenient for boats passing between them, but to explore its natural and cultural history in the flanking sandhill forests of pitch pine and oak you might prefer hiking.

The Atlantic Coastal Plain was good terrain for canal builders in the golden age of canals, before railroads and then trucks took over much of their business. Most of the canals are part of, or tributary to, the Atlantic Intracoastal Waterway. Perhaps most famous is the Chesapeake and Ohio Canal ("the C & O") from the Potomac River westward through Maryland, hiked along by Supreme Court judge-naturalist William O. Douglas to emphasize the importance of conserving it as a natural and cultural resource.

North of Trenton, New Jersey, is the Delaware and Raritan Canal. The Chesapeake and Delaware Canal crosses the Delmarva Peninsula as a segment of the Intracoastal Waterway; other segments include the Albemarle and Chesapeake Canal and the Dismal Swamp Canal in Virginia, and the Hamburg Ditch in North Carolina. You can take your little boat and mosquito repellent across southern Florida on the Caloosahatchee-Okeechobee-Lucie Canals and, being alert for heavy shipping, poke along the Gulf Intracoastal Waterway watching the fascinating bird life along the Gulf of Mexico. During spring migrations when tired birds arrive from South America they may rest in the shore shrubbery all around you. (Here is where I saw my first painted bunting, almost unbelievably beautiful.)

Like the railroads and superhighways that came after them, our waterways can take you through industrial complexes, farmlands and forests, and some of our most beautiful natural areas. They speak of the resources that, along with people-power, have made our nation great. Traversing the disparate areas, you will have much to see and think about. So why not travel them slowly with paddle, oar, and sail? If petroleum-powered, cut the motor and drift a while, and look for peaceful anchorages. Harken, sniff, and touch as well as look. Like your boat on its waterway, feel buoyant.

22 YARDS AND GARDENS

When traveling, it's fun to see how people relate to nature, as revealed by their planning and use of outdoor homespace. In cities you can watch for apartment window boxes and potted plants on fire escapes, where people living in rectangular buildings feel the need of growing things to make their domicile a home. What would cities be without geraniums?

Dwellers in ground-floor apartments sometimes have better opportunities to embrace nature. Brick, stone, concrete, or board steps fronting on a paved sidewalk and street may have a pot of coleus on them in good weather. A small back yard with little soil between trash cans and a clothes pole may still have a few well-cared-for plants; or a yard may be a jewel of a garden, a veritable Eden with both apple and fig trees beautifully tended even in the smallest of spaces. A grape arbor may grace a narrow concrete walkway hugging a house as it connects to the sidewalk. A clustering of hosta plants somehow survive at a corner of the building. People in such apartments may have lived there a long time; perhaps they were born there and their parents or grandparents came from the "old country" when they were first married. Longevity of residence can help a family relate closely to the land, growing perennial flowers instead of just annuals for instance. High inner-city mobility and change of ethnic groups increase people's difficulty in caring for nature around their homes.

After World War II, designers of rapidly spreading suburbs in America often favored *developments* with gracefully curved roads and little houses without evident boundaries between them. Presumably for sales reasons they were often called "estates" or "manors," without much regard for earlier meanings of the words. Some of these developments have maintained their lawns without any fences to indicate private ownership. Neighbors enjoy the commonality of their setting with greensward and here and there a Norway maple, pin oak, locust, magnolia, or palm and jacaranda, depending upon the climate and what the local nursery sells. Lawn mowers are in their element in such places. When people sit on the lawn they are apt to lay down a blanket first. For many residents (not all, by any means), nature is enjoyed at arm's length rather than embraced.

In some housing projects, however, hedges began to spring up in the 1950s, and even fences. "Doing one's own thing" became more in vogue than total conformity. Although original designers' plans for homespaces with the feel of lawned and landed gentry were abandoned, homeowners could now honestly express themselves and their feelings about nature in many different ways. More pedestaled bird baths and crystal balls appeared. Mowers of lawns apparently did not mind moving aside china ducks and flamingoes. Even statues of deer sometimes stood motionless in what had now become front yards. Back yards had more dog kennels and sand boxes, and some in warmer climates had blue-bottomed pools to compensate somewhat for loss of clean streams with swimming holes which the suburbs had polluted, filled with trash, and then often buried in culverts to flow unseen, as described by Robert Frost in his poem *A Brook in the City*. The trend was back to nature, in a civilized way. Big shade trees and swimming pools do not fit well in small yards, but dwarf fruit trees were a fair compromise and came into style. You may not spot them easily as you drive by in a car, but if you bicycle through post–World War II suburbs, happily you can see some now old enough to bear fruit.

By the 1970s many developers found land harder to come by, and many people could not afford a piece of land to call their own. Townhouses became prevalent, new manifestations of row houses in which homes share common exterior walls. Some were merely like old row houses with more electric appliances; others were designed around a courtyard, or even several connecting ones, and landscaped in a genteel manner with caretakers to keep them beautiful. Residents could enjoy manicured nature without having to be personally involved. The mostly peripheral parking lots, sometimes with promising young shade trees, held autos to take residents to the country if they had time and inclination to enjoy nature more intimately. Perhaps your tours start in such a place?

Cluster development was another response to the problem of more people and less land for homes. In cluster developments, single-family homes could be built closer together than many zoning regulations had previously allowed, *if* the development included undeveloped "open space" around or beside the houses. The amenities of a patch of woods and sometimes even a brook came with this modern version of the old-time "commons," the community pasture. These projects, though, were not designed for grazing sheep and cows. People moving from cities to suburbs are usually slow to learn the pleasures to be associated with the smell of farm animals. But less-mangled nature did thus come closer to homes. Bird feeders became more common as chickadees and titmice dared the flights from woods to windows. In such developments, you can look for tree houses and other evidence that suburban children can enjoy some of the ways of country children. But with their regulations, local ordinances, and insurance policies, are these developments limiting the kinds of experiences that can create a nature-educated society?

Both private and public gardens merit your attention while touring. Private gardens speak more of individuals and family life, of an area whose limits mark the boundaries of one's responsibilities. While touring you can note many ways that those boundaries are evidenced. Look for walls and fences. There are many kinds and designs. Many fences are mass-produced; others are delightfully home-designed and homemade.

You can have a great time traveling primarily to make photographs and/or sketches of fences; or you can play observation games en route, with rules made according to each region and its natural materials. For instance, in the New England countryside you can give different points to different kinds of walls, and the highest score wins: a glacial stone fence, 5 points; a crooked rail fence, 10 points; a concrete wall with broken bottles cemented in the top, 25 points. When my wife and I used to travel with our small children, one side of the car competed against the other to see who could count the most fields with baled hay. In some cities and suburbs, youngsters can learn a lot about people by looking for chain-link fences; count those with vines planted against them and those without. A sequel to this game gives points for different easily recognized kinds of vines, such as grape, wisteria, or bougainvillea, depending upon the region.

Hedges are planted by patient people who are willing to wait for nature's growth processes to complete closure. Patient but botanically ignorant folks may plant little shrubs too close together, while patient and impecunious people plant them too far apart. People who dig their own shrub plantings in the wild develop hedges without much uniformity but a good deal of character. In northern areas, people with enough money tend to buy evergreens for hedges, for year-round foliage and microclimate control; but people who use their vacation homes only in summer are quite happy with deciduous privet for privacy. You can bet that hedges will tell you a lot about people, though if you are doing competitive hedge-watching you may want to hedge your bets.

Screen plantings give more privacy than hedges, though tall hedges can be considered screen plantings. These dense rows of trees or tall shrubs may have been planted primarily to fend off cold and/or drying winds. On plains, Siberian or Chinese elm and Scots pine have often been used. Around vineyards east of the Great Lakes, Lombardy poplars have been favored. In Florida, feathery casuarina trees, also called "Australian pine," have given some protection from coastal winds, as have pitch pines and Japanese black pines along cooler shores. Screen plantings also give snug seclusion for outdoor living areas. When years have given them sufficient height they can even give privacy for second-floor bedrooms where houses are close together.

It is interesting to note how styles of hedges may relate to the lifestyles of people in different neighborhoods and regions. A New England cottage may have a lilac hedge or one of forsythia or Japanese barberry. A ranch on the American Great Plains may have a buffalo berry hedge, while one in South Africa may be of geraniums. A Victorian home with its intricate barge boards and other fancy trim may be bordered by rhododendrons and arborvitae.

Some hedges are meticulously sheared, maybe as many as three times a year, to keep them always trim; some are kept from getting unruly by having a haircut once a year; others grow wild and become quite untamable unless, with species that are quite shear-tolerant, they are mercilessly cut to their bases and given a fresh start. Watch for houses with design-conscious and horticulturally knowledgeable owners; the lines of their regularly trimmed hedge conform to those of the house so that the house and yard have a nice feeling of ordered unity. Others will use topiary (fancy-shearing) techniques to express their personal whimsy; for example a hedge of boxwood, privet, hemlock, or yew may be shaped to look like animals. Of course, topiary like that requires years of careful cutting as the plants grow.

Within the bounds of wall, fence, screen, hedge, or just a stretch of mown grass, gardens may glorify a piece of Planet Earth according to their place and season. Warm climates revel in riotous bloom all year, purpled with bougainvillea festooning walls while bird-of-paradise flowers, strelitzias, poke their elegant heads above beds of multicolored caladiums. A desert garden may, after a rare spring rain, boast a profusion of yellow blooms on a prickly-pear cactus as it stands confident in a spread of gravel and artfully placed stones, a piece of sandblasted gray "driftwood" near by. In northern climates, a brief flowering of sweet peas followed by daisies, day-lilies, and gladiolas may be preludes to goldenrods and asters before an early and long winter paints the gardens white.

Let us call it technique rather than nosiness to pause along a road to admire a stranger's garden. Personally I am not too shy to ring a cottage doorbell to ask the name of a plant of which the owner must certainly be proud. I'd rather, though, see a person working in his or her garden and just call out, "Pardon me, can you tell me the name of that plant?" Gardeners being the friendly sort they usually are, I have made delightful acquaintances with people who seem very glad to show me their gardens.

Fortunately there is a socially acceptable way to visit many of the grand private gardens designed by great gardeners. Garden clubs are apt to have garden tours or "open gardens" once a year or so when their members open their gardens for display to the public. Sometimes such events are free; sometimes there is a small charge. You may ask the staff at a community's library or post office whether it knows whom to contact at the local garden club. Visits to such gardens are well worth the effort of inquiry.

Public gardens welcome tourists during open hours. Parks, arboretums, and botanic gardens make great lingering places when you are tired, even if you do not know one plant from another. Neither the elderly Scottish gardener edging the turf nor the young college intern weeding the iris bed will care how much you know. You may get smiles from them, though, when you volunteer a compliment on their work. If a public garden is large, don't try to see everything and read every name on labeled plants. Watch for butterflies as well as blooms. Use your nose to explore fragrances. Listen to the birds and maybe the swish of a garden hose or the gritty scratch of a spade or trowel. Here— as in countless yards and gardens elsewhere—people are working with nature's gifts to make this world, our Planet Earth, this speck in space, a better place, to make it feel like home.

23   TOWNS AND CITIES

At least a bit of nature is close at hand wherever you are, even in the city. You may even be able to see sky between skyscrapers. If not, there should at least be changing daylight in the shaft above the areaway outside your window, and from it you can receive kitchen smells and sound from the occasional jangling of metal trash cans. The smells and sounds are borne by air; yes, there is certainly air out there. You can breathe some of it if the window can be opened.

Obviously you are not in the great outdoors with lots of sky and trees and birds. You are stuck in the city. But then again, you may be one of those people who feels happiest in a big city, not stuck at all. If so, how well have you explored urban nature? There are the parks you enjoy. Maybe you regularly take a walk to the nearest one, touring its paths and resting on its benches. You watch the people and the pigeons. And the ants?

One day I was outside the United Nations building on Manhattan's East Side, busy photographing caterpillar droppings that, at first glance, I thought were coffee grounds under a sidewalk plane tree ("sycamore"). Caterpillar droppings are beautifully organized little packages, often with designs worthy of french pastry in a Parisian patisserie. As I advanced my film, I noticed a disheveled man with uncertain steps obviously approaching me. "Hmm," I thought, "He certainly wants money for a drink." I started to turn away, as regretfully one often feels compelled to do.

"Pardon me," he said in a polite manner, "Did you know that pigeons eat meat?" He caught me for sure; I *didn't* know! This Eastsider was glad to meet another person with eyes for city nature. As we talked, he told how he had often shared his meager lunches with pigeons and had watched them carefully. Once one ate a piece of his bologna given him by a delicatessen, and he took the trouble to walk to the Museum of Natural History to report it to an interested staff. After a few minutes more of getting to know each other, he gave me an unforgettable 2-hour nature tour of the Lower East Side.

In many cities pigeons are plentiful. As we mentioned earlier, they are the descendants of immigrants themselves, European rock doves. You can also sometimes see racing pigeons wheeling high above in flocks, or pigeons some enterprising young person is raising for squab to eat or sell. House sparrows too add the movement of nature to a city. They proliferate noisily, making homes in odd niches and projections of buildings, gathering straws from vacant lots. Scientists have made many studies of these people-tolerant birds; they call them "commensals," animals feeding at our table. They are worth systematic watching as well as casual observation as we share each other's habitat in the city.

Starlings also decorate our cities with their forms and flutters, their squeals and squeaks, and their occasionally more melodious whistles. They also decorate cities with limey materials brought in from their daily excursions to the country to feed. Look for them as twilight approaches; then they flock to perches near warm air vents or where sun-baked bricks hold the day's heat on cool or cold nights, or where the underpinnings of bridges give protection. They know the city's microclimates and will reveal them to you if you watch. Listen for their early-morning awakenings on girders and gantries where they are safe from predators.

If your tour-city is on a river or coast, as most cities are, you will find that gulls are spirit-uplifters as well as garbage collectors. They give us their soaring wings to admire, next best to possessing them ourselves. And tails! Tails are no evolutionary afterthought. We can delightedly watch how the gulls' tails tip and spread as the birds hang-glide, hover, or sail gracefully away.

Insects in cities are certainly less plentiful than in the country, but you can find them if you look for them. Vacant lots are not really vacant; they usually have a host of insects. So do railroad yards and other weedy places. Parks too are good places to hunt for them. A street tree is probably never bug-free, though in winter the insects may be present only as eggs, larvae, or pupae, often protected underground, in litter, or inside weed stems. Wherever there are plants, nature will supply you with insects for your watching.

Where soil is bare and plants are rare, or even at first glance absent, look for ants. Even a pavement crack may be home to them and their myriad subway tunnels ("Dig we must") for subterranean foragings, feasts, munchies, and after-dinner naps. Where there are ants there may be ant-lions preying on them. Ant-lions, also called doodle bugs by children, dig conical pits in dry, sandy soil and lie hidden at their bottom. The slopes composed of sand particles lie at their natural angle of repose. When an ant steps into a pit, the sand becomes unstable and the ant slips back as it tries to climb out. Alerted by the commotion, the ant-lion thrusts up two big jaws that easily capture its dinner. Some kids feed ants to doodle bugs; others more in sympathy with ants just tickle the sandy cone with a straw and try to scratch out the ant-lion to see how big it is, and to watch it dig in again, backwards as dictated by its nature.

Cockroaches are unloved but admirable denizens of city basements and kitchens. Once I was the proud owner of a huge oriental cockroach from a city jail, obtained I might quickly add, by swapping with another student who coveted my Libellulid dragonfly. City cockroaches, unlike the little wood roaches, are dirty because they live in dirt, as do pigs who are poorly penned. Cockroaches surely do not think of themselves as bad; they just try to make a living cleaning up crumbs, fat, and whatever. We can admire their fleet-footedness and flat design, adapted to life in cracks, even while we try to keep down their numbers because we know they smell and we fear their disease-carrying proclivities. I find it harder to be charitable about the too-intimate lifestyles of fleas, bedbugs, and lice. With great patience they linger where any tourist from other infested accommodations or public conveyances may have unwittingly gathered them. I hope that in your travels you never meet them, beautiful as they are under a microscope in a laboratory.

The little gray house mouse, matching its drab basement habitat, can be tolerated and even made a pet; better that than allow it to proliferate and destroy food, garments, bedding, and any other nestible or edible materials. Brother Rat is less amenable to domestication except in laboratories. Your restaurant, warehouse, or domicile is *its* domicile, one to be defended if you corner it and thus arouse its territorial instincts. To enjoy urban rat-watching, it is best to give them room to do their thing. Sit around ends of sewers or beside dumps or river banks. Another but less natural way to admire these creatures is to visit a university's zoology or psychology department and ask permission to see the animal room. There is much to learn there as white beauties run through mazes and raise genetically proper progeny. However, all animal rooms are not open to the public. If you are not admitted, try the zoo.

Going to the zoo is the most popular way to see animals in a large city. There, however, you expect to see more exotic animals than city ones, often ones from other countries. For those of us who cannot journey afar, zoos are the next best way to meet fellow creatures from foreign lands. Some zoos take better care of their caged inmates than others. Those with adequate funding and staff play an important role in educating about animals and their conservation. They need tourist support. If you are at a zoo and just don't enjoy looking at caged animals, take pleasure in watching the ubiquitous house sparrows flit in and out of the bars to get their share of the animals' food.

City plants include the ubiquitous weeds, which grow in barren soil under extremes of heat and cold, downpour and drought. One must admire the ragweeds, plantains, and foxtail grasses of this world. They seemingly try to bring green beauty to the city-deserts we have made. We supplement their efforts with public parks, playgrounds, greenbelts, and street trees; privately we do what we can with backyard gardens and street-front window boxes to brighten our cities and bring back to them a little of the displaced greenery.

One of the encouraging social trends of this century's last quarter is the great expansion of community gardening, an outgrowth of the "Victory Gardens" begun during World War II. Look for community gardens in your travels. Their ability to bring people, soil, and growing things back together bodes well for greener cities in the future. We need urban areas where people have a greater understanding and deeper appreciation of the nature that supports them. Adding greenery helps.

As tourists we are not in a position to bring nature to a city, but we can appreciate the nature that we are sure to find there. We can wonder at the ways of pigeons and sparrows and stoop to take a closer look at the design inherent in a weed.

IV

TECHNIQUES

24 RECORDING YOUR OBSERVATIONS

Observation has been the theme of Parts I, II, and III, not just through sight but *with all our senses*. Nature has granted us a nervous system that brings us messages from our environment through eyes, ears, nose, tongue, and skin; this nervous system keeps us alive, leading us to the food and raw materials we need, protecting us from dangers, and in the process giving us some sorrow and much joy. Part IV deals with recording our observations, for four reasons.

First, acts of recording make us better observers. Making a written note challenges us to find the most fitting words to explain what we see, hear, and so forth. Making a quick sketch of a glimpsed bird sharpens our eyes to note such characteristics as the shape of its bill or the presence of a wing bar. Taking a photograph requires that we focus our attention. Recording sounds stimulates our listening. And making a pressed specimen of a plant requires that we choose an appropriate portion, looking over the possibilities carefully, selecting the best flowers, leaves, or other parts.

Second, records enable us to review our observations. Thus we learn by repeated stimulation of our brains, and we refresh our memories of places and happenings on our tours.

Third, our records serve for reference when we need to know what was where and when, what it was like, what it may have been doing, and so on. Perhaps the records may be of scientific importance when added to other bits of recorded knowledge, even though we may not consider ourselves scientists.

And finally, we can share our tours with those not fortunate enough to be along with us. Some of the greatest pleasures of a trip can come from its retrospective sharing. Sharing is an art well worth cultivating. Good records help in these several ways.

On a tour, making records is not necessary. You can have a wonder-filled trip without ever jotting a note, writing a postcard, or snapping a picture. Recording can be a bore, a nuisance, a chore, or worse, a sacrifice of that sense of freedom a tour can provide. On the other hand, recording can be a minor or major purpose of your tour and a great joy, as it has been to me and as I hope it may be for you. Therefore, the following suggestions:

Keep a Log, a chronological list of dates and places on your tour. It can be very simple. Or it can include hours of starting and stopping and distances traveled. If you are driving, an automobile record book from a stationery store works well and can include notes on purchases of fuel and any maintenance costs. This is practical, and in later years it can evoke many memories and suggest places to which you would like to return.

Keep a Journal, a day-by-day account in a bound notebook of significant facts—and likely some insignificant ones. For some of the less stable climates such as New England, I recommend daily weather notes. Early in the day note the weather, perhaps with a line about where and how you spent the night: "Tented again. Barred owl woke us at 2 A.M. but hard to hear over the mosquito chorus." Then each evening try faithfully to add comments about the day's places and events. Don't bother with complete sentences unless you want to; just

182

get some facts down on paper every evening. Who knows, they may become the basis for magazine articles or a book some day!

Keep a Diary, a bound notebook wherein you write whenever you feel like it about what seems interesting on your tour. You need not write every day; long lapses, though, are not helpful; if they occur, do get writing again when you have the urge. If you wish, a diary can be very personal, for no eyes but your own. Sacred. "Doug was unbearable this morning, until we had lunch at McDougal's. Maybe I wasn't much better. Gathered pinyon nuts for camp supper." And the next morning: "Sang around our small campfire last evening and listened to the down-canyon breeze jostle the aspen leaves as the almost-full moon rose. To sleeping bags around nine but reviewed the morning arguments and made resolves before sleep took over."

Write Letters, to folks at home, to friends, to anybody who will save your letters and give them back to you on your return. When you write to people who will *not* give them back, keep a copy if you think that the letter in retrospect will add to your other accounts of your tour. (I usually take a portable typewriter in our rig, which makes better carbon copies.) Maybe you will want to write your boss back on the job, or a legislator who should know of your concern about the latest pork-barrel "boondoggle" ruining the environment you are visiting. Whomever you write, give special attention to what it is about your trip that will be of interest to *them.*

Write Postcards, much as above. Buy commercial ones illustrating the places, flowers, animals, boats, or whatever you are experiencing. These can make you a pictorial record if they are returned. Sometimes instead I buy plain postcards at the post office. They save me money but cost me time making a sketch on one side and a message and address on the side with the printed stamp. The pictures are not as good as commercial ones of course, but the card is special, the only one of its kind, designed with a particular person in mind. Sometimes I get them returned later, though they may not be worth saving. Letters and postcards are fun to send when you know they will bring somebody a little happiness. (Of course you can also buy picture postcards and keep them for your own collection, without ever sending them.)

Write for Publication, or dreamed-of publication. Consider writing an article for a regional magazine in the area you are visiting, from a visitor's viewpoint. Or write some pages for a book related to your travels, as some of this book is being written on tour. For authors, a trip can be "H & H"—*h*ard work and *h*oliday combined.

Make Sketches, with pencil, pen, felt pen, or whatever. Usually you will draw in a sketchbook from a stationer's or art store, preferably the spiral-bound or similar kind that opens back so that both covers are under its leaves to give good support. Its size should be adapted to your carrying ability, for shirt pocket, fannypack, backpack, saddlebag, dashboard cubbyhole, or whatever. Be sure your name and address are on it in case you lose it, perhaps with a plea or promise of a reward if found and returned.

You may want your sketches on separate sheets of typewriter-sized paper for use on a clipboard. Have a heavy elastic to secure the lower end of the paper in a breeze. Keep the sheets in a file folder or other portfolio. Instead of sketchbook or paper, I use 3- by 5-inch file cards kept in a sturdy envelope that fits in a pocket or knapsack. On returning home, I can file my sketches by subject, such as *sky, landforms, plants, animals, people,* and *structures,* with various subsets indexed. That makes a useful reference file for my purposes, but the sketches scattered among various files do not make a readily found record of any one tour. Also, such small pictures must be quite simple. You may prefer 5- by 8-inch file cards. (For a few sketching techniques, see Chapter 7, "Wetlands.")

Paint Pictures, preferably with acrylics for convenience and flexibility of technique. The simplest technique is to use only black paint, white paint, and orange paint. The black, grays made with black and white, and the white can represent the *cool colors* of the spectrum (from blue-violet through blue to blue-green as shown in an artists' *color circle*) at whatever value (lightness or darkness) you want. Use the orange, suitably modified with black, grays, or white, to represent the *warm colors,* from red-violet through red to yellow-green, as shown in a color circle, at whatever value you want.

Of course added tubes of the primary colors (red, yellow, and blue) give more colorful and potentially more realistic pictures, but that increases your equipment. If you are a beginning painter, I recommend the aforementioned simpler technique as a starter because it gives excellent training in analysis of cool and warm colors and their values; also it can produce beautiful pictures. Then progress to a palette with black and white plus the primary colors, with which you can mix a great variety of other colors at many values and intensities. Intensity means brightness as distinct from lightness of value. If a beginner, you may want to take a how-to-paint book on tour to guide your efforts.

Make Photographs with the best camera you can afford that fits your needs. If you do not already have one, read a beginner's book on photography and then ask for advice from experienced persons at camera stores, when they are not too busy. A camera of small size and weight is convenient for touring. I like to carry my camera with me almost all the time when traveling, worn as surely as my pants, and have it right beside my sleeping bag at night. You never know what once-in-a-lifetime subject may suddenly present itself.

I favor a single-lens reflex camera (SLR), one with automatic controls for "grab shots" (ones when you don't have time to think of correct film exposure), but also with manual controls enabling you to tell the camera exactly what you want it to do. You improve your photography when you do take time to think about the size of lens opening and speed of shutter in order to gather just the right amount of light from a particular subject or to control the planes of focus. That is a large part of the art of photography, along with picture composition and a feeling for what makes a good picture that expresses what you want to portray.

Decide what kind of pictures you want to show people. Do you want to make 35-millimeter color transparencies for home slide shows and lectures? Do you want to make prints you can hand around or put in an album of your tour and/or send home or mail to friends? On-the-spot developing of prints by some cameras lets you evaluate your pictures as you take them and permits retaking when you think you can do better; sometimes also you may be so pleased with a picture that you wish immediately to take another of the same subject. You can also have prints made from your transparencies. Choose your best when they are returned from being professionally developed at a photo lab.

If you can afford two cameras and don't mind being encumbered by them, have one camera with slide film and one with print film.

Tours can be hard on cameras. I keep mine in its case with a broad-topped strap around my neck, and I open its case only to shoot, even though a photographer for *Life* magazine told me only silly amateurs would carry their cameras in a case! He was a news reporter, however, and not one likely to lie on his belly to take pictures of sand wasps or climb tall trees to photograph a hawk's nest. A restraining harness around your chest keeps your camera from swinging away from you if you bend over to look at a plant, stone, horned lizard, or some such, or if you are climbing rocks, trees, or a ship's rigging. When not wearing a harness and not actually shooting, I put one arm through the neck strap and thus sling my camera under my arm pit or sometimes farther around on my back to be out of my way (except in crowds where I like to have my precious camera in sight).

Some cameras are sold with a wrist strap instead of a neck strap. I don't like to see even an inexpensive camera swung around on one; it invites a damaging bang and may form a bad habit that can cause grief later with an expensive camera or with binoculars. Be sure to keep sand, dust, and water away from your camera at all times. When a lens must be cleaned, do it *gently* with a fresh tissue, not one which has been laid down on anything and might therefore have scratchy dust on it, or use a lens brush with attached air bulb to blow dust away.

A good-looking camera bag is tempting if you begin to acquire extra telephoto and wide-angle lenses, filters, tripod, and other equipment. I prefer, however, a container less enticing of attention and theft. When touring with a car, van, or truck, I keep my photographic gear in an old cardboard carton in which I have glue-gunned cardboard partitions to fit my camera, extra lenses, record book, pencil, insect repellent, lens tissues in an envelope, and the little lens brush. An old but clean garment on top adds to the camouflage and keeps off direct sunlight. However you package your camera, don't leave it in strong sunlight or a hot glove compartment of a car. Outdoors in subfreezing weather, your camera likes to be inside your zipped-up jacket, but be careful of any condensation forming on the lens (or even inside the camera) when it is brought out into the cold. An inexpensive sky filter kept on expensive lenses all the time protects them and improves many landscape shots. For hiking, I like an old canvas over-the-shoulder bag with vertical compartments made of milk cartons for carrying my photographic gear.

Photography can be as simple or as complex and challenging as you want, providing snapshots or great works of science and art. A zoom lens ranging from about 45 to 85 millimeters is a great help on tour, enabling you to compose good pictures. Closeup lenses, also called portrait attachments, are relatively inexpensive and great for pictures of flowers, insects, and other small objects of nature; use them also to copy local newspaper articles and maps pertinent to your tour; they will help you give interesting slide talks later. If you want good pictures of wildlife, you will want more powerful zoom telephoto lenses, as described in books on wildlife photography. A wide-angle lens will take in wide panoramas but usually makes objects look disappointingly small and far away; it is handy in tight places, as when taking pictures in a narrow street.

Do not try to take pictures of everything. Practice intelligent *seeing*. Then you can select the best subjects for good *photography*. Be sure not to become so engrossed with what you see through your camera lens that you miss the larger, unphotographable scenes and their significance. Also do not neglect sketching, as described above and in Chapter 7, for its ability to improve your photography as well as for its own sake. And pictures accompanied by writing can be worth a thousand wordless ones. So do not neglect written records; include both photographic data, descriptions, and sometimes your feelings.

Make Sound Recordings; they add an exciting dimension to a tour, sharpening the selectivity of your ears and helping afterwards to re-create happenings for yourself and others to enjoy. Modern battery-powered tape recorders can capture and also amplify nature's background music, including the swish or crash of waves, roaring of rapids and waterfalls; evergreen murmurs, aspen clatterings, and reed rustlings; cricket choruses, coyote concerts, and bird calls and songs. Sometimes I hear travel talks and nature programs that use canned music made with human instruments, often beautiful but somewhat disconcerting compared to nature's sounds. Many natural sounds can be the foreground of a presentation with pictures relegated to the background role, an interesting switch of the usual presentation. Perhaps you can stalk a singing thrush and then take background pictures of its remote haunts.

You can take a tour primarily for listening, as a sightless person must. Blind students of mine have taught me much about the joys of listening. I recommend it. And I strongly suggest traveling with a tape recorder. Let others hear what you have heard while you yourself get pleasure from hearing it again.

Videotape some passages of your tour with whatever recording device is suited to your finances and abilities. VCRs (video cassette recorders) can be used to take pictures with or without sound, or sound can be recorded separately. You can take pictures of maps of your travels with your route highlighted with a conspicuous color. Copies of current items from local newspapers add interest, especially if you have been personally involved, for instance attending a public event like a garden tour. You can photograph some of your own sketches too and incorporate them in the cassette record. Zoom lenses permit good closeup pictures of flowers, and supplementary lenses can allow even smaller natural items like insects to be recorded. The excellent records thus obtained will certainly need considerable editing before being shown to others. Inquire about editing procedures when you purchase equipment.

Collect Items as you tour, if you don't mind being encumbered by them on your trip or are willing to send them home by mail or express. Small objects are usually most practical, ones easily stowed or sent. Handmade articles of local natural materials are good souvenirs and gifts and their purchase often can be of financial help to local struggling artisans. Talk with them when they are not too busy to share their enthusiasm for and knowledge of their craft. Be appreciative as well as remunerative.

Picture postcards are also recommended collectibles, even if not sent to anybody. They are easily stowed. Stamps and coins from different countries often depict landscapes, plants, and animals. Brochures, posters, place mats, and maps help you learn as you visit places; they make interesting displays on your return when you report to family, friends, school, or club. Such items can be mailed home in a large envelope or mailing bag, so they do not become "stumblejunk" as you travel.

Natural objects are often free for the taking, but that does not free you from responsibilities. Always ask permission on other people's property before collecting anything. (That is one way to meet some mighty nice people.) Consider carefully whether removal of a stone, cone, shell, or other item may violate an environment or deplete its resources. Remember that if others see you collecting they may follow your example, but they may not be as careful as you are. Most parks do not allow collecting.

Collecting living organisms requires extra thought. You might think: "It is only a beetle." Yes, but it is the only life that beetle has. In my later years I have collected much less—and seen much more. I like to collect different kinds of cones, small dry fruits, and seeds. Each kind has its own wonderful design, and the seeds their own little genetic potentials. Most of the seeds never get planted; they make beautiful displays in glass olive jars, or useful reference specimens when stored in glass vials in a drawer. When collecting, first put them in paper envelopes or little kraft paper bags to dry thoroughly; label them with date and place, and preferably with habitat; add the name if you know it or can look it up in a field guide. If a plant may be rare, take only a few seeds, if any. Be conservative, always.

Collecting flowers for the record can be simply done. Pick only what you are sure nature can spare; when in doubt, just sketch and/or photograph them. Press them, gently arranged in nonglossy magazines or newspapers that absorb their moisture, changing to another as needed until the specimens are dry (not cool to the touch). Write collection data on the pressing pages conspicuously. When the flowers are dry, keep the pages ("field collecting sheets") together between two sheets of protecting corrugated cardboard or in a manila folder.

Best for collecting is a simply made press of two pieces of quarter-inch plywood with two buckling straps to apply pressure. Between these keep sheets of corrugated cardboard; their tubes promote passage of drying air. Between the cardboards put sheets of blotting paper to absorb moisture from the plants and pass it to the air tubes; and between the blotters put the paper sheets with the specimens. This sandwichy contraption can hold many layers of cardboards, blotters, and papers with specimens. When back home, carefully glue the pressed specimens onto sheets of heavy paper, probably white. Copy the collection data onto these mounting sheets. These can be used for display or reference.

One more collectible: fragrances gathered into little airtight containers. In later years one brief whiff can waft your mind back to where you first met sage brush, or burned eucalyptus wood in your fireplace, gathered seaweed, bedded down amid balsam firs, or accepted a proffered bit of lavender from a new acquaintance whose garden you stopped to admire over the sidewalk fence.

Don't make records just to appear busy. Don't collect just to satisfy an acquisitive greed. As with your whole tour, plan a worthy purpose and occasionally deviate from your plans when to do so seems wise and promises new adventures.

25 READING MORE

Pleasures of travel come in three phases: before, during, and after. This bibliographic chapter can enhance those pleasures. Some titles will stimulate your appetite for nature touring and prepare you to enjoy your trips because of advanced knowledge and the enthusiasms of authors who have delighted in the places to which you may go. Other titles are recommended for accompanying you or for the delight of retrospective reading.

Pretrip Books

Louis Pasteur said (freely translated): "In the field of observation, chance favors the mind that is prepared." You can of course have a wonderful time if you just start off on a tour unprepared, but your experiences will be far richer if you read about places beforehand.

A high school or college textbook may have an enlightening chapter on the area you will visit; a local teacher may have a copy to lend you. An encyclopedia, for example the *Americana* or *Britannica* at your public library, will probably have an overview of broad regions or political entities, often with more detailed information followed by a bibliography for further reading. A librarian can show you an index to back copies of *National Geographic*, leading you to articles carefully researched, popularly written, and beautifully illustrated, including maps, of regions you may plan to visit almost anywhere in the world. College and university libraries have scholarly periodicals such as the *Journal of Geography* for serious study. Choose your own level of reading, and perhaps then venture into one a bit beyond you to stretch your mind. Socrates said, as often quoted by my mother, "The more thou learnest to know and to enjoy, the more full and complete for thee will be the reward of living."

Many of the following books are still in print as of this writing. Look for them in bookstores, which can often order them if not in stock. They and out-of-print books can sometimes be found in libraries. I have included older books that have been of special use or interest to me, thinking they will sometimes be worth your diligent searching for them. You may wonder why I included some of the titles; that mystery may be solved if you can find the book! For instance Thollander's *Back Roads of New England* has exemplary sketches for those of you who wish to record your tour with pencil drawings. Some books about Native Americans have particular relevance to nature touring because they have lived so intimately with nature. Wigginton's series of *Foxfire* books tell of people in Appalachia who similarly are close to the land. . . . Enough. Let me not spoil the plot. Read on:

Travel Guides

AMERICAN AUTOMOBILE ASSOCIATION. *TourBooks* and *CampBooks*. Falls Church, VA: American Automobile Association, annual.

BARISH, F. *Frommer's A Guide for the Disabled Traveler: USA, Canada, & Europe*. New York: Frommer/Pasmantier, 1984.

BELOTE, J. *Guide to the Recommended Country Inns of the West Coast*. Chester, CT: The Globe Pequot Press, 1986.

CHAPIN, B. *Guide to the Recommended Country Inns of New York, New*

Jersey, Pennsylvania, Delaware, Maryland, Washington, D.C., Virginia, and West Virginia. Chester, CT: The Globe Pequot Press, 1985.

FISTELL, I. *America by Train: How to Tour by Train*. New York: Burt Franklin & Company, 1984.

FODOR. *Fodor's USA 1986*. New York: Travel Guides, 1986.

FOULKE, P., & R. FOULKE. *Daytrips and Budget Vacations in New England*. Chester, CT: The Globe Pequot Press, 1983.

FOULKE, P., & R. FOULKE. *Daytrips, Getaway Weekends, and Budget Vacations in the Mid-Atlantic States*. Chester, CT: The Globe Pequot Press, 1986.

GRIMES, P. *The New York Times Practical Traveler*. New York: Times Books, 1985.

HADLEY, L. *Traveling with Children in the USA: A Guide to Pleasure, Adventure, Discovery*. New York: William Morrow, 1977.

HARVARD STUDENT AGENCIES, eds. *Let's Go: The Budget Guide to Mexico*. New York: St. Martin's Press, 1985.

HARVARD STUDENT AGENCIES, eds. *Let's Go: The Budget Guide to the USA*. New York: St. Martin's Press, 1986.

HAWKINS, G. *U.S.A. by Bus and Train*. New York: Pantheon, 1985.

HECKER, H. *Travel for the Disabled: A Handbook of Travel Resources and 500 Worldwide Access Guides*. Portland, OR: Twin Peaks Press, 1985.

HILTS, L. *National Forest Guide*. Skokie, IL: Rand McNally, 1980.

KALS, W. *Land Navigation Handbook: The Sierra Club Guide to Map and Compass*. San Francisco: Sierra Club, 1983.

MARTINI, F. *Exploring Tropical Islands and Seas: An Introduction for the Traveler and Amateur Naturalist*. Englewood Cliffs, NJ: Prentice-Hall, Inc., 1984.

MOBIL OIL CORPORATION. *Mobil Travel Guides*. Chicago, IL: Rand McNally, annual.

MOHLENBROCK, R. *The Field Guide to U.S. National Forests, Region by Region, State by State*. New York: Congdon & Weed, Inc., 1984.

NATIONAL SCIENCE FOR YOUTH FOUNDATION. *Directory of Natural Science Centers*. New Canaan, CT: National Science for Youth Foundation, 1985.

PRATSON, F. *Consumer's Guide to Package Travel Around the World*. Chester, CT: The Globe Pequot Press, 1984.

RAND MCNALLY. *Campground and Trailer Park Directory—1986, USA, Canada, and Mexico*. Skokie, IL: Rand McNally, 1986.

SCHELLER, W. *Train Trips: Exploring America by Rail*. Charlotte, NC: The Eastwood Press, 1984.

SCOTT, D., & K. W. SCOTT. *Traveling and Camping in the National Park Areas—Eastern States*. Chester, CT: The Globe Pequot Press, 1979.

SCOTT, D., & K. W. SCOTT. *Traveling and Camping in the National Parks Areas—Mid-America*. Chester, CT: The Globe Pequot Press, 1978.

SCOTT, D., & K. W. SCOTT. *Traveling and Camping in the National Park Areas—Western States*. Chester, CT: The Globe Pequot Press, 1978.

SIERRA CLUB. *The Sierra Club Totebooks: Pocket-sized Wilderness Guides with Information on Trails, Campsites, and Natural Phenomena* (16 or more). San Francisco, CA: Sierra Club.

SQUIER, E. *Guide to the Recommended Country Inns of New England, ninth edition*. Chester, CT: The Globe Pequot Press, 1985.

STEVENS, F. *Nature Centers Have Trails*. Locally distributed by Baker & Taylor, 6 Kirby Ave., Somerville, NJ 08876. Parks and Nature, 1984.

SUNSET. *Sunset Travel Guides*. Menlo Park, CA: Lane Publishing Company.

TELANDER, G. *Wheeler's RV Resort & Campground Guide* (annual). Elk Grove Village, IL: Print Media Services Ltd., 1984.

WEISS, L. *Access to the World: A Traveler's Guide for the Handicapped*. New York: Facts On File, Inc., 1977.

YOUTH HOSTEL ASSOCIATION. *Youth Hosteler's Guide to Europe*. New York: Collier Books, 1973.

ZIMMERMAN, G. *The Complete Guide to Cabins and Lodges in America's State and National Parks*. Boston, MA: Little, Brown, 1985.

Many travel guides are useful for planning a tour, and then one or two of the smaller ones may travel with you. In addition to some of the above, the following can help plan trips.

Hikers, Bikers, Canoeists, Ski-tourers, and Campers, you can benefit from using *Sierra Club Guides* (1142 West Indian School Road, Phoenix, AZ), and the publications of The Appalachian Mountain Club (5 Joy St., Boston, MA 02108) are great too. For the Ozark Trail, write the Missouri Department of Conservation (Jefferson City, MO 65102). For Quetico-Superior canoe routes, contact the U.S. National Forest Supervisor, Box 338, Duluth, MN 55801.

Motorists, you will want oil-company maps such as those published for Mobil Oil Corporation by Rand McNally. You can buy them at bookstores or write Rand McNally (Travel Research Center, P.O. Box 7600, Chicago, IL 60680) for any of the seven regional guides for the United States. Rand McNally also publishes *Lodgings for Less*, by regions; its *Campground & Trailer Park Directory* for the USA, Canada, and Mexico is available by writing P. O. Box 728, Skokie, IL 60076. *Fodor's Modern Guides* (David McKay Company, Inc., 2 Park Avenue, New York, NY 10016) for dozens of regions in the USA and abroad, are available at bookstores and libraries.

Anybody, *you* may be able to resist such books as these, but *I* can't:

BERGON, F., ed. *The Wilderness Reader*. Los Angeles, CA: Times-Mirror, 1980.

BROWN, V. *Investigating Nature through Outdoor Projects*. Harrisburg, PA: Stackpole Books, 1983.

CORNELL, J. *Sharing Nature with Children*. Nevada City, CA: Ananda Publications, 1979.

DAVIDS, R. *How to Talk to Birds—And Other Uncommon Ways of Enjoying Nature the Year Round*. New York: Alfred A. Knopf, 1973.

DUBOS, R. *The Wooing of Earth*. New York: Charles Scribner's Sons, 1980.

GUINNESS, A. *Joy of Nature: How to Observe and Appreciate the Great Outdoors*. Pleasantville, NY: Reader's Digest Association, 1977.

HINES, F. *Introduction to Family Camping*. Charlotte, NC: Boy Scouts of America, 1984.

KATZ, A. *Naturewatch: Exploring Nature with Your Children*. New York: Addison-Wesley, 1986.

LAWRENCE, G. *A Field Guide to the Familiar*: *Learning to Observe the Natural World*. Englewood Cliffs, NJ: Prentice-Hall, Inc., 1984.

OWENS, MARK & DELIA. *Cry of the Kalahari—Seven Years in Africa's Last Great Wilderness*. Boston, MA: Houghton Mifflin, 1984.

WOOD, E. *Science from Your Airplane Window*. New York: Dover Publications, 1975.

If you are hiking, biking, cycling, canoeing, or ski-touring for a considerable distance and therefore traveling light, or planning such side trips from your auto route, select one field guide of special interest for that trip; next time choose another. When going by car or van, you may have room for several field guides. When going to a foreign country, you had probably best wait to buy field guides there, perhaps with a pocket dictionary to help you translate a foreign language.

When I began nature study in the pre-Peterson era, we had very few field guides; now a tantalizing quantity of high-quality guides challenges your selecting. I can include here only a few of my favorites. Some publishers have extensive series, for example Houghton Mifflin Company's *The Peterson Field Guide Series*; G. P. Putnam's Sons' *Putnam Nature Field Book*; The National Audubon Society's *Field Guides*; E. P. Dutton's *Dutton Nature Fieldbooks*; Little, Brown's *Stokes Nature Guides*; Golden Press's *Golden Nature Guides* and *Golden Regional Guides*; H. M. Gousha Company's *Explorer's Guides*; and also Prentice Hall Press's *PHalarope Books*. (Other countries also have excellent series.) You can look over nature guides at a nature-oriented bookstore, nature center, park visitor information center, public library, or maybe a private library of a naturalist friend. Make sure ones selected are designed for the region(s) you will be touring. Try not to get lost amid all these guides!

Some field guides "cover" a large area, perhaps even the whole United States. To do so, they must either be comprehensive and thick or very selective and thin. If you choose the former, you will have to be a patient scholar using them. If using the latter, be patient with the authors who had to decide what to leave out; realize that an item you are trying to identify may not have been included if it is not one of the most conspicuous and/or widely distributed. Be philosophical about leaving things unnamed yet enjoyed.

Relaxing Reading While on Tour

You will benefit from less utilitarian and more relaxing reading on route. Many a hiker carries a paperback up steep trails to read in a backpacked mountain tent by campfire. Henry David Thoreau advised reading the best books first, for otherwise there might not be time. Many classics, proven by time, weigh little in paperback editions. Take your pick. When you have finished one, give it away or swap it with another traveler. Next time in town, browse a bookstore and restock, perhaps alternating a classic with a breezy modern, thanking Thoreau for his advice but not necessarily following it.

I like to read a "good" book (that is, one *I* like) about the country I'm touring through. For instance, Willa Cather's *My Antonia* (Boston, MA: Houghton Mifflin) and John Janovy, Jr.'s *Keith County Journal* (New York: St. Martin's Press) certainly increased my pleasure when discovering Nebraska, so different from my native New England. *The Thorn Birds* by Colleen McCullough was perfect for my trip by the Indian-Pacific train across the Australian Outback from Perth to Sydney. (Perhaps my next book to write should be *Recommended Regional Reading: One Man's Meat?*) This chapter can only hint at the wonderful books to take with you.

Also recommended is a restful afternoon at a local library. As a tourist you will lack a library card for borrowing books, but librarians will delight in having a new person stay awhile to taste their wares. Ask about a novel or biography or autobiography by a native naturalist or other down-to-earth person. If in a studious mood, look for a reference on geology of the region or on native plants, animals, biotic communities, or crops. Your next day outdoors will be the richer for time thus spent.

Some Regional Books

The following national and regional books for nature-related reading and nature study (often merging) are suggestive of the countless ones you may wish to consider buying before your trip, or you may wish to wait and browse bookstores for these or others when you get to a different area. Those listed are mostly of two kinds. Many in my own library have proved their use and joy for me, so I hope they may for you. Others are recent titles I feel sure I would like to use before, during, or after a trip. I regret having had to omit so many excellent ones (including some written by people who I hope will remain friends after this omission!). And more good nature books are being published all the time. Do watch for them.

National

COUNTRY BEAUTIFUL. *America, from Sea to Shining Sea*. Waukesha, WI: Home Library Series of *Country Beautiful*, 1976.

FOLSOM, F. & M. *America's Ancient Treasures*, 3rd rev. Albuquerque, NM: University of New Mexico Press, 1983.

FROME, M. *Promised Land: Adventures and Encounters in Wild America*. New York: Morrow, 1985.

HILOWITZ, B., & S. GREEN (eds.). *Natural Wonders of America*. New York: Simon & Schuster, 1980.

HILTZ, L. *National Forest Guide*. Skokie, IL: Rand McNally, 1980.

JACKSON, J. *American Space—The Centennial Years: 1865–1876*. New York: W. W. Norton, 1972.

JENSEN, KAREN. *America: Land of Wildlife*. Washington, DC: National Wildlife Federation, 1984.

JORDAN, E. *Nature Atlas of America*. Maplewood, NJ: Hammond Incorporated, 1972.

KANE, J., & G. ALEXANDER. *Nicknames and Sobriquets of U.S. Cities,*

States, and Counties. Metuchen, NJ: Scarecrow Press, Inc., 1979.

LANDI, V. *The Great America Countryside: Field Notes on Animals, Plants, Historic Sites, and the Natural Environment.* New York: Macmillan, 1982.

NATIONAL GEOGRAPHIC SOCIETY. *A Guide to Our Federal Lands.* Washington, DC: National Geographic Society, 1985.

NATIONAL GEOGRAPHIC SOCIETY. *Our Threatened Inheritance—Natural Treasures of the United States.* Washington, DC: National Georgraphic Society, 1985.

NATIONAL PARKS AND CONSERVATION ASSOCIATION. *Guide and Map: National Parks of the United States.* Washington, DC: Superintendent of Documents, U.S. Government Printing Office, 1984.

NATIONAL PARK FOUNDATION. *The Complete Guide to America's National Parks.* New York: Viking Press, 1984.

READER'S DIGEST. *America from the Road: A Motorist's Guide to Our Country's Natural Wonders and Most Interesting Places.* Pleasantville, NY: Reader's Digest Association, Inc., 1982.

READER'S DIGEST. *Our National Parks—America's Spectacular Wilderness Heritage.* Pleasantville, NY: Reader's Digest Books, 1985.

READER'S DIGEST. *Scenic Wonders of America: An Illustrated Guide to Our Natural Splendors.* Pleasantville, NY: Reader's Digest Association, Inc., 1981.

RILEY, L., & W. RILEY. *Guide to the National Wildlife Refuges.* New York: Doubleday, 1981.

SHANKS, B. *This Land Is Your Land—The Struggle to Save America's Public Lands.* San Francisco: Sierra Club Books, 1984.

SHELFORD, V. *Naturalist's Guide to the Americas.* Baltimore: Williams and Wilkins, 1926.

STEGNER, W. & P. *American Places.* New York: E. P. Dutton, 1981.

STILGOE, J. *Common Place Names of America.* New Haven, CT: Yale University Press, 1982.

VECSEY, C., & R. VENABLES (eds.). *American Indian Environments: Ecological Issues in Native American History.* Syracuse, NY: Syracuse University Press, 1980.

Regional

Appalachian Mountains

GINNS, P. *Snowbird Gravy and Dishpan Pie: Mountain People Recall.* Chapel Hill, NC: University of North Carolina Press, 1982.

GLIMM, J. *Flatlanders and Ridgerunners: Folktales from the Mountains of Northern Pennsylvania.* Pittsburgh, PA: University of Pennsylvania Press, 1983.

MURLLES, D., & C. STALLINGS. *Hiker's Guide to the Smokies.* San Francisco: Sierra Club ToteBooks, 1973.

SHERMAN, S., & J. OLDER. *Appalachian Odyssey: Walking the Trail from Georgia to Maine.* Brattleboro, VT: The Stephen Greene Press, 1977.

WIGGINTON, E. (ed.). *Foxfire 6.* Garden City, NY: Doubleday, 1980.

Great Basin

CASEY, R. *Journey to the High Southwest: A Traveler's Guide.* Seattle, WA: Pacific Search, 1985.

HART, J. *Hiking the Great Basin: The High Desert Country of California, Oregon, Nevada, and Utah.* San Francisco: Sierra Club ToteBooks, 1981.

McPHEE, J. *Basin and Range.* New York: Farrar, Straus, Giroux, 1981.

NICHOLS, J. *On the Mesa.* Salt Lake City: Peregrine Smith Books, 1986.

PERRY, J. & J. G. PERRY. *The Sierra Club Guide to the Natural Areas of New Mexico, Arizona, and Nevada.* New York: Random House, 1986.

PERRY, J. & J. G. PERRY. *The Sierra Club Guide to the Natural Areas of Colorado and Utah.* New York: Random House, 1985.

ROGERS, G. *Then and Now: A Photographic History of Vegetation Change in the Central Great Basin Desert.* Salt Lake City, UT: Utah University Press, 1982.

Great Plains

BARR, C. *Jewels of the Plains: Wild Flowers of the Great Plains Grasslands and Hills*. Minneapolis, MN: University of Minnesota Press, 1983.

BRAUN, L. *Grasslands* (Audubon Society Nature Guide). New York: Knopf, 1985.

DIPPIE, B. *Remington and Russell: The Sid Richardson Collection*. Austin, TX: University of Texas Press, 1982.

DOIG, I. *This House of Sky: Landscapes of Western Mind*. New York: Harcourt Brace Jovanovich, 1980.

EHRLICH, G. *The Solace of Open Places*. New York: Viking Penguin, 1985.

HUND, D. *Legacy of the West*. Lincoln, NE: University of Nebraska Press, 1982.

ISE, J. *Sod and Stubble*. Lincoln, NE: University of Nebraska Press, 1936.

JANOVY, J. *Keith County Journal*. New York: St. Martin's Press, 1978.

JANOVY, J. *Back in Keith Country*. New York: St. Martin's Press, 1981.

JONES, J. ET AL. *Mammals of the Northern Great Plains*. Lincoln, NE: University of Nebraska Press, 1983.

MADSON, J. *Where the Sky Begins: Land of the Tallgrass Prairie*. Boston: Houghton Mifflin, 1982.

Mid-Atlantic States

AMOS, W. *Atlantic & Gulf Coasts* (Audubon Nature Guides). New York: Knopf, 1985.

HALLA, L. *Spring in Washington*. New York: William Sloane Associates, Inc., 1947.

LAWRENCE, S. *The Audubon Society Guide to the Natural Places of the Mid-Atlantic States: Coastal*. New York: Pantheon Books, 1984.

LAWRENCE, S., & B. GROSS. *The Audubon Society Guide to the Mid-Atlantic States: Inland*. New York: Pantheon Books, 1984.

McPHEE, J. *The Pine Barrens*. New York: Farrar, Straus & Giroux, 1967.

PERRY, B. *A Sierra Club Naturalist's Guide to the Mid-Atlantic Coast: Cape Hatteras to Cape Cod*. New York: Random House, 1985.

ROTHROCK, J. & J. *Chesapeake Odysseys: An 1883 Cruise Revisited*. Centreville, MD: Tidewater Publishers, 1983.

YEADON, D. *Secluded Islands of the Atlantic Coast*. New York: Crown Publishers, Inc., 1984.

Midwest

ARCHER, M. *Reading for Young People: The Upper Midwest*. Chicago, IL: American Library Association, 1981.

FULLER, W. *The Old Country School: The Story of Rural Education in the Middle West*. Chicago, IL: University of Chicago Press, 1982.

HUBBELL, S. *A Country Year: Living the Questions*. New York: Random House, 1986.

LAYCOCK, G. & E. *The Ohio Valley: Your Guide to America's Heartland*. Garden City, NY: Doubleday, 1983.

RABAN, J. *Old Glory: An American Voyage*. New York: Simon & Schuster, 1981.

RAFFERTY, M. *The Ozarks Outdoors: A Guide for Fishermen, Hunters, and Tourists*. Stillwater, OK: University of Oklahoma Press, 1985.

ROOT, R. & J. *Interstate 90: A Guide to Points of Interest You Can See—Without Stopping*. Brooksville, ME: Travel*Vision, 1984.

Northeast

DIETZ, L. *The Allagash: History of a Wilderness River in Maine*. Thorndike, ME: Thorndike Press, Reprint 1985.

GODIN, A. *Wild Mammals of New England: Field Guide Edition*. Chester, CT: The Globe Pequot Press, 1983.

HOAGLAND, E. *Walking the Dead Diamond River*. Berkeley, CA: 1973.

IRLAND, L. *Wildlands and Woodlots: The Story of New England Forests*. Hanover, NH: University Press of New England, 1982.

JOHNSON, C. *The Nature of Vermont: Introduction and Guide to a New England Environment*. Hanover, NH: University Press of New England, 1980.

JORGENSEN, N. *A Guide to New England's Landscape*. Chester, CT: The Globe Pequot Press, 1977.

JORGENSEN, N. *Southern New England, A Sierra Club Naturalist's Guide*. San Francisco: Sierra Club Books, 1978.

KULIK, S., P. SALMANSON, M. SCHMIDT & H. WELCH. *The Audubon Society Field Guide to the Natural Places of the Northeast: Coastal*. New York: Pantheon Books, 1984.

KULIK, S., P. SALMANSON, M. SCHMIDT & H. WELCH. *The Audobon Society Field Guide to the Natural Places of the Northeast: Inland*. New York: Pantheon Books, 1984.

LANNON, M. *Maine Forever—A Guide to Nature Conservancy Preserves in Maine*. Brunswick, ME: Maine Chapter, The Nature Conservancy, 1984.

McNAIR, S. *New England 1985—Fisher Annotated Travel Guide*. New York: New American Library, 1984.

NISS, B. *New England Naturally*. Portland, ME: Guy Gannett Publishing Company, 1983.

PRATSON, F. *Guide to Eastern Canada, second edition*. Chester, CT: The Globe Pequot Press, 1986.

ROOT, R. & J. *Interstate 90: A Guide to Points of Interest You Can See—Without Stopping*. Brooksville, ME: Travel*Vision, 1984.

RUSSELL, H. *Indian New England before the Mayflower*. Hanover, NH: University Press of New England, 1983.

STEELE, F. *At Timberline: A Nature Guide to the Mountains of the Northeast*. Boston: Appalachian Mountain Club, 1982.

THOLLANDER, E. *Back Roads of New England*. New York: Crown Publishers, 1974.

THOMAS, E. *Pocket Guide to the Maine Outdoors*. Thorndike, ME: Thorndike Press, 1985.

THOMPSON, B. *The Changing Face of New England*. Boston: Houghton Mifflin, 1977.

WEBSTER, H. *Trips with Children in New England.* Dublin, NH: Yankee Publishing Company, 1982.

Northwest

ALASKA TRAVEL. *Alaska, Yukon, British Columbia Travel Guide.* Salt Lake City, UT: Alaska Travel Guide, annual.

ALT, D., & D. HYNDMAN. *Roadside Geology of Washington.* Missoula, MT: Mountain Press Publishing Co., 1984.

BOYD, E. *Wolf Trail Lodge.* Anchorage, AK: Alaska Northwest Publishing Co., 1984.

BULEY, R. *The Old Northwest: Pioneer Period 1815–1840,* 2 vols. Bloomington, IN: Indiana University Press, 1983.

CONRADER, J. & C. *Northwoods Wildlife Region.* Happy Camp, CA: American Wildlife Region No. 9, Naturegraph Publishers, Inc., 1982.

DARVILL, D. *Hiking the North Cascades.* San Francisco: Sierra Club ToteBooks, 1982.

DOIG, I. *Winter Brothers: A Season at the Edge of America.* New York: Harcourt Brace Jovanovich Publishers, 1982.

EPPENBACH, S. *Alaska's Southeast: Touring the Inside Passage.* Seattle, WA: Pacific Search, 1985.

HOAGLAND, E. *Notes from the Century Before: A Journal from British Columbia.* San Francisco, CA: North Point Press, 1982.

JOHNSON, B. *Yukon Wild.* Stockbridge, MA: Berkshire Traveler Press, 1984.

KOZLOF, E. *Seashore Life of the Northern Pacific Coast.* Seattle, WA: University of Washington Press, 1983.

LEESON, T., P. LEESON & R. STEELQUIST. *The Olympic Peninsula.* Port Washington, NY: Independent Publishers Group, 1984.

McCONNAUGHEY, B., & E. McCONNAUGHEY. *Pacific Northwest* (Audubon Society Nature Guide). New York: Knopf, 1985.

McGINNIS, J. *Going to Extremes* (In Alaska). New York: Alfred A. Knopf, 1980.

PERRY, J. & J. *The Sierra Club Guide to the Natural Areas of Oregon and Washington*. San Francisco: The Sierra Club. 1983.

SCHWARTZ, S. *Nature in the Northwest: An Introduction to the Natural History and Ecology of the Northwestern United States from the Rockies to the Pacific*. Englewood Cliffs, NJ: Prentice-Hall, Inc., 1983.

SHANE, S. *Discovering Mount St. Helens: A Guide to the National Volcanic Monument*. Seattle, WA: University of Washington Press, 1985.

STANWELL-FLETCHER, T. *Driftwood Valley*. Boston: Little, Brown, 1950.

YOUNG, R. *My Lost Wilderness—Adventures of an Alaskan Hunter and Guide*. Piscataway, NJ: New Century Publishers, 1983.

Rocky Mountains

BAARS, D. *The Colorado Plateau*, rev. Albuquerque, NM: University of New Mexico Press, 1983.

BAKER, W., E. LARRISON, C. YOKUM & I. BAXTER. *Wildlife of the Northern Rocky Mountains*. Healdsburg, CA: The Naturegraph Company, 1961.

HALKA, C. *Time, Rocks, and the Rockies—A Geologic Guide to the Roads and Trails of Rocky Mountain National Park*. Missoula, MT: Mountain Press Publishing Co., 1984.

HASSELSTROM, L. *Journal of a Mountain Man: James Clyman* (Classics of the Fur Trade Series). Missoula, MT: Mountain Press, 1984.

HAWTHORNE, H., & E. MILLS. *Enos Mills of the Rockies*. Boston: Houghton Mifflin, 1935.

MILLS, E. *The Rocky Mountain Wonderland*. Boston: Houghton Mifflin, 1915.

PORSILD, A. *Rocky Mountain Wildflowers*. Chicago: University of Chicago Press, 1978.

WOLF, J. *Guide to the Continental Divide Trail, Vol. 1: Northern Montana*. Missoula, MT: Mountain Press Publishing Co., 1982.

Sierra Nevada

BROWN, V. *The Sierra Nevadan Wildlife Region*. Healdsburg, CA: The Naturegraph Company, 1954.

LEOPOLD, A. *Wild California: Vanishing Lands, Vanishing Wildlife*. Berkeley, CA: University of California Press/The Nature Conservancy, 1985.

MUIR, J. *The Mountains of California*. New York: Viking Penguin, 1985.

WHITNEY, S. *A Sierra Club Naturalist's Guide to the Sierra Nevada*. San Francisco: Sierra Club, 1979.

South

AMOS, W., & S. AMOS. *Atlantic & Gulf Coasts* (Audubon Nature Guides). New York: Knopf, 1985.

BROWN, C. *Wildflowers of Louisiana and Adjoining States*. Baton Rouge, LA: Louisiana State University Press, 1972.

COWDREY, A. *This Land, This South*. Lexington, KY: University of Kentucky Press, 1983.

GRAVES, J. *Hard Scrabble: Observations on a Patch of Land*. Austin, TX: Texas Monthly Press, 1974.

GRAVES, J. *From a Limestone Ledge*. Austin, TX: Texas Monthly Press, 1980.

KEATING, B. *The Gulf of Mexico: Exxon Shorelines of America Series; A Studio Book*. New York: Viking Press, 1972.

LOCKWOOD, C. *The Gulf Coast: Where the Land Meets the Sea*. Baton Rouge, LA: Louisiana State University Press, 1984.

SCHUELER, D. *Adventuring along the Gulf of Mexico: The Sierra Club Travel Guide to the Gulf Coast of the United States and Mexico from the Florida Keys to Yucatan*. New York: Random House, 1986.

SHELDON, R. *Roadside Geology of Texas*. Missoula, MT: Mountain Press Publishing Co., 1979.

WARTON, M., & R. BARBOUR. *A Guide to the Wildflowers and Ferns of Kentucky*. Lexington, KY: University of Kentucky Press, 1971.

WILLIS, M., & H. IRWIN. *Roadside Flowers of Texas*. Austin, TX: University of Texas Press, (1961) 1975.

Southeast

BENNER, B. *Carolina Whitewater: A Canoeist's Guide to the Western Carolinas*. Ann Arbor, MI: Thomas Press, 1981.

FEDERAL WRITERS PROJECT. *Georgia: A Guide to Its Towns & Country-side*. Clair Shores, MI: Somerset Publishers, (1940) 1981.

FOSHEE, J. *Alabama Canoe Rides and Float Trips*. Huntsville, AL: Strode Publishers, 1976.

MCNAIR, S. *Florida and the Southeast 1985: Fisher Annotated Travel Guide*. New York: New American Library, 1984.

SPRUNT, A., & J. DICK. *Carolina Low Country Impressions*. Old Greenwich, CT: Devin-Adair Co., Inc., 1964.

Southwest

ABBEY, E. *Desert Solitaire*. New York: Ballantine Books, (1968) 1983.

ALCOCK, J. *Sonoran Desert Spring*. Chicago, IL: University of Chicago Press, 1985.

ANNERINO, J. *Hiking the Grand Canyon* (Sierra Club Tote Book). New York: Random House, 1986.

CALVIN, R. *Sky Determines: An Interpretation of the Southwest*. Albuquerque, NM: University of New Mexico Press, (1948) 1965.

COCKRUM, E. *Mammals of the Southwest*. Tucson, AZ: Arizona University Press, 1982.

DUTTON, B. *American Indians of the Southwest*. Albuquerque, NM: University of New Mexico Press, 1983.

GANCI, D. *Hiking the Southwest: Arizona, New Mexico and West Texas*. San Francisco: Sierra Club ToteBooks, 1983.

GEHLBACK, F. *Montain Islands and Desert Seas: A Natural History of the U.S.–Mexican Borderlands*. Bryan, TX: Texas A. & M. University Press, 1982.

KIRK, R. *Desert: The American Southwest.* Boston: Houghton Mifflin, 1973.

NIEHAUS, T. *A Field Guide to Southwestern and Texas Wildflowers.* Boston: Houghton Mifflin, 1984.

WAGNER, F. *Wildlife of the Desert.* New York: Harry N. Abrams, Inc., 1980.

West Coast

GOUSHA CO. *Explorer's Guide to the West: Rivers and Lakes.* San Jose, CA: H. M. Gousha Co., 1972.

HESSE, G. *California and the West 1985—Fisher Annotated Travel Guide.* New York: New American Library, 1984.

JAEGER, E., & A. SMITH. *Introduction to the Natural History of Southern California.* Los Angeles: University of California Press, (1966) 1971.

PERRY, J. & J. *The Sierra Club Guide to the Natural Areas of California.* San Francisco: Sierra Club, 1983.

SCHULTHEIS, R. *The Hidden West: Journeys in the American Outback.* San Francisco: North Point Press, 1983.

Bibliography

A Sampling of Travels and Travelers

BACH, JR, O. *Hiking the Yellowstone Backcountry*. Phoenix, AZ: Sierra Club ToteBooks, 1973.

BANKS, J. *Journal of the Right Honourable Sir Joseph Banks during Captain Cook's First Voyage*. Saint Clair Shores, MI: Scholarly Press, Inc., 1976.

BARTRAM, W. *Travels*. Salt Lake City, UT: Peregrine Smith, Inc., 1980.

BELT, T. *The Naturalist in Nicaragua*. Chicago: University of Chicago Press, 1874, 1985.

BERKELEY, E. & D. *The Life and Travels of John Bartram: From Lake Ontario to the River St. John*. Tallahassee, FL: University Presses of Florida, 1982.

BROOKS, P. *Speaking for Nature*. San Francisco: Sierra Club Books, 1983.

CARRIGHAR, S. *Home to the Wilderness*. Boston: Houghton Mifflin, 1973.

CHATWIN, B., & P. THEROUX. *Patagonia Revisited*. Boston: Houghton Mifflin, 1986.

DANNENFELDT, K. *Leonhard Rauwolf: Sixteenth-century Physician, Botanist, and Traveler*. Cambridge, MA: Harvard University Press, 1968.

DARWIN, C. (L. ENGEL, annotator). *The Voyage of the Beagle*. Garden City, NY: Doubleday, 1962.

DURANT, M., & M. HARWOOD. *On the Road with John James Audubon*. New York: Dodd, Mead, 1980.

GANNETT, L. *Sweet Land*. Garden City, NY: Doubleday, 1934.

GIBBONS, E. *Stalking the Faraway Places and Some Thoughts on the Best Way to Live*. New York: David McKay Company, Inc., 1973.

GOLDSMITH, J. *Voyage in the Beagle.* London, ENG: Chatto & Windus, 1978.

HANLEY, W. *Natural History in America: From Mark Catesby to Rachel Carson.* New York: New York Times Book Company, 1977.

HOMER. (W. SHEWRING, trans.). *The Odyssey.* New York: Oxford University Press, 1980.

HONOUR, H. *The New Golden Land: European Images of America from the Discoveries to the Present.* New York: Pantheon Books, 1976.

HUDSON, W. *Idle Days in Patagonia.* Berkeley, CA: Creative Arts Books, 1979.

HUMBOLDT, A. *Personal Narrative of Travels to the Equinoctial Regions of America during the Years 1799–1804* (3-vol. reprint of 1951 ed.). New York: Arno Press, 1969.

KELSEY, J. *Climbing and Hiking in the Wind River Mountains.* Phoenix, AZ: Sierra Club ToteBooks, 1980.

LAWRENCE, P. *Hiking the Teton Backcountry.* Phoenix, AZ: Sierra Club ToteBooks, 1973.

LUCE, D., & L. ANDREWS. *Francis Lee Jacques: Artist-Naturalist.* Minneapolis, MN: University of Minnesota Press, 1982.

MELVILLE, H. (C. FEIDELSON, JR., ed.). *Moby Dick.* Indianapolis, IN: Bobbs-Merrill, 1964.

MILLS, E. *The Adventures of a Nature Guide.* Boston: Houghton Mifflin, 1932.

MOON, W. *Blue Highways: A Journey into America.* Boston: Little, Brown, 1982.

MORRIS, J. *Journeys.* New York: Oxford University Press, 1984.

MUIR, J. *A Thousand-mile Walk to the Gulf.* Boston: Houghton Mifflin, (1916) 1981.

RABAN, J. *Old Glory: An American Voyage.* New York: Simon & Schuster, 1981.

RUSHO, W. *Everett Ruess: A Vagabond for Beauty.* Salt Lake City, UT: Gibbs M. Smith, Inc., 1983.

SCHULTZ, J., E. SILLIMAN (ed.). *James Willard Schultz (Apikuni).* Norman, OK: University of Oklahoma Press, 1982.

SEVERIN, T. *Tracking Marco Polo.* New York: Harper, 1986.

STEINBECK, J. *Travels with Charlie: In Search of America.* New York: Viking Press, 1962.

STODDARD, H. *Memoirs of a Naturalist.* Norman, OK: University of Oklahoma Press, 1969.

TEALE, E. *The Wilderness of John Muir.* Boston: Houghton Mifflin, 1954.

TEALE, E. *North with the Spring; Journey into Summer; Autumn across America; Wandering through Winter.* New York: Dodd, Mead, 1981.

TEALE, E. *Springtime in Britain.* New York: Dodd, Mead, 1970.

TURNER, F. *Rediscovering America.* New York: Viking, 1985.

VAN DOREN, M. *Travels of William Bartram.* New York: Dover Publications, 1928.

Please see also Chapter 25, "Reading More," section on "Pre-trip Books." Note also the following:

Chapter 1

ATTENBOROUGH, D. *The Living Planet.* Boston: Little, Brown, 1984.

BROWN, V. *The Amateur Naturalist's Handbook.* Englewood Cliffs, NJ: Prentice-Hall, Inc., 1980.

BROWN, V. *Investigating Nature through Outdoor Projects.* Harrisburg, PA: Stackpole Books, 1983.

CORNELL, J. *Sharing Nature with Children.* Nevada City, CA: Ananda Publications, 1979.

DAVIDS, R. *How to Talk to Birds and Other Uncommon Ways of Enjoying Nature the Year Round.* New York: Alfred A. Knopf, 1973.

DUBOS, R. *The Wooing of Earth.* New York: Charles Scribner's Sons, 1980.

DURRELL, G., WITH L. DURRELL. *A Practical Guide for the Amateur Naturalist.* New York: Alfred A. Knopf, 1983.

ELLIOTT, R., & A. GARE (eds.). *Environmental Philosophy.* University Park, PA: Pennyslvania State University, 1983.

GUINNESS, A. (ed.). *Joy of Nature—How to Observe and Appreciate the Great Outdoors*. Pleasantville, NY: Reader's Digest Association, 1977.

HIGGINS, W. *TourPlay* (games of observation and hobbies and collection). New York: The William Frederick Press, 1949.

HINES, F. *Introduction to Family Camping*. Charlotte, NC: Boy Scouts of America, 1984.

KATZ, A. *Naturewatch: Exploring Nature with Your Children*. New York: Addison-Wesley, 1986.

LAWRENCE, G. *A Field Guide to the Familiar: Learning to Observe the Natural World*. Englewood Cliffs, NJ: Prentice-Hall, Inc., 1984.

PALMER, E., & H. SEYMOUR. *Field Book of Natural History*, 2nd ed. New York: McGraw-Hill, 1974.

PEPI, D. *Thoreau's Method: A Handbook for Nature Study*. Englewood Cliffs, NJ: Prentice-Hall, Inc., 1985.

SISSON, E. *Nature with Children of All Ages—Activities and Adventures for Exploring, Learning, and Enjoying the World around Us*. Englewood Cliffs, NJ: Prentice-Hall, Inc., 1982.

THOMAS, K. *Man and the Natural World—A History of the Modern Sensibility*. New York: Pantheon Books, 1984.

Chapter 2

BAKER, T. *A Field Guide to American Windmills*. Norman, OK: University of Oklahoma Press, 1985.

BATTAN, L. *Weather in Your Life*. New York: W. H. Freeman, 1983.

BEYER, S. *The Star Guide: A Unique System for Identifying the Brightest Stars in the Night Sky*. Boston: Little, Brown, 1985.

CALDER, N. *The Weather Machine—How Our Weather Works and Why It Is Changing*. New York: Viking Press, 1974.

CALVIN, R. *Sky Determines: An Interpretation of the Southwest*. Albuquerque, NM: University of New Mexico Press, (1948) 1965.

EDINGER, J. *Watching for the Wind: The Seen and Unseen Influences on Local Weather*. Garden City, NY: Anchor Books, Doubleday, 1967.

Bibliography

GROSSINGER, R. *The Night Sky: The Science and Anthropology of the Stars and Planets.* San Francisco: Sierra Club Books, 1981.

KALS, W. *How to Read the Night Sky.* New York: Doubleday, 1974.

LAWRENCE, G. *A Field Guide to the Familiar—Learning to Observe the Natural World.* Englewood Cliffs, NJ: Prentice-Hall, Inc., 1984.

LEHR, P., R. BURNETT & H. ZIM. *Weather: A Guide to Phenomena and Forecasts.* New York: Golden Press, 1962.

LOCKWOOD, J. *World Climatology—An Environmental Approach.* New York: St. Martin's Press, 1974.

MAYALL, R., M. MAYALL & J. WYCKOFF. *The Sky Observer's Guide: A Handbook for Amateur Astronomers.* New York: Golden Press, 1971.

MEINEL, A. & M. *Sunsets, Twilights, and Evening Skies.* New York: Cambridge University Press, 1983.

MOORE, P. *Stargazing: Astronomy without a Telescope.* Woodbury, NY: Barron's, 1985.

PEPI, D. *Thoreau's Method—A Handbook for Nature Study.* Englewood Cliffs, NJ: Prentice-Hall, Inc., 1985.

PETRIE, F., & J. SHAW. *The Watercolorist's Guide to Painting Skies.* New York: Watson-Guptill Publications, 1984.

RAYMO, C. *365 Starry Nights: An Introduction to Astronomy for Every Night of the Year.* Englewood Cliffs, NJ: Prentice-Hall, Inc., 1983.

REIFSNYDER, W. *Weathering the Wilderness: The Sierra Club Guide to Practical Meteorology.* San Francisco: Sierra Club, 1980.

RONAN, C. *The Skywatcher's Handbook: Night and Day, What to Look for in the Heavens Above.* New York: Crown, 1985.

RUBIN, L., & J. DUNCAN. *The Weather Wizard's Cloud Book—How You Can Forecast the Weather Accurately and Easily by Reading the Clouds.* Chapel Hill, NC: Algonquin Books of Chapel Hill, 1984.

SCHAEFFER, V. *A Field Guide to the Atmosphere.* Boston, MA: Houghton Mifflin, 1981.

SLOANE, E.. *Eric Sloane's Weather Book.* New York: Duell, Sloan and Pearce, 1952.

WHITNEY, C.. *Whitney's Star Finder: A Field Guide to the Heavens.* New York: Alfred A. Knopf, 1981.

WIRTH, D., & J. YOUNG. *Ballooning—The Complete Guide to Riding the Wind.* New York: Random House, 1984.

Chapter 3

ABBEY, E. *Beyond the Wall: Essays from the Outside.* New York: Holt, Rinehart and Winston, 1984.

ALT, D., & D. HYNDMAN. *Roadside Geology of Oregon.* Missoula, MT: Mountain Press Publishing, 1978.

ALT, D., & D. HYNDMAN. *Roadside Geology of Northern California.* Missoula, MT: Mountain Press Publishing, 1975.

APPLETON, J. *The Experience of Landscape.* London, ENG: William Clowes & Sons, Ltd., 1975.

BECKEY, F. *Mountains of North America.* San Francisco: Sierra Club Books, 1982.

BIRD, J. *The Natural Landscapes of Canada—A Study in Regional Earth Science.* Toronto, CAN: Wiley Publishers of Canada, 1972.

FARB, P. *The Face of North America.* New York: Harper & Row, 1968.

GUSSOW, A. *A Sense of Place—The Artist and the American Land.* San Francisco: Friends of the Earth, 1974.

HART, J. *The Look of the Land.* Englewood Cliffs, NJ: Prentice-Hall, Inc., 1975.

HEINTZELMAN, O., & R. HIGHSMITH, JR. *World Regional Geography,* 4th ed. Englewood Cliffs, NJ: Prentice-Hall, Inc., 1973.

JORGENSEN, N. *A Guide to New England Landscapes.* Chester, CT: The Globe Pequot Press, 1977.

MCPHEE, J. *In Suspect Terrain.* New York: Farrar, Straus, Giroux, (1982) 1984.

MEINIG, D. W. (ed.). *Interpretations of Ordinary Landscapes.* New York: Oxford University Press, 1979.

NAVEH, Z., & A. LIEBERMAN. *Landscape Ecology: Theory and Application.* New York: Springer-Verlag New York, Inc., 1984.

NELSON, G. *How To See—A Guide to Reading Our Manmade Landscape.* Boston: Little, Brown, 1979.

STEWART, G. *Names on the Land: The Classic Story of American Place-naming.* San Francisco: Lexikos, (1967) 1982.

THOMPSON, B. *The Changing Face of New England.* Boston: Houghton Mifflin, 1977.

TREFIL, J. *Meditations at 10,000 Feet: A Scientist in the Mountains.* New York: Scribner's, 1986.

TUNNARD, C. *A World with a View—An Inquiry into the Nature of Scenic Values.* New Haven, CT: Yale University Press, 1978.

USDA SOIL CONSERVATION SERVICE. *Land Resources Regions and Major Land Resource Areas of the United States.* Agricultural Handbook 296. Washington, DC: Superintendent of Documents, Government Printing Office, (1972) 1981.

WATTS, M. *Reading the Landscape of America.* New York: Collier Books, 1975.

ZELINSKY, W. *The Cultural Geography of the United States.* Englewood Cliffs, NJ: Prentice-Hall, Inc., 1973.

ZUBE, E. *Landscapes: Selected Writings of J. B. Jackson.* Minneapolis, MN: University of Minnesota Press, 1970.

Chapter 4

ABBEY, E. *Desert Solitaire.* New York: Ballantine Books, 1983.

ANDERSON, W. *Geology of Iowa: Over Two Billion Years of Change.* Iowa City, IA.: University of Iowa Press, 1983.

BELL, P., & D. WRIGHT. *Rocks and Minerals.* New York: Macmillan/Collier, 1985.

CHRONIC, H. *Pages of Stone: Geology of Western National Parks and Monuments.* Seattle, WA: Mountaineers, 1985.

CVANCARA, A. *A Field Manual for the Amateur Geologist.* Englewood Cliffs, NJ: Prentice-Hall, Inc., 1985.

HARRINGTON, J. *Dance of the Continents: Adventures with Rocks and Time.* Boston: Houghton Mifflin, 1983.

HEADSTROM, R. *Suburban Geology: An Introduction to the Common Rocks and Minerals of Your Back Yard and Local Park*. Englewood Cliffs, NJ: Prentice-Hall, 1985.

LEIPER, H. (comp. and ed.). *The Agates of North America*. San Diego, CA: The Lapidary Journal, Publishers, 1966.

MACDONALD, J. *The Fossil Collector's Handbook—A Paleontology Field Guide*. Englewood Cliffs, NJ: Prentice-Hall, Inc., 1983.

MACMAHON, J. *Deserts* (Audubon Society Nature Guide). New York: Knopf, 1985.

MCPHEE, J. *In Suspect Terrain*. New York: Farrar, Straus, Giroux, (1982) 1984.

OJAKANGAS, R., & C. MATSCH. *Minnesota's Geology*. Minneapolis, MN: University of Minnesota Press, 1982.

RAYMO, C. *The Crust of the Earth—An Armchair Traveler's Guide to the New Geology*. Englewood Cliffs, NJ: Prentice-Hall, Inc., 1983.

WEAVER, D. *For Pebble Pups—A Collecting Guide for Junior Geologists*. Chicago, IL: Chicago Natural History Museum, 1955.

WYCKOFF, J. *Rock Scenery of the Hudson Highlands and Palisades: A Geological Guide*. Glens Falls, NY: Adirondack Mountain Club, 1971.

Chapter 5

BRADY, N. *The Nature and Properties of Soils*, 9th ed. New York: Macmillan, 1984.

CARTER, V., & T. DALE. *Topsoil and Civilization*. Norman, OK: University of Oklahoma Press, (1955) 1974.

DONAHUE, R., R. MILLER & J. SHICKLUNA. *Soils: An Introduction to Soils and Plant Growth*. Englewood Cliffs, NJ: Prentice-Hall, Inc., 1983.

FOTH, H. *Fundamentals of Soil Science*, 6th ed. New York: John Wiley & Sons, 1978.

FULLER, W. *Soils of the Southwest*. Tucson, AZ: The University of Arizona Press, 1975.

HUNT, C. *Geology of Soils*. New York: W. H. Freeman, 1972.

KELLOGG, C. *The Soils that Support Us*. New York: Macmillan, 1943.

KOLLMORGEN CORP. *Munsell Soil Color Chart*. Baltimore: Macbeth Division of Kollmorgen Corporation, 1975.

PRITCHETT, W. *Properties and Management of Forest Soils*. New York: John Wiley & Sons, 1979.

UNITED STATES DEPARTMENT OF AGRICULTURE. *Atlas of American Agriculture*. Washington, DC: U.S. Government Printing Office, 1936.

UNITED STATES DEPARTMENT OF AGRICULTURE. *Soils and Men (Part V): 1938 Yearbook of Agriculture*. Washington, DC: U.S. Government Printing Office, 1938.

UNITED STATES DEPARTMENT OF AGRICULTURE. *Soils—The 1957 Yearbook of Agriculture*. Washington, DC: Superintendent of Documents, U.S. Government Printing Office, 1957.

UNITED STATES DEPARTMENT OF AGRICULTURE ET AL. *Soil Taxonomy—A Basic System of Soil Classification for Making and Interpreting Soil Surveys*. New York: John Wiley & Sons, 1983.

Chapter 6

ARNO, S., & R. HAMMERLY. *Timberline: Mountain and Arctic Forest Frontiers*. Seattle, WA: Mountaineers, 1984.

BROOKS, P. *The Pursuit of Wilderness*. Boston: Houghton Mifflin, (1962) 1971.

CAULFIELD, C. *In the Rainforest*. New York: Knopf, 1985.

CLAPHAM, W. *Natural Ecosystems*. New York: Macmillan, 1973.

COSTELLO, D. *The Prairie World*. New York: Thomas Y. Crowell, 1969.

DASMANN, R. *A Different Kind of Country*. New York: Macmillan, 1968.

DAVIS, M. *The Near Woods*. New York: Alfred A. Knopf, 1974.

DICE, L. *Natural Communities*. Ann Arbor, MI: University of Michigan Press, 1952.

INTERNATIONAL UNION FOR THE CONSERVATION OF NATURE. *The World's Greatest Natural Areas: An Indicative Inventory of Natural Sites of World Heritage Quality*. Gland, Switzerland: IUCN Commission on National Parks and Protected Areas, 1982.

KUCHLER, A. *Potential Natural Vegetation of the Conterminous United States*. New York: American Georgraphical Society, 1964.

LINDSEY, A., D. SCHMELZ & S. NICHOLS. *Natural Areas in Indiana and Their Preservation*. West Lafayette, IN: Indiana Natural Areas Survey, Purdue University Press, 1969.

PEATTIE, D. *A Natural History of Trees of Eastern and Central North America*. New York: Crown Publishers, (1948) 1966.

PERRY, J. & J. *The Sierra Club Guide to the Natural Areas of California*. San Francisco: Sierra Club, 1983.

PERRY, J. & J. *The Sierra Club Guide to the Natural Areas of Oregon and Washington*. San Francisco: Sierra Club, 1983.

RADFORD, A. ET AL. *Natural Heritage: Classification, Inventory, and Information*. Chapel Hill, NC: University of North Carolina Press, 1981.

RICHARDSON, J. *Wild Edible Plants of New England*. Chester, CT: The Globe Pequot Press, 1981.

ROTH, C. *The Plant Observer's Handbook—A Field Botany Manual for the Amateur Naturalist*. Englewood Cliffs, NJ: Prentice-Hall, Inc., 1984.

ROUECHE. *What's Left of a Diminishing America*. Boston: Little, Brown, (1962) 1968.

SCOTT, J. *Botany in the Field—An Introduction to Plant Communities for the Amateur Naturalist*. Englewood Cliffs, NJ: Prentice-Hall, Inc., 1984.

SUTTON, A., & M. SUTTON. *Eastern Forests* (Audubon Society Nature Guide). New York: Knopf, 1985.

WHITNEY, S. *Western Forests* (Audubon Society Nature Guide). New York: Knopf, 1985.

ZWINGER, A. & B. WILLARD. *Land above the Trees: A Guide to American Alpine Tundra*. New York: Harper & Row, 1972.

Chapter 7

CADUTO, M. *Pond and Brook: A Guide to Nature Study in Freshwater Environments.* Englewood Cliffs, NJ: Prentice-Hall, Inc., 1985.

CARRIGHAR, S. *One Day on Teton Marsh.* New York: Pyramid Books, (1947) 1968.

COWARDIN, L., V. CARTER, F. GOLET, & E. LaROE. *Classification of Wetlands and Deepwater Habitats of the United States.* Washington, DC: Superintendent of Documents, U.S. Government Printing Office, 1979.

HOTCHKISS, N. *Common Marsh, Underwater, & Floating-leaved Plants of the United States and Canada.* New York: Dover Publications, 1972.

JOHNSGARD, P. *Waterfowl: Their Biology and Natural History.* Lincoln, NE: University of Nebraska Press, 1968.

NIERING, W. *The Life of the Marsh.* New York: McGraw-Hill, 1966.

NIERING, W. *Wetlands* (Audubon Society Nature Guide). New York: Knopf, 1985.

PRESCOTT, G. *How to Know the Aquatic Plants.* Dubuque, IA: William C. Brown Company, 1969.

SMARDON, R. (ed.). *The Future of Wetlands—Assessing Visual-Cultural Values.* Totowa, NJ: Allanheld, Osmun, 1983.

TINER, R. JR. *Wetlands of the United States—Current Status and Recent Trends.* Washington, DC: Superintendent of Documents, U.S. Government Printing Office, 1984.

URSIN, M. *Life in and around the Salt Marshes—A Handbook of Plant and Animal Life in and around the Temperate Atlantic Coastal Marshes.* New York: Thomas Y. Crowell, 1972.

WELLER, M. *Freshwater Marshes—Ecology and Wildlife Management.* Minneapolis, MN: University of Minnesota Press, 1981.

Chapter 8

BARDACH, J. *Downstream: A Natural History of the River.* New York: Harper & Row, 1964.

BURMAN, B. *Look down that Winding River—An Informal Profile of the Mississippi.* New York: Taplinger Publishing Company, 1973.

COKER, R. *Streams, Lakes, and Ponds.* New York: Harper & Row, 1968.

COUSTEAU, JACQUES-YVES, & M. RICHARDS. *Jacques Cousteau's Amazon Journey.* New York: Abrams, 1984.

CURRY, J. *The River's in My Blood.* Lincoln, NE: University of Nebraska Press, 1983.

CZAYA, E. *Rivers of the World.* New York: Van Nostrand Reinhold, 1983.

DAVIS, N. *The Father of Waters—A Mississippi River Chronicle.* San Francisco: Sierra Club Books, 1982.

DIETZ, L. *The Allagash: History of a Wilderness River in Maine.* Thorndike, ME: Thorndike Press, 1985 reprint.

FRATER, A., ed. *Great Rivers of the World.* Boston: Little, Brown, 1984.

GABLER, R. *New England White Water River Guide.* New Canaan, CT: Tobey Publishing Company, Inc., 1975.

GRAVES, J. *Goodby to a River.* New York: Alfred A. Knopf, 1961.

HUSER, V. *River Reflections—An Anthology.* Charlotte, NC: The Eastwood Press, 1984.

JONK, C. *River Journey.* New York: Stein and Day, 1964.

KIMBROUGH, E. *Better than Oceans.* New York: Harper & Row, 1976.

LOPEZ, B. *River Notes: The Dance of Herons.* New York: Avon Books, 1980.

LOPEZ, B. *The Dance of the Herons.* New York: Avon Books, 1979.

MANN, R. *Rivers in the City.* New York: Praeger, 1973.

MIGEL, J. *Stream Conservation Handbook.* New York: Crown Publishers, 1974.

MORISWA, M. *Streams, Their Dynamics and Morphology.* New York: McGraw-Hill, 1968.

NEEDHAM, P. *Trout Streams—Conditions that Determine Their Productivity and Suggestions for Stream and Lake Management.* San Francisco: Holden-Day, 1969.

OGLESBY, R., C. CARLSON & J. MCCANN. *River Ecology and Man.* New York: Academic Press, 1972.

PERRY, J. & J. *Exploring the River*. New York: Whittlesey House, 1960.

RUSSELL, R. *River Plains and Sea Coasts*. Berkeley, CA: University of California Press, 1967.

SWENSON, P. *Secrets of Rivers and Streams*. Portland, ME: Guy Gannet Publishing Co., 1982.

THEROUX, P. *Sailing Through China*. Boston: Houghton Mifflin, 1984.

Chapter 9

ANGEL, H., & P. WOLSELEY. *The Water Naturalist*. New York: Facts on File, Inc., 1982.

BROOKS, P. *Roadless Area*. New York: Alfred A. Knopf, 1966.

FASSETT, N. (rev. by E. OGDEN). *A Manual of Aquatic Plants*. Madison, WI: University of Wisconsin Press, (1940) 1969.

FISHER, R. *Still Waters, White Waters: Exploring America's Rivers and Lakes*. Washington, DC: National Geographic Society, 1977.

FREY, D. *Limnology in North America*. Madison, WI: University of Wisconsin Press, 1966.

HUNT, C., & R. GARRELS. *Water—The Web of Life*. New York: W. W. Norton, 1972.

MARSHALL, A. *Still Waters*. New York: William Morrow, 1978.

SETON, E. *The Arctic Prairies*. New York: Harper Colophon Books, (1911) 1981.

TAUB, F. *Lakes and Reservoirs*. Amsterdam, NY: Elsevier Scientific Publishing Co., 1984.

THOMPSON, G., & J. COLDREY. *The Pond*. Cambridge, MA: M.I.T. Press, 1984.

WETZEL, R. *Limnology*. Philadelphia, PA: W. B. Saunders, 1975.

Chapter 10

AMOS, W., & S. AMOS. *Atlantic & Gulf Coasts* (Audubon Society Nature Guide). New York: Knopf, 1985.

ARNOLD, A. *The Sea Beach At Ebb-tide*. New York: Dover Publishers, (1901) 1968.

BASCOM, W. *Waves and Beaches*. Garden City, NY: Anchor Books, Doubleday, (1964) 1980.

BESTON, H. *The Outermost House: A Year of Life on the Great Beach of Cape Cod*. New York: Rinehart and Company, 1949.

BERRILL, M. & D. *The North Atlantic Coast—Cape Cod to Newfoundland*. San Francisco: Sierra Club Books, 1981.

CARSON, R. *The Edge of the Sea*. Boston: Houghton Mifflin, (1955) 1979.

CLANCY, E. *The Tides: Pulse of the Earth*. Garden City, NY: Anchor Books, Doubleday, 1969.

COULOMBE, D. *The Seaside Naturalist: A Guide to Nature at the Seashore*. Englewood Cliffs, NJ: Prentice-Hall, Inc., 1984.

GUINNESS, A. (ed.). *Joy of Nature—How to Observe and Appreciate the Great Outdoors*. Pleasantville, NY: Reader's Digest Association, 1977.

FINCH, R. *Common Ground: A Naturalist's Cape Cod*. Boston: David R. Godine, Publisher, 1981.

FOX, W. *At the Sea's Edge: An Introduction to Coastal Oceanography for the Amateur Naturalist*. Englewood Cliffs, NJ: Spectrum Books, Prentice-Hall, Inc., 1983.

GIBBONS, E. *Stalking the Blue-eyed Scallop*. New York: David McKay Company, Inc., 1964.

GOSNER, K. *A Field Guide to the Atlantic Seashore*. Boston: Houghton Mifflin, 1978.

HAY, J. *The Great Beach*. New York: W. W. Norton, 1980.

HAY, J., & P. FARB. *The Atlantic Shore: Human and Natural History from Long Island to Labrador*. New York: Colophon Books, Harper & Row, 1966.

KOPPER, P. *The Wild Edge: Life and Lore of the Great Atlantic Beaches*. Alexandria, VA: Time/Life Books, 1979.

KOZLOFF, E. *Seashore Life of the Northern Pacific Coast: An Illustrated Guide to Northern California, Oregon, Washington, and British Columbia*. Seattle, WA: University of Washington Press, 1983.

LIPPSON, R., & A. LIPPSON. *Life in the Chesapeake Bay*. Baltimore: Johns Hopkins, 1984.

NATIONAL GEOGRAPHIC SOCIETY. *America's Seashore Wonderlands*. Washington, DC: National Geographic Society, 1985.

RICCIUTI, E. *The Beachwalker's Guide: The Atlantic Shore from Maine to Florida*. Garden City, NY: Doubleday, 1982.

ROMASHKO, S. *The Complete Collector's Guide to Shells and Shelling*. Miami, FL: Windward Publishing, 1984.

RUDLOE, J. *The Erotic Ocean: A Handbook for Beachcombers and Marine Biologists*. New York: E. P. Dutton, 1984.

STRAHLER, A. *A Geologist's View of Cape Cod*. Garden City, NY: The Natural History Press, 1966.

TEAL, J. & M. *Life and Death of the Salt Marsh*. New York: Ballantine Books, 1969.

TREFIL, J. *A Scientist at the Seashore*. New York: Charles Scribner's Sons, 1984.

WERTHEIM, A. *The Intertidal Wilderness*. New York: Random House, 1985.

WATERS, J. *Exploring New England Shores: A Beachcomber's Handbook*. Lexington, MA: Stone Wall Press, 1974.

UNIVERSITY OF FLORIDA. *Florida's Sandy Beaches: An Access Guide*. Gainesville, FL: University of Florida, 1985.

Zinn, D. *The Handbook for Beach Strollers from Maine to Cape Hatteras, second edition*. Chester, CT: The Globe Pequot Press, 1985.

Chapter 11

AMERICAN ASSOCIATION OF SCIENTIFIC WORKERS. *Science from Shipboard*. Washington, DC: Science Service, 1943.

BAILEY, M. & M. *Second Chance*. New York: David McKay Company, Inc., 1977.

BALCOMB, K. *The World's Whales—The First Complete Illustrated Guide*. New York: W. W. Norton, 1984.

CARSON, R. *The Sea around Us*. New York: Oxford University Press, 1951.

COKER, R. *This Great Wide Sea*. Chapel Hill, NC: University of North Carolina Press, 1947.

CUSHING, D., & J. WALSH (eds.). *The Ecology of the Seas*. Philadelphia, PA: W. B. Saunders, 1976.

DARRACH, C. *From a Coastal Schooner's Log*. Halifax NS: Nova Scotia Museum, 1979.

DUNCAN, R., & J. WARE. *A Cruising Guide to the New England Coast*. New York: Dodd, Mead, 1972.

HALEY, D. (ed.). *Sea Birds of Eastern North Pacific and Arctic Waters*. Santa Barbara, CA: Pacific Press, 1984.

HARDY, A. *The Open Sea* (2 vols.). Boston: Houghton Mifflin, 1971.

HARRISON, P. *Seabirds: An Identification Guide*. Boston: Houghton Mifflin, 1983.

HEYERDAHL, T. *Kon-tiki*. Chicago, IL: Rand McNally, 1950.

HEYERDAHL, T. *The Tigris Expedition: In Search of Our Beginnings*. Garden City, NY: Doubleday, 1981.

KNIGHT, K. *Atlantic Circle*. New York: W. W. Norton, 1985.

KOTSCH, W. *Weather for the Mariner*. Annapolis, MD: Naval Institute Press, 1983.

LOFGREN, L. *Ocean Birds*. New York: Alfred A. Knopf, 1984.

MARX, W. *The Frail Ocean*. New York: Ballantine Books, 1967.

MAXTONE-GRAHAM, J. *Liners to the Sun*. New York: Macmillan, 1985.

MENARD, H. *Ocean Science: Readings from Scientific American*. San Francisco: W. H. Freeman, 1977.

NARANJO, R. *Wind Shadow West*. West Caldwell, NJ: Hearst Marine Books, 1983.

PAYSON, H. *You Can't Blow Home Again*. West Caldwell, NJ: Hearst Marine Books, 1984.

ROSS, W. *Sail Power: The Complete Guide to Sails and Sail Handling*. New York: Alfred A. Knopf, 1984.

SCARR, D. *Touch the Sea*. New York: Avon Books, 1984.

SCHEFFER, V. *The Year of the Whale*. New York: Charles Scribner's Sons, 1969.

STONEHOUSE, B. *Sea Mammals of the World*. New York: Penguin, 1985.

THORSON, G. *Life in the Sea*. New York: World University Library, McGraw-Hill, 1971.

VAN TJEERD, A. *Science at Sea—Tales of an Old Ocean*. San Francisco: W. H. Freeman, 1981.

WINN, L., & E. H. WINN. *Wings in the Sea: The Humpback Whale*. Hanover, NH: University Press of New England, 1985.

Chapter 12

ALLEN, D. *The Life of Prairies and Plains*. New York: McGraw-Hill, 1967.

ANGEL, T., & K. BALCOMB III. *Mammals and Birds of Puget Sound*. Seattle, WA: University of Washington Press, 1982.

BERNSTEIN, C. *The Joy of Birding—A Guide to Better Birdwatching*. Santa Barbara, CA: Capra Press, 1984.

BONNER, W. *Seals and Man*. Seattle, WA: Washington Sea Grant Program, University of Washington Press, 1982.

CADE, T. *The Falcons of the World*. Ithaca, NY: Cornell University Press, 1981.

CADIEUX, C. *Coyotes—Predators and Survivors*. Harrisburg, PA: Stackpole Books, 1983.

COCKRUM, E. *Mammals of the Southwest*. Tucson, AZ: Arizona University Press, 1982.

COVELL, JR., C. *A Field Guide to the Moths*. Boston: Houghton Mifflin, 1984.

CURTIS, B. *The Life of the Fish—His Manners and Morals*. New York: Dover Publications, 1949.

DE CARLI, F. *The World of Fish*. New York: W. H. Smith Publishers, Inc., 1975.

DUNNING, J. *The Loon: Voice of the Wilderness*. Dublin, NH: Yankee Books, 1985.

EVANS, H. *Life on a Little-known Planet*. Chicago, IL: University of Chicago Press, 1966.

EVANS, H. *The Pleasures of Entomology: Portraits of Insects and the People Who Study Them*. Washington, DC: Smithsonian Institution Press, 1985.

FORSYTH, A. *Mammals of North America*. Columbia, SC: Camden House, 1985.

GIBBONS, W. *Their Blood Runs Cold: Adventures with Reptiles and Amphibians*. University, AL: University of Alabama Press, 1983.

GORMLEY, G. *A Dolphin Summer*. New York: Taplinger, 1985.

HAYES, H. *The Last Place on Earth*. New York: Stein and Day, 1976, 1983.

HAZARD, E. *The Mammals of Minnesota*. Minneapolis, MN: University of Minnesota Press, 1982.

HAWKINS, A. ET AL. *Flyways—Pioneering Waterfowl Management in North America*. Washington, DC: Superintendent of Documents, U.S. Government Printing Office, 1984.

JENSEN, KAREN. *America: Land of Wildlife*. Washington, DC: National Wildlife Federation, 1984.

JOHNSGARD, P. *A Guide to North American Waterfowl*. Bloomington, IN: Indiana University Press, 1982.

McMANUS, P. *The Grasshopper Trap*. New York: Holt, Rinehart and Winston, 1985.

McNAMEE, T. *The Grizzly Bear*. New York: Knopf, 1984.

OWEN, D. *Camouflage and Mimicry*. Chicago, IL: University of Chicago Press, 1982.

PETERS, R. *Dance of the Wolves*. New York: McGraw-Hill, 1985.

PETERSON, R. *Field Guide to Western Birds*. Boston: Houghton Mifflin, 1972.

PETERSON, R. *Field Guide to the Birds—A Completely New Guide to All the Birds of Eastern and Central North America*. Boston: Houghton Mifflin, 1980.

PETERSON, R., G. MOUNTFORT & P. HOLLOM. *A Field Guide to Birds of Britain and Europe*, 4th ed. rev. Boston: Houghton Mifflin, 1983.

PETTINGILL, JR., O. *A Guide to Bird Finding East of the Mississippi*, 2nd ed. Boston: Houghton Mifflin, 1980.

PETTINGILL, JR., O. *A Guide to Bird Finding West of the Mississippi*. New York: Oxford University Press, 1981.

PRESTON-MAFHAM, R. *Spiders of the World*. New York: Facts on File, 1984.

ROTH, C. *The Wildlife Observer's Guidebook*. Englewood Cliffs, NJ: Prentice-Hall, Inc., 1984.

SENDERS, J. *Shells: A Collector's Color Guide*. New York: Hippocrene Books, Inc., 1984.

THOMAS, B. *Talking with the Animals: How to Communicate with Wildlife*. New York: Morrow, 1985.

VAN GELDER, R. *Mammals of the National Parks*. Baltimore: Johns Hopkins University Press, 1982.

WAGNER, F. *Wildlife of the Deserts*. New York: Harry N. Abrams, Inc., 1980.

WATKINS, W. *The Tracker: The Story of Tom Brown, Jr*. New York: Berkeley Books, 1978, 1985.

WHITE, R. *A Field Guide to the Beetles*. Boston: Houghton Mifflin, 1983.

WOOD, R. *Wood Notes—A Companion and Guide for Birdwatchers*. Englewood Cliffs, NJ: Prentice-Hall, Inc., 1984.

WOOTEN, A. *Insects of the World*. New York: Facts on File, 1984.

Chapter 13

FLETCHER, W., & C. LITTLE. *The American Cropland Crisis*. Bethesda, MD: American Land Forum, 1982.

JONES, B. *The Farming Game*. Lincoln, NE: University of Nebraska Press, 1982.

MACFADYEN, J. *Gaining Ground—The Renewal of America's Small Farms*. New York: Holt, Rinehart and Winston, 1984.

McALESTER, V. & L. *A Field Guide to American Houses*. New York: Alfred A. Knopf, 1984.

SCHULER, S. *American Barns*. Exton, PA: Schiffer Publishing, Ltd., 1984.

SLOANE, E. *Eric Sloane's America*. New York: Galahad Books, 1982.

UNGER, D. *Leaving the Land*. New York: Harper & Row, 1984.

Chapter 14

BARR, C. *Jewels of the Plains*: *Wild Flowers of the Great Plains Grass-lands and Hills*. Minneapolis, MN: University of Minnesota Press, 1983.

BRAUN, L. *Grasslands* (Audubon Society Nature Guide). New York: Knopf, 1985.

DOIG, I. *The House of Sky: Landscapes of a Western Mind*. New York: Harcourt Brace Jovanovich, 1980.

JONES, JR., J., D. ARMSTRONG, R. HOFFMAN & C. JONES. *Mammals of the Northern Great Plains*. Lincoln, NE: University of Nebraska Press, 1983.

MADSON, J. *Where the Sky Began: Land of the Tallgrass Prairie*. Boston: Houghton Mifflin, 1982.

PHILLIPS PETROLEUM. *Pasture and Range Plants*. Bartlesville, OK: Phillips Petroleum Company, 1963.

SEARS, P. *Lands beyond the Forest*. Englewood Cliffs, NJ: Prentice-Hall, Inc., 1969.

STUBBENDIECK, J., S. HATCH & K. KLAR. *North American Range Plants*. Lincoln, NE: University of Nebraska Press, 1982.

YOUNG, P., & N. YOST (ed.). *Back Trail of an Old Cowboy*. Lincoln, NE: University of Nebraska Press, 1983.

Chapter 15

ARNO, S., & R. HAMMERLY. *Timberline: Mountain and Arctic Forest Frontiers*. Seattle, WA: Mountaineers, 1984.

BROCKMAN, C. *Trees of North America*: *A Field Guide to the Major Native and Introduced Species North of Mexico*. New York: Golden Press, 1968.

CARAS, R. *The Forest*. Boston: Houghton Mifflin, 1979.

CAULFIELD, C. *In the Rainforest*. New York: Knopf, 1985.

COLLINGWOOD, G., & W. BRUSH. *Knowing Your Trees*, 31st ed. Washington, DC: American Forestry Association, 1984.

CONRADER, J. & C. *Northwoods Wildlife Region*. Happy Camp, CA: Naturegraph Publishers, Inc., 1982.

DAVIS, M. *The Near Woods*. New York: Alfred A. Knopf, 1974.

FISK, E. *Parrot's Wood*. New York: Norton, 1985.

FORSYTH, A., & K. MIYATA. *Tropical Nature—Life and Death in the Rain Forests of Central and South America*. New York: Charles Scribner's Sons, 1984.

HOWES, P. *This World of Living Things*. New York: Duell, Sloan, and Pearce, 1959.

IRLAND, L. *Wildlands and Woodlots: The Story of New England's Forests*. Hanover, NH: University of New England Press, 1982.

NASH, R. *Wilderness and the American Mind*, 3rd ed. New Haven, CT: Yale University Press, 1982.

PEATTIE, D. *A Natural History of Trees of Eastern and Central North America*, 2nd ed. New York: Bonanza Books, 1964.

PEATTIE, D. *A Natural History of Western Trees*. New York: Bonanza Books, 1953.

PETRIDES, G. *A Field Guide to Trees and Shrubs*, 2nd ed. Boston: Houghton Mifflin, 1972.

PYNE, S. *Fire in America: A Cultural History of Wildland and Rural Fire*. Princeton, NJ: Princeton University Press, 1982.

STONE, R. *Dreams of Amazonia*. New York: Viking Press, 1985.

SUTTON, A., & M. SUTTON. *Eastern Forests* (Audubon Society Nature Guide). New York: Knopf, 1985.

WALKER, L. *Trees—An Introduction to Trees and Forest Ecology for the Amateur Naturalist*. Englewood Cliffs, NJ: Prentice-Hall, Inc., 1984.

WHITNEY, S. *Western Forests* (Audubon Society Nature Guide). New York: Knopf, 1985.

Chapter 16

CRAMPTON, F. *Deep Enough: A Working Stiff in the Western Mine Camps*. Norman, OK: University of Oklahoma Press, 1982.

SELTZER, C. *Miners and Managers in the American Coal Industry*. Lexington, KY: University of Kentucky Press, 1984.

YOUNG, P., & N. YOST (ed.). *Back Trail of an Old Cowboy*. Lincoln, NE: University of Nebraska Press, 1983.

Chapter 17

AINSWORTH, F. *Snowmobile Safety and You*. Seattle, WA: Outdoor Empire Publishing, Inc., 1982.

ARMINGTON, S. *Trekking in the Nepal Himalaya*. Berkeley, CA: Lonely Planet Publications, 1985.

BRIDGE, R. *America's Backpacking Book*. New York: Charles Scribner's Sons, 1973.

BROWN, T. *Tom Brown's Field Guide to Nature Observation and Tracking*. New York: Berkley Books, 1983.

BUNNELLE, H. *Food for Knapsackers and Other Trail Travelers*. San Francisco: Sierra Club ToteBooks, 1971.

BUNNELLE, H., & S. SARVIS. *Cooking for Camp and Trail*. San Francisco: Sierra Club Outdoor Activities Guides, 1972.

CHAMBERLAIN, L., & T. CHAMBERLAIN. *Guide to Cross-Country Skiing in New England*. Chester, CT: The Globe Pequot Press, 1985.

DOAN, M. *Starting Small: The Sierra Club Outdoors Guide for Families*. San Francisco: Sierra Club, 1979.

DROTAR, DAVID. *Hiking, Pure and Simple*. Piscataway, N.J.: Winchester Press, 1984.

ELSER, S., & B. BROWN. *Packin' in on Mules and Horses*. Missoula, MT: Mountain Press Publishing Co., 1980.

FLETCHER, C. *The Complete Walker III*. New York: Alfred A. Knopf, 1984.

GARD, W. *The Chisholm Trail*. Norman, OK: University of Oklahoma Press, 1984.

GEORGE, J. *The American Walk Book: An Illustrated Guide to the Country's Major Historic and Natural Walking Trails from New England to the Pacific Coast*. New York: E. P. Dutton, 1979.

HART, J. *Hiking the Bigfoot Country*. San Francisco: Sierra Club ToteBooks, (1975) 1984.

HART, J. *Walking Softly in the Wilderness: The Sierra Club Guide to Backpacking.* San Francisco: Sierra Club, (1977) 1984.

HILLABY, J. *Journey Home—A Walk about England.* New York: Holt, Rinehart & Winston, 1983.

JENKINS, P. *A Walk across America.* New York: William Morrow, 1979.

JENKINS, P. & B. *The Walk West: A Walk across America 2.* New York: William Morrow, 1981.

JONES, J.S. *Tramping in Europe: A Walking Guide.* Englewood Cliffs, NJ: Prentice-Hall, Inc., 1984.

KALS, W. *Land Navigation Handbook: The Sierra Club Guide to Map and Compass.* San Francisco: Sierra Club, 1983.

LAWRENCE, P. *Snowmobiler's Handbook.* Berkeley, CA: Ross Books, 1974.

LUMMIS, C. *Tramp across the Continent.* Lincoln, NE: University of Nebraska Press, 1982.

LUND, M., & B. WILLIAMS. *The Snowmobiler's Bible.* Garden City, NY: Doubleday, 1974.

MUIR, J. *A Thousand-mile Walk to the Gulf.* Boston: Houghton Mifflin, (1916) 1981.

NEW YORK–NEW JERSEY TRAIL CONFERENCE. *Catskill Trails.* New York: New York–New Jersey Trail Conference, 1983.

OLMSTEAD, N. *To Walk with a Quiet Mind.* San Francisco: Sierra Club ToteBooks, 1975.

QUINN, J. *The Winter Woods.* Old Greenwich, CT: The Chatham Press, 1976.

RIVIERE, W., & L.L. BEAN. *The L.L. Bean Guide to the Outdoors.* New York: Random House, 1981.

ROWELL, G. *High and Wild: Essays on Wilderness Adventure.* San Francisco: Lexikos, 1983.

RUSSELL, H. *Winter Search Party—A Guide to Insects and Other Invertebrates.* New York: Thomas Nelson, Inc., 1971.

STOKES, D. *A Guide to Nature in Winter.* Boston: Little, Brown, 1976.

SUSSMAN, A., & R. GOODE. *The Magic of Walking.* New York: Simon & Schuster, 1967.

TEJADA-FLORES, L. *Backcountry Skiing—The Sierra Club Guide to Skiing off the Beaten Track.* San Francisco: Sierra Club Outdoor Activities Guides, 1981.

231

TEJADA-FLORES, L. *Wildwater: The Sierra Club Guide to Kayaking and Whitewater Boating.* San Francisco: Sierra Club Outdoor Activities Guides, 1978.

TRELEASE, W. *Winter Botany—An Identification Guide to Native Trees and Shrubs.* New York: Dover Publications, 1967.

WARREN, M., & S. KOCHER. *Appalachian Trail.* Portland, OR: Graphic Arts Publishing Co., 1979.

WILLIAMS, T., & T. MAJOR. *The Secret Language of Snow.* New York: Pantheon Books, 1984.

Chapter 18

ANGELILLO, P. *Short Bike Rides on Long Island, second edition.* Chester, CT: The Globe Pequot Press, 1983.

BAUER, F. *How Many Miles to Hillsboro?* Old Tappan, NJ: Hewitt House, 1969.

BRIDGE, R. *Bike Touring: The Sierra Club Guide to Outings on Wheels.* San Francisco: Sierra Club Activities Guides, 1979.

CUYLER, L. *Short Bike Rides in the Berkshires.* Chester, CT: The Globe Pequot Press, 1979.

FERGUSON, G. *Freewheeling Bicycling: The Open Road.* Seattle, WA: Mountaineers-Books, 1985.

MULLEN, E., & J. GRIFFITH. *Short Bike Rides in Connecticut, second edition.* Chester, CT: The Globe Pequot Press, 1983.

MULLEN, E., & J. GRIFFITH. *Short Bike Rides on Cape Cod, Nantucket, & the Vineyard, second edition.* Chester, CT: The Globe Pequot Press, 1984.

STONE, H. *Short Bike Rides in Greater Boston and Central Massachusetts.* Chester, CT: The Globe Pequot Press, 1982.

STONE, H. *Short Bike Rides in Rhode Island.* Chester, CT: The Globe Pequot Press, 1980.

Chapter 19

BRAINERD, J. *Working with Nature—A Practical Guide.* New York: Oxford University Press, 1973.

LEWIS, D., & L. GOLDSTEIN (eds.). *The Automobile and American Culture*. Ann Arbor, MI: University of Michigan Press, 1983.

LUXENBERG, S. *Roadside Empires—How the Chains Franchised America*. New York: Viking Press, 1985.

POND, B. *A Sampler of Wayside Herbs*. Riverside, CT: The Riverside Press, 1974.

RAYMO, C. *Reading the Landscape along Interstate 80: The Rock Beneath, the Land above*. Northbrook, IL: Hubbard Scientific, 1982.

ROOT, R. & J. *Interstate 90: A Guide to Points of Interest You Can See without Stopping; Guide Number 1, Boston to Ohio*. Box 245 Brooksville, ME 04617: Travel*Vision, 1984.

ROOT, R. & J. *Interstate 90: A Guide to Points of Interest You Can See without Stopping; Guide Number 2, Ohio to Wisconsin*. Box 245 Brooksville, ME 04617: Travel*Vision, 1984.

SHAPIRO, J. *Meditations from the Breakdown Lane: Running Across America*. Boston: Houghton Mifflin, 1982.

Chapter 20

GIES, J. *Bridges and Men*. New York: Grosset & Dunlop, 1963.

Chapter 21

ANDERSON, H. & L. *Canals and Inland Waterways of Maine*. Portland, ME: Maine Historical Society, 1982.

DARWIN, A. *Canals and Rivers of Britain*. Ardmore, PA: Hastings Books, 1977.

FISHER, JR., A. *America's Inland Waterways—Exploring the Atlantic Seaboard*. Washington, DC: National Geographic Society, 1973.

GARRITY, R. *Canal Boatman—My Life on Upstate Waterways*. Syracuse, NY: Syracuse University Press, 1977.

HAHN & SPRINGER. *Canal Boat Children on the C & O, Pa., & New York Canals*. York, PA: American Canal & Transport Center, 1977.

KIMBROUGH, E. *Better than Oceans.* New York: Harper & Row, 1976.

PAYNE, R. *The Canal Builders: The Story of Canal Engineers Through the Ages.* New York: Macmillan, 1959.

PORTEOUS, D. *Canal Ports—The Urban Achievement of the Canal Age.* New York: Academic Press, 1977.

SWANSON, L. *Canals of Middle America.* Moline, IL: Swanson Publishing Company, 1964.

WILLIAMS, E. *Canal Country.* Utica, NY: H. M. Cardamone, 1982.

Chapter 22

DUBKIN, L. *The Natural History of a Yard.* Chicago: Henry Regnery Co., 1955.

LEES, C. *Plants and Man.* Englewood Cliffs, NJ: Prentice-Hall, Inc., 1970.

McHARG, I. *Design with Nature.* Garden City, NY: Doubleday, (1969) 1971.

MITCHELL, J. H. *Ceremonial Time: Fifteen Thousand Years on One Square Mile.* New York: Warner Books, 1984.

MITCHELL, J. H. *A Field Guide to Your Own Back Yard.* New York: Norton, 1985.

PRATT, C., & W. MAXWELL. *Garden and the Wilderness.* Freemont, CA: Horizon Books, 1980.

SMYSER, C. *Nature's Design: A Practical Guide to Natural Landscaping.* Emmaus, PA: Rodale Press, 1982.

STONE, D. *The Great Public Gardens of the Eastern United States: A Guide to Their Beauty and Botany.* New York: Random House, 1982.

TEALE, E. *Near Horizons: The Story of an Insect Garden.* New York: Dodd, Mead, 1943.

Chapter 23

BARNET, S. *The Rat: A Study in Behavior,* rev. ed. Chicago, IL: University of Chicago Press, 1984.

BATES, M. *A Jungle in the House: Essays in Natural and Unnatural History.* New York: Walker & Company, 1979.

CADUTO, M., & L. MANN. *Ann Arbor Alive: The Ecology of a City.* Ann Arbor, MI: Ecology Center of Ann Arbor, 1981.

GEORGE, C., & D. MCKINLEY. *Urban Ecology: In Search of an Asphalt Rose.* New York: McGraw-Hill, 1974.

GILL, D., & P. BONNETT. *Nature in the Urban Landscape: A Study of City Ecosystems.* Baltimore: York Press, 1973.

HEADSTROM, R. *Suburban Wildflowers: An Introduction to the Common Wildflowers of Your Back Yard and Local Park.* Englewood Cliffs, NJ: Prentice-Hall, Inc., 1984.

HEADSTROM, R. *Suburban Wildlife: An Introduction to the Common Animals of Your Back Yard and Local Park.* Englewood Cliffs, NJ: Prentice-Hall, Inc., 1984.

KIERNAN, J. *Footnotes on Nature.* New York: Doubleday, 1952.

KNOWLER, D. *The Falconer of Central Park.* New York and London: Bantam Books, 1984.

MCALESTER, V. & L. *A Field Guide to American Houses.* New York: Alfred A. Knopf, 1984.

MUTHESIUS, S. *The English Terraced House.* New Haven, CT: Yale University Press, 1982.

RUBLOWSKY, J. *Nature in the City.* New York: Basic Books, 1967.

SMITH, A. *The American House Styles of Architecture Coloring Book.* New York: Dover Publications, 1983.

WADE, R., ed. *Wild in the City: The Best of ZOONOOZ.* San Diego, CA: Zoological Society of San Diego, 1985.

Chapter 24

ARCO. *Sight, Light, and Color—An Illustrated Encyclopedia.* New York: Arco Publishing Company, 1984.

BAGER, B. *Nature as Designer—A Botanical Art Study.* New York: Van Nostrand Reinhold, 1961.

BROWN, V. *The Amateur Naturalist's Diary.* Englewood Cliffs, NJ: Prentice-Hall, Inc., 1983.

CLARK, K. *Landscape into Art*. New York: Harper & Row, 1976.

DE FIORE, G. *Learning to See and Draw*. New York: Watson-Guptill Publications, 1984.

FREEMAN, M. *The Wildlife & Nature Photographer's Field Guide*. Cincinnati, OH: Writers Digest Books, 1984.

GUSSOW, A. *A Sense of Place: The Artist and the American Land*. San Francisco: Friends of the Earth, 1972.

KILHAM, L. *A Naturalist's Field Guide*. Harrisburg, PA: Stackpole Books, 1981.

LEONARD, E. *Painting the Landscape*. New York: Watson-Guptill Publications, 1984.

LESLIE, C. *Nature Drawing—A Tool for Learning*. Englewood Cliffs, NJ: Prentice-Hall, Inc., 1980.

LESLIE, C. *Notes from a Naturalist's Sketchbook*. Boston: Houghton Mifflin, 1981.

LESLIE, C. *The Art of Field Sketching*. Englewood Cliffs, NJ: Prentice-Hall, Inc., 1984.

MACFARLANE, R. *Collecting and Preserving Plants for Science and Pleasure*. New York: Arco Publishing, Inc., 1984.

MAIR, E. *A Field Guide to Personal Computers for Bird-watchers and Other Naturalists*. Englewood Cliffs, NJ: Prentice-Hall, Inc., 1985.

MAYE, P. *Field Book of Nature Photography*. Phoenix, AZ: Sierra Club ToteBooks, 1974.

MERRIAM, J. *The Garment of God: Influences of Nature in Human Experience*. New York: Charles Scribner's Sons, 1943.

OSOLINSKI, S. *Nature Photography: A Guide to Better Outdoor Pictures*. Englewood Cliffs, NJ: Prentice-Hall, Inc., 1981.

PETRIE, F. *Drawing Landscapes in Pencil*. New York: W. W. Norton, 1984.

PETRIE, F., & J. SHAW. *The Watercolorist's Guide to Painting Skies*. New York: Watson-Guptill Publications, 1984.

RUE, L. *How I Photograph Wildlife and Nature*. New York: W. W. Norton, 1984.

SWENEY, F. *The Art of Painting Animals*. Englewood Cliffs, NJ: Prentice-Hall, Inc., 1983.

Bibliography

THOLLANDER, E. *Back Roads of New England.* New York: Crown Publishers, Inc., 1974.

WILSON, D. *In the Presence of Nature.* Amherst, MA: University of Massachusetts Press, 1978.

INDEX

This index is designed to be both practical and fun. Purposely this book was built from widely scattered bits, ecologically related ones to which the index can guide you. Don't be disappointed if you don't find much specific information about any one indexed item when you locate it, for the purpose of the book is to help you appreciate *relationships*. Look for each item's context in the text and then be aware of its place in this wonderful nature-patterned and people-patterned world.

Try reading down a column somewhere in the index. Are you perplexed by such sequences as "bobolinks, bogs, books," and "doodle bugs, double-nickel"? Such items can be intriguing, perhaps to you or your youngster. Kids can have a treasure hunt with this index, for instance seeing how many names of mammals or kinds of scientists they can find in it. Furthermore, although items in the illustrations are not indexed, children can have fun seeing how many objects they can identify in each environment pictured in the chapter headings.

Aborigines, 126, 127
Abutments, stone or concrete bridge, 159
Acacia trees, in savanna, 113
Acadia National Park, ME, cobble beach, 78
Acid, from pine needles, 39; from granite, 54; bogs, 57; leaching from mines, 131
Accommodations, 145. *See also* Inns; Motels
Acorns, 56, 96
Africa, 42, 44, 113, 127, 128, 129, 171
Agates, 36–37, 82
Agriculture, 29. *See also* Farming
Alaska, wetlands, 50; muskeg and permafrost, 57
Alders, in shrubswamps, 55
Alfalfa, 109, 118
Algae, 70, 83, 84

Alkali, in deserts, 41
Alligator, in cypress swamps, 55
Alluvial fans, 62, 63, 107
Alpacas, on rangelands, 112; shrubs on ranges of, 114
Alps, 26, 107, 108, 120; forests, 123
Amazon, 50, 61, 65, 120, 126
Amerindians (*see* Native Americans)
American Museum of Natural History, 174
Amphipods, 77
Andes, 26, 33, 108
Angle of repose, of soil, 27; of beach sand, 76
Antarctic cruise, 87
Antelopes (*see* Pronghorns)
Anthropologists, 127, 133
Ant-lions (*see* Doodle bugs)
Ants, 3, 4, 5, 11, 93, 173

Appalachian Mountain Club, 141
Appalachians, 30
Appalachian Trail, between Maine and Georgia, 140
Aqueducts, 159
Aquifers, windmills pumping from, 114
Arboretums, travelers relaxing in, 172
Arborvitae, planted around Victorian homes, 171
Arctic, muskeg in, 57
Argentina, pampas of, 116
Arid regions, 29, 30, 41
Arizona, 29, 41, 45, 160
Armadillos, 95
Arnheimland, Australia, forest home of aborigines, 127
Artisans, 125
Artists, 41, 57, 110, 124, 127
Ash, sedimented igneous rock, 34
Ash trees, 56, 125
Asia, 42, 127
Aspens, 121, 130–31, 183
Asters, in autumn garden, 171
Atlantic Intracoastal Waterway, 165
Atlantic Ocean, 77, 80, 164
Atmosphere, at sunset, 25
Audubon Societies, source of information about trails, 141
Australia, 22–23, 27, 113, 116, 117, 118, 126, 127, 142
Austria, 107, 123
Autumn, 53, 56, 57, 97, 119, 130, 138, 139
Avalanches, 73, 120, 123

Back country, 63
Backpacking, 7
Backwash, sound of, 85
Backwaters on floodplains, 63
Bald-cypress, 45, 54, 100, 122, 151
Balsam fir, 190
Banks, 61, 62, 129, 152, 160, 161
Banner marks, used to identify birds, 95
Barberry, hedges of Japanese, 171
Bare feet, where safe, 10–11, 69, 77
Barns, 106, 109, 110, 111
Barrenlands, clothes suitable for, 10
Barrier beaches (*see* Beaches, barrier)
Basalt, from volcanoes, 34

Bavaria, Germany, farms in Black Forest, 107
Bayberry on dunes, 80
Bay trees, 55
Bayou, 63
Beaches, barrier, 52, 71, 72, 75, 76, 78–82, 85, 97–98
Beach grass, 38, 80
Beach-heather stabilizing dunes, 80
Beach plum on dunes, 80
Bedding, of sedimentary rock, 34. *See also* Sleeping bags
Bedrock, 31, 33, 34, 64
Beech in bottomland hardwood swamps, 56
Bees, serving farmers, 105
Beetles, 51, 65, 95, 98, 189
Bicycles, 143, 145–48. *See also* Cycling
Biking (*see* Bicycles; Cycling)
Billows with whitecaps, 91
Binoculars, 13, 76, 89, 146
Biologists, 127
Birch, 56, 68
Birds, 44; watching, 76, 81, 82, 95, 97, 98, 138, 143–45, 160, 161, 165, 169
Bison, 112, 116
Black-bellies, 23, 25, 114, 156–57
Blackbirds, 54, 95, 118, 130
Black Forest, Germany, farms in, 107
Black Hills, South Dakota, 34
Blind, sound recording for and with, 188
Blinds (*see* Hides)
Blizzards, 110, 113
Bloodsuckers (*see* Leeches)
Blueberries, 54
Bluestem grass, 118, 119
Bluffs, 62, 80
Boats and ships, 85, 163, 164. *See also* Canoes
Bobolinks, 118
Bogs, 57
Books, 146, 185, 187, 191–96, 197–205
Borrow pit, 130, 152
Botanic gardens, 172
Botanists, 7, 126, 132
Bottomlands, 56, 74
Bougainvillea, 170, 171
Boulders, 72, 156
Boxelder, 109

Boxwood for topiary, 171
Brazil, 124, 126. *See also* Amazon
Breaches in levees, 63
Breeze, 22, 76, 130, 183. *See also* Wind
Bridges, 66, 155, 174
Bridges and causeways, 158–59, 160
Bronze Age archeological dig, 133
Brook, 60, 61, 66, 163
Buffalo berry, Great Plains hedges of, 171
Buildings, 106, 108, 114, 117, 126, 167, 169, 171, 173
Bulrushes, 51, 69
Bunting, painted, in Gulf Coast shrubbery, 165
Burreeds in marshes, 51
Butterflies, 6, 160, 172
Buttonbush, 51, 54

Cactus, 171
Caladiums, 171
California, 74, 82, 119, 127, 140, 141
Camargue, 50
Cameras, 14, 58, 140, 147, 185–87, 186. *See also* Photographing
Camouflage, 10, 161, 162
Campgrounds, 22, 44, 81, 123, 130, 141, 146. *See also* Accommodations; Inns
Camping, 8, 11, 22, 29–30, 66, 136, 145, 156, 157, 183
Camps, nature trails at established, 141
Canada, 33, 53, 56, 57, 70, 71, 73, 76, 77–78
Canadian Rockies, with glacial landscapes, 73
Canals, 164, 165, 166
Canoes, 10, 44, 53, 65, 68, 84, 141
Canopy of forest with red-eyed vireos, 96
Cape Cod, MA, 40, 57, 70, 80, 165
Cape Cod National Seashore, 80
Cape of Good Hope, 91
Cape Hatteras National Seashore, 80
Cape Horn, winds south of, 91
Caribbean Sea, 55–56, 81
Cascade Ranges, OR, 26, 73
Casuarina trees as windbreaks in Florida, 170
Cataract, 61, 65
Cattails, 44, 51, 53, 57, 69, 130, 161

Cattle, 112, 114, 115, 118, 119, 120
Causeways, 161
Caverns, 65, 73, 82
Cayuga Lake, New York, 72
Censuses, 7, 138, 143–45
Central America, 42, 44
Central Lowland of United States, physiographic region, 30
Central Valley, CA, physiographic region, 30; rangelands, 119
Channel, 62, 63, 64, 83
Chemicals used in monocultures, 124
Chernozem soils of Great Plains, 41
Chess and checkers, 13
Chestnut soils of the southern Great Plains, 41
Chickadees, 169
Chicopee River, MA, remnant of great Glacial River Chicopee, 71
Children, 4, 5, 15, 37, 50, 69, 100, 101, 111, 123, 136, 140, 151, 162, 164, 169, 175. *See also* Games
Chile's seabird colonies, 84
China, 127, 158
Choctaw Indians, 63
Cincinnati Dome, geological uplift in Ohio and Kentucky, 34
Cirque (*cwm* in Welsh), made by mountain glacier, 73
Cities, 9, 21, 24, 50, 100, 101, 106, 128, 141, 155, 159, 167, 173, 174–77
Civilizations, 66, 127
Civil War, 118
Cladophora, 83
Clams and clam worms, 83
Clays, 71
Cliffs on rocky shores, 84
Climates, 23, 34, 40, 41, 73, 74, 106, 108, 109, 111, 113, 114, 115, 116, 117, 119, 122, 124, 127–28, 168, 171
Clipboards, 132–33, 139, 147
Clones of cottonwoods, 131
Clothing, 10–11, 79, 83, 113, 146, 150–51
Clouds, 23, 57, 70, 79, 89, 90, 96, 114
Clover, 95, 160
Cluster development preserving open space, 169
Coal, 131, 133
Coastal Plain, 51, 165

Coast Ranges of California, physiographic region, 30
Cobblestones, 77, 78, 85, 150, 156
Cockroaches, 101, 175
Cold, 95, 124, 174
Coleus, 167
Collecting, 95, 125, 181, 182, 183, 188–98, 190
Colorado Plateau with cattle rangelands, 119
Colorado River, 141
Colors, 23, 25, 35, 36, 40, 41, 56, 72, 77, 94, 117, 119, 122, 147, 160, 161, 184
Columbia Plateau, of igneous rock, 34
Commensals, 174
Commons, old-time and new, 169
Community gardens, 177
Companions, 4–5, 55, 75
Compass, 24, 137
Cones, 189
Conglomerate rocks, with gravels, 35
Connecticut Valley, 41, 71, 110
Consumers of energy, 74
Continentality of climates, 113
Coot, 57
Coral beaches and reefs, 81
Cordgrasses in salt marshes, 52, 83
Corn, 23, 44, 109, 117, 122
Cottonwoods, 108, 113, 117, 118, 130–31, 133, 135
Cousteau, Jean Jacques, 86, 126
Cover, 95, 96, 134
Countryside, 106, 159
Coves at Olympic and Gaspe Peninsulas, 84
Cowboys and cowgirls, 112
Cows, 107, 109, 142
Coyotes, 117, 145
Crafts, 125, 188–89
Cranberries, 57, 80
Creosote bush in desert rangelands, 114
Crickets, 44, 94, 95
Croplands, 42, 118
Crops, 106, 107, 108, 114
Crown of roads, 181
Cruises, 9, 87
Culverts, 23, 154–55, 161, 168
Culture, 42, 106, 126, 151, 165
Currents, 60–61, 71, 76, 77, 80, 122, 156, 164

Cycling, 7–8, 9, 15, 32, 44, 51, 58, 106, 143–44, 168
Cypress swamps of Gulf Coast, 55

Dams, 61, 66, 74, 164
Daisies, 171
Day-lilies, 171
DOR (animals dead on road), 95
Deccan, of ancient rocks, 33
Deepwater habitats, 51
Deer, 95, 168
Delmarva Peninsula, crossed by Intracoastal Waterway, 165
Deltas, 53, 63, 71, 72, 81
Deposition, 62. See also Sedimentation
Deserts, 41, 44, 52, 74, 97, 113–14, 122, 127, 128, 156–57, 160, 171
Desertification of farm and grazing land, 42, 127
Development, 106, 119, 168–69
Diary, keeping a, 183
Dikes, 35, 162
Dinosaur footprints, 41
Directions, 24, 137
Ditches, 108, 151, 152
Divides between watersheds, 153
Dogs, 106, 138
Dogwood bushes in shrubswamps, 54
Doodle bugs, 93, 175
Double-nickel on superslab, 95, 96
Douglas fir, 45, 83, 125
Douglas, William O., 165
Doves, 95, 159, 160, 174. See also Pigeons
Dragonflies, 69, 98, 175
Drawing (see Sketching)
Dreaming, 6, 10
Dredging, 153
Driftwood, 77, 83
Driving, 8, 9, 28, 58, 93–94, 106
Drought, 117
Dry washes in desert valleys, 156
Ducks, 51, 56, 57, 168
Dumfrieshire, Scotland, with hide overlooking merse, 162
Dunes, 76, 77, 79, 80, 82
Dust, 114, 117, 144, 186

Earth (see Planet Earth)
Earth colors for clothing, 10, 161

Earthworms, 39, 55, 95
Ecologists, 131, 134
Eddies in potholes, 64
Eden in city, 167
Eelgrass, 76
Eiders seen from dune, 79
Elderberries, 54
Elderly people, touring with, 12–15
Elms, 56, 109, 113, 150, 164, 170
Enclosures compared to exclosures, 120
Energy, 62, 71, 78, 79, 108, 131, 132, 134
Engineers, 151, 152, 163
England, 77, 112, 159, 162, 164
Enteromorpha, 83
Entomologists, 4, 7
Environmental education using nature trails, 141
Equipment, 8, 58, 184, 185–86
Environmentalists concerned about road-building, 152
Erosion, 9, 28, 42, 107–8, 109, 117, 123
Eucalyptus, 96, 118, 127, 190
Eurasia, 113, 122
Europe, 44, 140
Evening (*see* Twilight)
Everglades in Florida, 81, 108
Everglades National Park, 52, 55, 81
Exclosures compared to enclosures, 120

Falcons, 134
Fallow farmlands, 42
Farmers, 74, 94, 105, 106, 109
Farms, 42, 71, 74, 105, 107, 108, 117
Fencerows, 97. *See also* Hedgerows
Fences, 95, 107, 118, 119, 162, 168, 169, 170. *See also* Walls
Fens, 57
Ferns, 65
Ferries, 9, 23, 66
Fertility, 83, 106, 109, 124. *See also* Manure
Fetch, 82, 91
Fetterbush of Southeastern Coastal Plain, 55
Field, 25, 94, 107
Field glasses (*see* Binoculars)
Field guides, 95, 97, 98, 146, 195–96
Fig, 106, 167
Fiji, 125, 126

Film for cameras, 185–86
Finger Lakes, NY, 72, 165
Fire, 109, 114, 123, 133, 158, 183
Fire Island National Seashore, NY, seaside forests, 80
First aid kit, 8, 146
Fish, 56, 64, 69, 97, 99, 131, 153
Fishermen, 56, 65, 74, 100
Fish hatchery, 100
Fishing, 64, 65, 70, 74
Flash floods, 30, 156–57
Flatlands, 63, 108, 125, 142
Flatwater, 74, 164
Flies, 98, 114
Flint Hills of Kansas, 49, 118
Flood control, 56, 63, 74, 121
Flooding to protect soil from subtropical sun, 108
Flood plains, 29, 56, 61, 62, 63, 164
Floods, 62, 63, 64, 123, 124, 131
Floodway, 29, 62, 131
Florida, 44, 52, 55, 73, 80, 81, 108, 119, 165, 170
Flowerbeds, 106, 121
Flowers, 189–90
Flowwater fishermen, 74
Flycatchers, 69, 119
Flyways, 97, 98
Fodder, 110, 115
Fog, 23, 84, 85, 90
Folkways of farmers, 42, 106
Foods, 11, 14
Footpaths (*see* Trails)
Footwear, planning for, 10
Forbs, 116, 117, 134, 160
Fords, 66, 155–56
Forests, 39, 41, 44, 45, 56, 63, 80, 82, 95, 96, 116, 121, 122, 123, 125–26, 127, 134, 164. *See also* Woodlands; Reforestation
Forsythia, 171
Foxtail grasses, 176
France, 50, 100, 164
Friends, 145. *See also* Companions
Friends of the Earth, 46–47
Frigate birds on Gulf Coast, 56
Frogs, 55, 100
Front Range of Rockies, 27
Frost, 124, 129, 152
Frost, Robert, 61, 164, 168

Fruit trees, 168
Fungus diseases in monocultures, 124

Gabions holding stones for erosion
    control, 63
Games, 13, 14, 43, 60, 61, 77, 78, 111,
    154–55, 163, 170
Garden clubs, 172
Gardeners, 121, 172
Gardens, 101, 105, 107, 169, 171, 172,
    177
Garnet, pink sand from, 76
Gaspe Peninsula, 84
Geese, 57, 81
Geneticists, 124, 131
Geoducks from Pacific Northwest
    mudflats, 83
Georgia, segment of Appalachian Trail
    in, 140
Geraniums, 167, 171
Germany, forest recreation in Alps, 123
Glacial Lake Agassiz compared to Great
    Lakes today, 71
Glacial Lake Maumee, 71
Glacial Lake Missoula, 71, 72
Glacial Lake Saginaw, 71
Glacial Lake Springfield in Connecticut
    River Valley, 71
Glacial River Chicopee, 71
Glaciation, 39, 57, 71, 72–73
Glacier National Park, MT, with alpine
    glaciation, 73
Gladiolas, 171
Goats, 107, 112
Goatsbeard, windblown seeds of, 96
Gold, dredging gravel for, 153
Gold Beach, OR, coast north to Astoria,
    82
Goldenrods, 171
Gophers, 39, 96–97, 116
Grain, 150. *See also* Corn; Wheat
Granite, 31, 32, 54
Grapes, 106, 164, 167, 170
Grassed waterways, 42
Grasses, 40, 43, 51, 53, 56, 94, 112, 113,
    117, 118, 119, 132, 137, 142
Grasshoppers, 94
Grassland, 96, 97, 112, 113
Gravel, 71, 107, 108, 130, 132, 144,
    152–53, 171

Gravel pit (*see* Borrow pit)
Grazing lands, 42, 112, 117, 120
Great Basin, 30, 52, 74, 119
Great Lakes, 23, 71, 72, 132, 133, 164,
    170
Great Plains, 22, 30, 52, 53, 94, 96, 109,
    113, 116, 117, 118, 133, 152, 170
Great Smoky Mountains National Park,
    44
Green Mountains, VT, 140
Greenwich, England, 113
Ground squirrels, 97
Groundwater, 53, 56, 69, 114
Grouse moors in Scotland, 116
Grove, 108, 121, 138
Guano of seabird colonies, 84
Gulf Coast, 55, 165
Gulls, 23, 85, 89, 91, 164, 175
Gum trees, 56, 96, 118

Habitats, 96, 147
Hackberries by watercourses on plains,
    118
Hammocks amid the sawgrass everglades,
    81
Handicapped people, 7, 15–16, 148, 188
Hand lens, 13, 76, 146
Hand specimen of rock, 36
Hans Brinker, 164
Harbor, 87, 91
Hats, 84, 113, 146
Hawks, 95, 97, 98, 162
Hay, 107, 109
Haystacks made by meadow voles, 94
Heat, 94, 95
Hedges, 94, 168, 170
Helmet (*see* Hats)
Hemlock for topiary, 171
Hemp for lashing reed boats, 92
Herbs, 51, 116
Herbicides killing woody plants, 115
Herders, 107, 140
Herons, 3, 50, 53, 84, 100, 164
Herpetologists, 55
Hide-and-seek, 13
Hides for watching wildlife, 162
Hickories in upper middle latitudes, 122
Highlands of Scotland, 116
High latitudes, 57, 122

Highways, 95, 108, 119, 157. *See also* Roads
Hiking, 28, 58, 137, 165. *See also* Walking
Hilltops, 3, 25, 30, 79, 83, 98
Himalayas, 33, 108, 128
Hinterlands, 52, 62, 63, 64
History, 6, 66, 70, 71
Holly trees in dune hollows, 80
Hops barns, round, disappearing, 110
Horizon, 88
Hornblende making black sand, 76
Horse flies, 76
Horse latitudes, 90
Horses, 110, 111, 119
Hosta planted by sidewalks, 167
Howling Fifties in southern hemisphere, 91
Hudson River, 164
Humid regions, 39, 73, 119
Humus, 39, 74, 124, 134
Hundredth meridian, 113
Hunting, 96, 100
Hurricanes, 55

Ice, 160. *See also* Glaciation
Icebergs, 72, 87
Iceboating, 74
Ice sheet, 76. *See also* Glaciation; Pleistocene
Igneous rocks, 34
Illinois shrubswamps, 54
India, 33, 120
Indian cultures, 41
Indian Ocean, 81, 87
Indian Reservations, 36
Infrastructures, 66, 151
Inland Waterway, barrier beaches along, 81
Inns, 25, 96, 145
Insect repellents, 58, 76, 165
Insects, 69, 98, 98–99, 124, 144, 145, 160, 164, 173–74, 175
International government agencies, for natural area information, 46
International Union for the Protection of Nature and Natural Resources, 46
Intertidal zone, 74, 83
Intracoastal Waterway of Atlantic Coastal Plain, 165

Iowa, 41, 48, 53
Iron, 132, 150, 159
Irrigation, 74, 114, 118, 119, 132

Jacaranda trees, 168
Jack rabbits, 95, 116
Jellyfish, 76
Jetsam, 70
Job's tears, of volcanic glass, 34
Jogging on beach, 77
Journal, keeping a, 182. *See also* Magazines
Journal of Geography, 192. *See also* Magazines
Junipers with pinyon pines in Southwest, 122

Kansas, 27, 34, 49, 113, 117, 118
Karst topography on limestone, 73
Kauri trees in New Zealand, 49
Kelp, 76
Kentucky, 34, 140
Kettle holes with sphagnum bogs, 57
Kettles of migrating hawks, 98
Keys, Florida, 81
Kingfishers, 100, 164
Kississimi Prairie rangelands in Florida, 119
Klamath River, CA, 141
Knife for sharpening pencils, 57, 147
Koala, 96

Lagoons, 82
Lake beds, 29, 39, 41, 71
Lake Okeechobee, FL, rangelands north of, 119
Lakes, 62, 70, 71, 72, 73, 74, 164
Lake Superior, 72
Landforms, 28, 62, 132
Landmarks, 137, 140
Landscapes, 45, 56, 63, 68, 72, 91, 95, 105, 106, 108, 109, 110, 111, 118, 119, 127, 130, 131, 132, 133, 134, 149, 157, 159, 164, 165, 168–69, 170, 188
Landscaping, 161, 168–69
Landslides, 123
La Push, WA, wild shores of, 83
Larch, 56, 123
Laterites, 40, 126

Lava, 34
Lavender, 190
Lawns, 144, 168
Lay of the land, 26–30. *See also*
    Topography
Leaching, 52, 131
Lead poisoning, 66–67
Leatherleaf bogs, 57
Leeches in lakes, 68, 70
Legumes (pulses), 40
Levee, 29, 62, 63
Lewis and Clark Trail, 140
Lianas, 49, 96, 158
Libraries, 45, 48, 146, 192
Life preservers, 84
Lightning, 70, 109. *See also*
    Thunderstorms
Limestones, 32, 35, 65, 73, 80–81, 118
Laurentian Shield of ancient rocks in
    Canada, 33
Lichens on walls, 32
Listening, 61, 68, 69, 70, 84–85, 96, 101,
    118, 172, 181, 183
Litter of natural organic matter, 39
Llamas, 112, 114
Loam, 108
Locks of canals, 66, 164
Locust trees, 134, 150–51, 168
Log, keeping a written, 182
Logs, 150–51
Longhorns, 119
Long Trail, along Green Mountains in
    Vermont, 140
Looking (*see* Observation)
Losing your way, to avoid, 137–38
Loons, 7
Low Countries, canals and windmills in,
    164
Lower middle latitudes, forests of, 122
Low latitudes (tropics), 40, 122, 124

Magnifying glass, binoculars used as, 14
Magnolias, 168
Maine, 35, 40, 45, 68, 77, 78, 79, 86,
    125, 136, 140, 141
Maori seeing changes in New Zealand,
    127
Mallow growing on spent shale, 132
Mammals, 95, 97

Mangrove swamps, 45, 55–56, 81
Manitoba, 71, 113
Manure, 105, 106, 110. *See also* Fertility
Maples, 56, 121, 122, 123, 128, 143, 164,
    168
Maps and charts, 65, 87, 98, 113, 114,
    144, 187, 188
Marmots, 97
Marshes, 51, 52–53, 80, 81, 161
Marsh gas, methane, 70
Marsh-marigolds, 60
Marsh wrens, watching, 51
Massachusetts, 41, 57, 78, 80, 165
Mature stream, 29, 61, 62
Mayflies, 98, 99
Meadow in late summer with orthopteran
    chorus, 94
Meadowlarks, 95, 118
Mediterranean, 74, 87
Meltwater numbing, 69
Memory, 138, 182
Meridian, prime, 113
Merrimac River, 80
Merses (*see* Salt marshes)
Mesas, colors of, 35
Mesopotamia, 66
Metamorphic rocks, 35, 78
Mice, 176
Michigan, 57, 71, 152
Microclimates, 15, 106, 124, 130, 160,
    174
Microorganisms, 39, 70
Middle latitude climates, 124. *See also*
    Upper and Lower middle latitude
    climates
Migrations, 97, 165
Minerals, 36, 76
Mineralogist, 36
Mines, 131–32, 133, 134, 135, 153
Minnesota, 41, 53, 71, 132, 141
Minnows, 56, 69, 83, 84
Mississippi Lowlands, 23, 30, 56
Mississippi River, 61, 63, 65, 81
Missouri River, 74
Moisture (*see* Rain; Water)
Monadnocks, 34
Montana, 22, 73
Monkeys, 96
Monocular field glass, 13, 146

Monocultures of hybrid trees, 124–25, 127
Moon, 83, 89
Moose, 57
Moraines deposited by glaciers, 73
Mosquitoes, 57, 58, 69, 76, 98, 165, 182
Moss, 56, 57
Motels (*see* Inns)
Motion sickness, 5, 88
Motorcycles, 8. *See also* Cycling
Mountains, 26, 27, 28, 33, 115, 123
Mud, 31–32, 69, 144, 151, 163
Mudflats, 83, 84
Mudstones (*see* Shales)
Mulches, 40, 42
Museums, 141, 174. *See also* Nature centers
Music, 69, 78, 94, 96, 99, 100, 121, 124, 143, 146
Muskeg vegetation, 56–57
Muskrats, 51

Natchez Trace, 140
National Audubon Society, 47
National Geographic, 192. *See also* Magazines
National government agencies, 46
National Parks, 44, 82–83, 140
National Parks and Conservation Association, 47
National Seashores, 80, 82
National Wildlife Federation, 47
National Wildlife Refuges, 80, 81, 165
Native Americans, 41, 42, 118, 125, 133, 140, 150
Natural communities protecting plants and animals, 44
Natural areas, 44–45, 116, 126, 133–34
Naturalists, 7, 152, 159, 161, 165
Natural vegetation, 39, 42, 49, 107, 116, 118, 119, 126, 140. *See also* Vegetation, Natural
Nature, need for more understanding of, 177
Nature centers, 48, 141, 142, 146
Nature Conservancy, The, 48, 133
Nature study, books for, 12
Nature trails, 141, 142
Near East, deserts of, 127

Nebraska, 113, 117, 141
Neptune, game challenging, 77
Netherlands, 164–65
Nevada, 52, 74, 119
New England, 110, 130, 152, 171
New England Wild Flower Preservation Society, 48
New Hampshire, 78
New Jersey, 40, 57, 80, 141, 165
New Orleans, 81
Newspapers, 144, 187–88
New York, 54, 72, 80, 110, 123, 124, 164, 165, 174
New Zealand, 49, 127
Night, 25, 77, 89, 128, 145
Niobrara River, NB, 141
Nipped bank, 62, 64
North Carolina, 51, 80, 165
North Dakota, 53, 108, 113
Notebook, 147
Notes, 139
Nurseries, 123, 131, 168
Nutria in bald-cypress swamps, 55

Oak, 56, 93, 119, 122, 138, 164, 165, 168
Observation, 3, 21, 61, 84, 91, 94, 137, 138, 161–62, 181–90
Obsidian, 34
Ocean, 87, 98. *See also* Seas
Odors, 23, 24, 45, 70, 109, 121, 172, 173, 190
Ohio, 34, 71, 133, 134
Oil shale crushed for hydrocarbons, 131
Oklahoma, 113, 117, 118
Open country, 96, 97, 118, 120, 144
Open space, 144, 168, 169
Opossum, 95
Orchids, 57
Ore from mines, 131
Oregon, 57, 73, 74, 77, 82, 140, 141
Organic matter, 39, 108
Ornithologists, 96, 134, 159
Orthopteran symphony, 94
Osprey, 97, 100, 162
Outback, Australian, 27, 116, 118
Outcrops of rock, 31, 33, 34
Outdoor recreation, 29
Overgrazing, 115, 123
Oxen, 32, 64, 111, 126

Pacific Ocean, 82, 113
Packing, 8, 14
Painting, 6, 57, 58, 61, 77, 91, 127, 129, 162, 184–85
Palmettos, 119
Palms, 81, 168
Pampas, Argentina, 41, 116
Panther, 55
Paper, 127, 139
"Paper chase" using pea pods, 14
Parking lots, 27, 29, 62, 63, 169
Parks, 7, 29, 36, 44, 123, 141, 142, 144, 172, 173, 175, 176
Passes through mountains, 33, 153, 157
Pasteur, Louis, 191
Pasture, 107, 112, 169
Paths, tow, 164. *See also* Trails
Patterns, 114, 119, 120, 132, 134
Peat, 57, 116, 152
Pebbles, 31–32, 37, 41, 85, 152
PCBs, 12
Pedologists, 39
Pelicans, 56, 82
Penguins, 87
Periwinkle snails, 75
Permafrost, 57
Perth, Australia, with gallery of aboriginal art, 127
Pheasants, 100
Phoebe, 69
Photographing, 6, 11, 57, 61, 70, 77, 84, 87, 91, 114, 125, 126, 147, 159, 170, 173, 181, 185–86, 187
Phreatophytes, 115
Physiographic regions, 30
Picnic, 14, 25, 50, 137
Piedmont, 30, 63
Pigeons, 101, 159, 160, 173, 174, 177. *See also* Doves
Pineapple fields, 107
Pine Barrens, NJ, 141
Pines, 40, 55, 69, 109, 122, 123, 124, 125, 127, 134, 142, 165, 170
Pinyon nuts, 183
Pioneers, 33, 49, 114, 119, 140, 150
Pitcher plants in bogs, 57
Plains, 49, 74, 96, 114. *See also* Great Plains; Coastal Plains
Planet Earth, 9, 25, 92, 106, 171, 172

Plane trees, 44, 173
Planning, records as part of purpose of tour, 190
Plateaus, 28
Plantains, 176
Plantations, 116, 123, 124, 125, 127
Plant presses, making and using, 189–90
Plants, 138, 142, 189–90
Playas, 29, 52, 74
Pleistocene, 71, 72, 73
Plovers, 76, 98
Plum Island, MA, 78, 80
Pocosin swamps, 51, 55
Podzols, 40, 41
Poetry, 61, 168
Poison-ivy, 69
Poisons, 12, 53, 116, 131
Point-bar deposits by streams, 62
Polders pumped by windmills, 164
Pond-lilies, 137
Ponds, 70, 145. *See also* Lakes; Pools
Pony, 112, 113, 120
Pools, swimming, 168
Poplars, 106, 124, 130, 134, 170
Population, 36, 44, 100, 117, 127, 128, 143, 144, 169
Pore-spaces with air and water in soil, 38
Potatoes, 106, 107
Potholes, 53, 64, 72, 156
Potomac River, 165
Poultry, 110, 112
Power, 74, 116, 165
Prairie dogs, 97, 116
Prairies, 41, 42, 44, 48, 49, 53, 74, 113, 114, 116–17, 118, 119
Predators, 96, 174
Privet, 171
Progress, 99
Pronghorns, 96, 116
Publications, writing for, 184
Pulloffs (*see* Rest stops)
Pumice, 34
Puriri trees, 49
Put-and-take game management, 100
Pyrenees, 142

Quarries and mines, 31, 129, 130, 131, 132, 133–34, 135
Quietness, 70, 161–62, 166

Rabbits, 39, 95
Rabbitbrush, 115
Rafting down river, 65
Ragweed, 176
Railroads, 138, 144, 159, 165, 175
Rain, 53, 74, 113, 121, 122, 139, 145
Rainforests, 49, 50, 96, 127
Ranches, 109, 114
Ranchers, 115, 116
Rangelands, 113–19
Rats, 97, 176
Reading while waiting for wildlife, 162
Reclamation, 125, 131, 132, 133–34. *See
    also* Reforestation
Recorder, 124, 146
Recording your observations, 147,
    181–83, 184–90
Recreation, 29, 74
Recreational vehicles, 8–9, 29, 44
Redbed formations with dinosaur
    footprints, 41
Red-cedar, 151
Red maple floodplain swamps, 56
Red maple seepage swamps, 56
Red-winged blackbirds, 54
Redwood, 151
Redwood National Park, CA, 44
Reeds, 92, 161
Reforestation, 116, 120, 123–24, 125, 128
Relaxation, 23, 45, 146, 157, 172, 196–97
Reservoirs, 74
Rest stops, 95, 157, 160
Revegetation (*see* Reclamation;
    Reforestation)
Rhododendrons, 171
Rice, 106
Ridge roads along divides of watersheds,
    153
Ridges, 98, 153
Rills beginning to form gullies, 42
Riprap, 40, 63, 160
Rivers, 50, 61, 63, 65, 74, 81, 126, 141.
    See also Streams
River bank (*see* Banks)
Roadcuts, 33, 40
Roads, 29, 65, 95, 143, 144, 149–53,
    154–56, 157
Road scraper, 151
Roaring Forties in southern hemisphere's

prevailing westerly winds, 91
Robin, 95, 138–39
Rock fences (*see* Stone walls)
Rockpiles, 97
Rocks, 31, 34, 35, 36, 63, 84–85, 131,
    160
Rock slides, 73
Rocky Mountains, 26, 27, 30, 33, 108
Rocky shores, 84–85
Rodents, 96, 97, 116–17
Romans, 66–67, 150, 158–59
Roots, 39, 115
Rosewood, 124
Rowboat, 23
Runoff of water, 29
Rushes, 51, 53, 130
Russian thistle, 115
Rut-water, 162

Sagebrush, 115, 198
Saguaro cactus, 45
Sahel, 120, 128
Sailors, 24
Saint Francis of Assisi, 97
St. Mark's National Wildlife Refuge,
    FL, 81
Salmon, 153
Salt marshes, coastal and inland, 52;
    behind barrier beaches, 79; mud,
    83; by canoe, 84; merse at
    Dumfrieshire, 162
Sanctuaries, 44–45; 141. *See also*
    Wildflower sanctuaries; Wildlife
    sanctuaries
Sand, 69, 71, 75, 76, 82, 122, 175
Sand dunes (*see* Dunes)
Sandhill cranes, 119
Sand paintings by Native Americans, 42
Sandpipers, 53, 76, 98, 130
Sandstones, 35
Sand worms, 77
Savanna with scattered trees, 113
Sawgrass, 45, 81, 108
Scandinavia, 72
Schools, 125, 126, 141, 142
Science, 4, 126
Scientist, 61, 64, 138, 139, 182
Scissor-tailed flycatcher, 119
Scotland, 116, 162

Scree, 28
Screen plantings for privacy, 170
Scrub-shrub wetlands with scattering of
    shrubby trees, 55
Scuba diving, 70
Sea anemones, 84
Sea caves with sea lions, 82
Sea-grapes, 81
Sea legs, 88
Sea lions, 82, 85
Sea palms in tide pools, 84
Seas and oceans, 88, 89–90, 91, 92
Seascape, 91
Seashores, 75–76, 77, 78, 78–79, 80–82,
    83–85
Seasons, 89, 94, 96, 130, 141, 144, 145,
    151, 163. *See also* Climates
Sea turtle, 87
Sea wall of cobblestones, 78
Seaweeds, 76, 83, 190
Sedges, 51, 53, 56
Sedimentary rocks, 34, 35, 78
Sedimentation, 9, 42, 55, 71, 72, 107,
    108, 123
Seedlings, 121, 130
Seeds, 95, 113, 130, 189
Selenium poison in some brackish water,
    53
Senior citizens, 6, 15–16, 87, 148
Senses, 3, 61, 69, 84, 181. *See also*
    Odors; Listening
Sewers, 176
Shade, 108, 121, 123, 130
Shadows, 58, 64, 77, 95, 96
Shale, 32, 35, 132
Shapes, 21–30, 129
Sharing, 182, 188
Sharks, 76
Sheep, 107, 112, 114, 116, 117, 120
Shells, 81, 153
Shelterbelt on Great Plains, 109
Shepherds, 112
Shingle, 78, 85
Shorebirds, 83
Shortgrass plains of Texas panhandle,
    119
Shrubbery, 43, 95, 109, 115, 164
Shrublands, 97, 115, 116
Shrubs, 115, 134

Shrubswamps, 50, 53, 54–55, 161
Sidewalks, 167, 173
Sierra Club, 48, 140, 141
Sills in rocks, 35
Silos, 109
Silt, 42, 71
Sink hole lakes in karst topography, 73
Sitka spruce, 45
Sketching, 7, 9, 57, 76, 84, 91, 159, 170,
    181, 183, 184, 192. *See also* Painting
Skiing, 66, 123
Skunks, 95
Sky, 21, 22, 23–24, 25, 77, 88, 89, 95,
    96, 97, 113, 114, 157, 173
Sleeping bags, 14, 25, 77, 145, 146, 183
Sleeping out, 145
Slide shows, 185, 187
Slipoff slope, 62, 64
Slopes, 27, 62, 108, 120, 129
Snakes, 55, 68, 95, 157
Snorkeling, 70
Snow, 101, 113, 114, 122, 123, 139, 152
Snowshoe hare tracks, 141
Socrates, 192
Sod, 115
Soils, 29, 39, 40, 42, 54, 56, 71, 106,
    108, 124
Solar radiation, 76
Solitude, 5, 75, 77
Sounds, 84, 181, 187, 188
South America, 42, 113, 126, 130
Southey, Robert, 60–61
Southwestern United States, 74
Souvenirs, 125, 188
Spaniards, 119, 140
Spanish-moss, 55
Sparrows, 12, 95, 176, 177
Specimens (*see* Collecting)
Sphagnum bogs, 57
Spiders, 37, 94
Spoilbanks, 131, 133, 134
Spring, 64, 74, 97, 98–99, 138, 163
Spruce, 40, 56, 57, 69, 83, 107, 122, 123,
    124
Squall, 70, 90
Squirrels, 95, 96
Stables with stalls, bays, and tack rooms,
    110
Stalactites, 65

Stalagmites, 64
Stalking, 43, 96
Starlings, 95, 174
Stars, 25, 44, 70, 89
Steinbeck, John, 4
Stephenson, Robert Louis, 4
Stone Age, 42, 127, 158
Stones, 63, 158, 160, 166, 171
Storms, 78, 79, 85, 88, 91, 117, 160. *See
also* Thunderstorms; Rain
Stove, 145
Streak plate for testing minerals, 36
Streambank, 39, 62, 63, 64
Streambed cut down by youthful
streams, 64
Streams, 29, 61, 62, 63, 64, 65, 66–67,
74, 118, 123, 153–55, 159
Street trees, 121, 173, 175, 176
Strelitzias, 171
Students, 4, 144
Subsoils, 39
Subtropical forests, 45, 49
Suburbs, 144, 168–69
Sugar cane fields, 106, 108
Sumac, poison, 54
Summer, 57, 68, 76, 77, 94, 98–99, 108,
113, 127
Sun, 25, 89, 96, 108, 142, 144
Sunbathing, 76
Sundews, 57
Sunscreen lotion, 76, 84
Sunset, 13, 24, 25, 51, 89, 99, 138
Surf, 79, 82, 84, 85
Swales with red-winged blackbirds, 118
Swallows, 97, 98, 129, 164
Swamps, 53–57, 63, 81, 133, 143
Swash marks on beaches, 77
Swimming, 66, 68, 70, 76, 168
Switzerland, 107, 120, 123–24
Sycamores, 56, 150, 164, 173–74

Tallgrass prairie of eastern plains, 113
Talus slopes of tumbled rock, 28
Tape recording, 6, 84, 99, 139, 140,
187–88
Tarn, 73
Tasman Sea, 23, 117
Teachers, 4, 144
Telescope, 13, 146

Tent, 145, 146
Terrace, 30, 56, 62, 107
Texas, 27, 81, 113, 119
Thatch, 39, 162
Thrushes, 96, 99, 188
Thunderstorms, 23, 30, 49, 64, 70, 108,
113, 114, 115
Tide, 75, 83, 84
Timber, 56, 127
Time, 94, 146, 149, 157
Titi, 55
Titmice, 169
Toads, 100, 101
Tobacco, 110
Topiary, 171
Topography, 28, 73, 98, 106, 137. *See
also* Lay of the land
Topsoil, 42, 117, 134, 152
Tornado, 23, 161
Touring, 12, 191, 192–94. *See also*
Driving; Cycling; Hiking
Towns and cities, 174–77. *See also* Cities
Tracks, 96, 129
Trade routes, touring along, 133
Trailers (*see* Recreational vehicles)
Trails, 43, 65, 81, 123, 136, 137, 138,
139, 140, 141
Transport, public, 9–10
Travel agencies, 5, 87
Travel guides, 192–94
Tree ferns, 49
Treeline, 96
Treeswamps, 51, 55–56
Triassic Era with redbeds, 41
Tributaries of streams, 153
Tropics, 40, 41, 90, 125, 126. *See also*
Low latitudes
Trout, 64, 152
Truck farms near cities, 106
Tules, 51, 57, 69
Tumbleweeds, 115
Tundra, 140
Twilight, 25, 96, 98–99, 145, 174

Underpasses and overpasses influencing
landscapes, 159
Undertow, 76
Uranium hazard in water, 12
Upper middle latitude forests, 122

United States Biological Survey, 99
United States Bureau of Land
    Management, 46
United States Fish & Wildlife Service,
    46, 50, 51
United States Forest Service, 46, 123,
    124, 141
United States Government Printing
    Office, 46
United States National Park Service, 46

Vacant lots, 144, 174, 175
Valleys, 64, 65, 72, 73, 107, 131, 153
Veery, 143
Vegetation, 39, 79, 115, 139, 152. *See
    also* Natural Vegetation
Verge, 95, 96
Vernal pools, 74, 139
Viburnum bushes, 54
Victory gardens (*see* Community gardens)
Videotaping, 188
Villages, 107, 144, 164
Vines sought in travel game, 170
Vineyards, 164, 170
Vireo, 93, 96, 101, 141
Volcano, 26, 27, 28, 73
Voles, 94
Volunteering, 142
Voyagers, 49, 65
Vultures, 97

Wading, 64, 65, 68, 69
Wagons, 33, 150, 151
Walking, 6, 7, 84, 106, 137. *See also*
    Hiking; Trails
Walls, 32, 36, 107, 134, 169, 171. *See
    also* Fences
Warblers, 55, 69, 97
Wasatch Range, uplifted, 28
Wasps, 98
Water, 11–12, 52, 53, 64, 76, 78, 84, 89,
    97, 111, 113, 114, 131–32, 134, 141
Waterfront, 21, 144
Watersheds, 74, 123, 155
Water snakes, 68, 70
Water striders, 64, 65

Water supply, 74, 107, 111
Water ouzel, 66
Water table, 51, 78, 108, 115
Watts, May T., 68
Waves, 78, 82, 90, 91
Waterfowl, 53
Weather, 98, 110, 137, 145, 146, 182,
    186. *See also* Storms
Weeds, 3, 95, 105, 106, 132, 175, 176,
    177
Well house, 111
Wetlands, 50, 51, 58–59, 152
Whales, 87, 92
Wheat, 106, 108, 117, 144
Wheels, 146, 150, 163
White-cedar, 151
Whooping cranes, 81
Wilderness, 7, 44, 82
Wilderness Society, 48
Wildflowers, 44, 74, 122, 164
Wildflower sanctuaries with native
    vegetation, 45
Wildflower societies, 141
Wildlife, 51, 56, 63, 82, 95–96, 99, 123,
    124, 126, 134, 138, 140, 144, 161
Wildlife sanctuaries and refuges, 29,
    44–45
Willows, 54, 56, 58, 164
Wilson's thrush (*see* Veery)
Windbreaks, 42, 109, 119, 170
Windmills, 114, 118, 164
Window boxes, 167, 177
Wind, 22, 23, 69, 76, 78, 79, 82, 85, 88,
    89, 90, 91, 109, 111, 114, 115, 117,
    124, 145, 160, 164, 170
Winter, 66, 74, 79, 82, 96, 114, 122, 127,
    128, 171, 175
Wisteria, 170
Wood, 150, 151
Woodchucks, 39, 97
Woodcock, 55
Woodlands, 113, 122. *See also* Forests
Wool, 142
Words, 60, 181
Worms, 83, 95
Writing, 9, 61, 144, 145, 162, 181, 183,
    187

Yards and gardens, 3, 4, 27, 106, 138,
    167–68, 168–69, 170–71
Yazoo streams entering mature streams,
    63
Yellowlegs, 98
Yellow Pages, 148

Yew, 171

Zephyr, 70
Zoning, 169
Zoologists, 95
Zoos, 176

ABOUT THE AUTHOR

John W. Brainerd, Harvard A.B. and Ph.D., worked for the U.S. Forest Service and the U.S. Fish & Wildlife Service before teaching biology and conservation for thirty-two years at Springfield College in Massachusetts. He has written many articles and books, including *Working with Nature* and *Nature Study for Conservation*, and his articles have appeared in *Audubon Nature Bulletin, National Parks Bulletin, American Nature Study, Nature Conservancy News,* and *Elementary School Science Bulletin.*

Dr. Brainerd is past president of the American Nature Study Society, a Fellow of the Association of Interpretive Naturalists and American Association for the Advancement of Science, an honorary life member of the Appalachian Mountain Club, and a charter member of the American Land Resource Association. He has received the John F. Kennedy Award for Conservation from the Izaak Walton League and a Massachusetts Audubon "A" for Conservation Award.

He and his wife, who now live in Maine, have toured in forty-eight states and in Canada, Europe, and Australia.